MISSING PERSONS

a writer's guide to finding the lost, the abducted and the escaped

Fay Faron

WRITER'S DIGEST BOOKS
CINCINNATI, OHIO

The examples within these pages are all cases which have come across the desk of The Rat Dog Dick Detective Agency, either directly or through the "Ask Rat Dog" column. The names, locales, sexes and physical descriptions have routinely been changed to protect the parties involved.

01   00   99   98   97   5   4   3   2   1

Library of Congress Cataloging-in-Publication Data

Faron, Fay.
　　　Missing persons / by Fay Faron.
　　　　　p.　cm.
　　　Includes index.
　　　ISBN 0-89879-790-X
　　　1. Missing persons—Investigation—United States. 2. Private investiga-
tors—United States. I. Title.
　　　HV6762.U5F37　　1997
　　　363.2'3360—dc21　　　　　　　　　　　　　　　　　　96-51861
　　　　　　　　　　　　　　　　　　　　　　　　　　　　　　　　CIP

Content edited by Roseann Biederman
Production edited by Patrick Souhan
Interior designed by Jannelle Schoonover
Cover designed by Chad Planner
Cover illustration by Chris Spollen

Dedication

For Dad,
who is still sorely missed

Acknowledgment

Thanks to Ann Flaherty, Chief Investigator of The Rat Dog Dick Detective Agency, for doing the real work

About the Author

Fay Faron runs the Rat Dog Dick Detective Agency in San Francisco, specializing in tracking missing persons. She writes a syndicated column titled "Ask Rat Dog," which appears in more than thirty newspapers across the country. In the column she gives advice on tracking missing—or misplaced—persons. She has appeared on *The Oprah Winfrey Show* to track down lost loves and relatives for the studio audience. She has been a guest expert on other television shows, such as *Larry King Live, Joan Rivers, Good Morning America* and *The Jenny Jones Show*. Articles about her have appeared in many newspapers, including *USA Today*, the *San Francisco Examiner* and *Arizona Republic*. She has written two instructional books for investigators: *A Private Eye's Guide to Collecting Bad Debt* (1991) and *The Instant National Locator Guide* (1991), now in a second edition. She also hosted an instructional video on skip tracing titled *People Tracking* (1992). A regular guest on radio talk shows across the country, she also speaks at conferences for investigators. She recently completed her first mystery novel, *Lily Kills Her Client*. She lives in San Francisco.

Table of Contents

Introduction

Back in the fifth grade, my teacher passed out a deck of cards, each describing a career I could look forward to, should I ever escape elementary academia. Being a "people person," I easily narrowed my career choices down to two: psychiatrist, thinking I could hear juicy gossip on a regular basis, and elevator operator, because then I could drop out of school immediately and get on with my life. If a private investigator card was in that pack, I undoubtedly discarded it (either I perceived the job as too dangerous or I sensed I'd spend a lot of my time viewing dead bodies).

The fact is, most days, gumshoes do pretty much the same things one does in any business: typing, filing, research, working on computers, searching out new clients and just plain thinking. Most days here at The Rat Dog Dick Detective Agency, you'd think you were in an insurance office. But that's most days. Every once in a while, I find myself somewhere like St. Thomas, hanging out in a jeep, searching for a playboy husband who ran away with the girl who made the sandwiches on his yacht. Then I say, "This is why I do this for a living."

Another misconception about this industry is that the law allows private investigators some special dispensation in order for us to do our jobs. Imagine my chagrin the first time I had a shoot-out and found myself handcuffed to the fellow who robbed the local Safeway. Or when I tried to explain why I was going seventy-five miles an hour in a school zone to a cop who thought there was no law against a husband cheating on his spouse. Or when I was chased through the alley by one of those neighborhood watch committees yelling nasty names, such as stalker, at me. It doesn't take long for a fledgling investigator to realize what he has is a *business* license and he's got no more police power than, say, Leona Helmsley.

Why It's (Sometimes) Easier to Write a Mystery Than to Solve One in Real Life

- Things usually don't work out as planned.
- People hardly ever do what you want.

- The protagonist isn't always inherently brave or smart.

That's what's different in real life. What's the same, I just discovered while penning this book: to pull off a scam (e.g., find out where someone lives, works, sleeps . . .), it takes writing a "script," being careful that the beginning leads toward a desirable end. Unlike a novel, however, in real life, the protagonist has only limited control over the other characters, so his skills are sorely tested. If his script works, he learns what he wants; if not, the story continues until he does.

The Focus of This Book

Already on the market are many books targeted at professional and amateur sleuths that give some basic idea of how to *skip trace*—or locate people. Because those readers are interested in finding a specific person or persons, a great portion of the content of those books consists of addresses to write to for information—federal agencies, DMVs, courthouses and the like. While essential to a working investigator, these pages are of little use to the mystery writer. This book, instead, deals with the *process* of locating missing persons: who they are, who's looking for them and what their reactions are once they're found. We'll talk about the resources PIs use in locating people and how a gumshoe can work those resources to get the most out of them. Whenever possible, points will be illustrated with real-life cases from the files of The Rat Dog Dick Detective Agency.

You'll also learn about the indexes available within the county courthouse complex, the most powerful databases used by the industry today, the world of "confidential" informants, the kinds of scams and surveillance techniques real PIs use to get information and, of course, the pitfalls of relying on your client as a resource for intelligence.

How I Came to Be Rat Dog

The year was 1982. I'd just bought a Sausalito houseboat and it was sinking fast. I mean really. I can't bear to tell the whole sorry story, but suffice to say, I'd been mugged two days prior, at which time I'd lost my purse, keys, makeup and the uninterrupted continuity of my facial features. Now, with the houseboat gurgling from the bottom of Richardson Bay, my home, furniture, clothes and entire equity were gone as well. It was a really bad couple of days.

Since I'd owned the houseboat only six weeks, I went back to the seller and informed him that the reason the boat had floated with one corner lower than the other was *not* because of the heavy fireplace in the corner, as I'd been told, but because there was water in the hull, which I had not been told. The seller explained about the whole act of god and seventy-mile-an-hour wind thing and said if I had a problem with that, I should talk to The Man Upstairs. I did and He told me to go see my attorney.

The lawsuit was put in motion and we waited. My attorney told me that if I could find the guy who lived in my houseboat for the two years before I bought it, he could testify as to the progressiveness of the listing and I could possibly reach a more favorable settlement. So I found the guy. In two days. Even though he had moved to a cave and changed his name.

After that, my attorney started hiring me to find people. We looked up the law and found I could be a skip tracer if I stuck to locating people through public records. I was doing that just fine when the Department of Consumer Affairs set me up by acting as a client and asking how I worked. I said through public records, which was the right answer. The shill on the phone then said since he was searching for a fifteen-year-old girl, that just wouldn't work. Finally he goaded me into saying I'd probably go talk to the neighbors. Soon afterward came the cease and desist letter.

Instead of ceasing and/or desisting, I took their silly little test to get my PI license and passed. By answering 101 multiple choice questions about how many folks it takes to be declared a riot, I was now able to interview people rather than just look them up in public records. When the clerk asked what I wanted my agency to be called, I inquired as to whether The Rat Dog Dick Detective Agency had been taken. It hadn't.

Immediately, I got on the mailing lists. Since I was specializing in the collection of court judgments—this was before I found out that wasn't possible—I looked for a book on that subject. When there wasn't one, I wrote it. First entitled *Take the Money and Strut!*, it was sold through mail order, mostly to PIs. It was then repackaged for the bookstores under the title

A Nasty Bit of Business, and later, *A Private Eye's Guide to Collecting a Bad Debt*. My first mystery novel, *Lily Kills Her Client* has just been completed.

People liked writing about "the detective who finds people like a rat dog finds rats," so I got some notoriety from programs like *Good Morning America*, *Larry King Live*, *20/20* and *The Oprah Winfrey Show*, as well as periodicals, such as *USA Today*, *Vanity Fair*, *Entrepreneur, Inc.* and *Money*. In 1993, King Features syndicated my "Ask Rat Dog" column. In 1996, I was accepted into Marcus's upcoming edition of *Who's Who*. Jack Olsen, an Edgar Award-winning true crime writer, is penning a book on one of my cases, due out in 1998; and I've even been asked to co-host a reality-based television program for Lifetime, depicting some of the adventures we've had around here. All because that darn houseboat sank back in 1982.

As for the agency, it's now a two-person operation; my trusty chief investigator, Ann Flaherty, has taken over many of the detecting endeavors, leaving me time to consult, write, lecture, play TV personality and count the money. We specialize in finding people—adoptions, lost loves, missing relatives, old friends, scoundrels—whoever needs finding. Our clients are people who know of us through various TV shows, the column or a local radio show on which I appear monthly.

Writing this book seems a natural outcome of that combined experience. In it, I've told everything I know of the elusive folks who have come to that point in their lives when they must be labeled "missing persons."

Glossary

To save time and space, certain terms have been abbreviated in this book. Others are colloquialisms used around our office.

PI = private investigator
MP = missing or misplaced person
MO = modus operandi
DOB = date of birth
YOB = year of birth
SSN = Social Security number
DL# = driver's license number

DMV = Department of Motor Vehichles

NCIC = FBI's National Criminal Information Center database

Scoundrel = an especially ornery or irritating MP

Him, he, his, himself, guys, fellows = same and/or her, she, hers, herself. I'm just not getting into that whole thing.

WHO MAKES UP THIS POPULATION CALLED INVESTIGATORS?

A woman once wrote me about her aborted love affair. It seems her boyfriend, Benny, had lost his job (and therefore his apartment)—both in short order. Benny claimed he could not continue their relationship as he was so distraught he was moving away. Yet months later, through friends, our heroine learned her ex had managed to meet and get engaged to someone else.

Sherry may have been a woman scorned, but she was not one without ideas. Against all odds, she tracked her ex-love to Arizona, alas three months too late. Two years later, Benny called and admitted he'd made a mistake and it was Sherry he loved and wanted, not some other broad. They talked for about an hour but then he forgot to call back.

So Sherry hit her ex's trail again. Calling his employer, she learned Benny was—yes, again—out of a job. She finagled his home address, but after never seeing his car in the parking lot, she concluded his new girlfriend had probably kicked him out. Her suspicions were confirmed when her certified/restricted letter was forwarded and Benny picked it up. Still, he chose not to continue the relationship.

After this admirable job of ratdogging, Sherry decided she should become a private investigator. Her question to me was whether the state licensing committee would give her credit for the two years of tracking she'd already done on the trail of hapless Benny.

And who would sign off her hours? The Ben Man?

Curiously, I get many such letters. People get such a kick out of their own lives that they erroneously assume someone else's troubles will consume them thusly. Now as much as I applaud turning one's own dysfunctional relationship into an interesting career twist, should our Sherry actually pursue this reckless dream, I fear she would surely find that someone else's doomed love affair isn't nearly as compelling as her own.

Still, Sherry has the kind of curiosity and persistence that makes a good investigator. Those who do the smart thing when choosing this field work for someone else, thereby insuring they'll get paid even on the days when the phone does not ring. The rest of us muddle through somehow, never really making the $40 to $150 per hour we claim we make because it's just too embarrassing—and useless—to turn in a time sheet declaring we looked for Benny for two years (that's four thousand hours times $95 per hour), and the bill is therefore $380,000. Please pay in thirty days. Thanks so.

Types of Investigators

We're everywhere—police detectives, FBI special agents, district attorney investigators, fire inspectors, private eyes. We all detect; some of us just get paid more than others.

Government Jobs

The best jobs in detectivedom are held by those happy souls employed by the government. The FBI, CIA, DMV (Department of Motor Vehicles), police department, city attorney, district attorney, public defender, public administrator, coroner and departments of internal revenue, welfare and consumer fraud—all of them hire investigators. These people get paid even when crime is at an all-time low. What makes them so popular is that the public astutely figures they are already on retainer via our tax dollars. A client *chooses* a private investigator over the FBI only when the FBI has told the client to go fish.

Investigative Careers Not Necessarily Requiring a License

Adoption searchers, information brokers, heirfinders, collection skip tracers, people who buy judgments—all of them skirt licensing requirements by restricting their activities to re-selling information without indulging in the interviewing, surveillance, car chases and shoot-outs we PIs are famous for. To insist these folks obtain private investigators' licenses would be akin to requiring a librarian to do the same before he headed to the stacks for a 1952 edition of *McCall's*. Of course, necessity often dictates these professionals occasionally step over the line and interview someone along the way, but then, hey, that's necessity for you.

Many PIs, myself included, consider *adoption searchers* among the best detectives working in the investigative field today. What other sleuths routinely find people without so much as a name to go on? They accomplish this through tedious hours of scouring public records and charge anywhere from nothing to a fair price and beyond for their efforts. Birth parents and children still suffering Sudden Birth Separation Syndrome are among the most impassioned consumers an investigator encounters, and often the searcher must counsel the patron not only through the process, but long after the case is solved.

Information brokering is a fairly new profession, whereby data is retrieved from an online service and resold to someone who has no access to that database. These guys are the tourist information of the intelligence superhighway and a resource PIs use almost daily to gain entry to some of the more obscure databases they just can't justify signing on to. Many times, in many cases, PIs themselves act as nothing more than information brokers for savvy clients, usually attorneys.

What *heirfinders* do is scour eye-blinding microfiche for names of folks due some amount of unclaimed funds worth the

PI's time pursuing. They then expend their own resources and energy searching for the beneficiaries and praying to God no other heirfinder locates them first. That task completed, the heirfinders then must cajole the would-be clients' signatures onto contracts and then worry whether said clients will actually cough up once the claims are delivered as promised. For this they charge anywhere from 25 to 50 percent of the take. Heirfinding, for some undeterminable reason, is considered by outsiders to be "easy money," primarily because of a book some clown wrote entitled *How to Make $100,000 in Fifteen Minutes Without Even Sitting Upright in Bed*, or something like that. It's not easy money. Heirfinding is a tough job requiring a combination of skills ranging from genealogy to skip tracing, and although big scores are possible, amateurs are crushed in the wake as competent searchers rush toward the lucky recipients.

The *skip tracing* of collection accounts is a specialty requiring a quick tongue and a heart of stone. Working usually without sophisticated databases (budget, I guess) the skip tracers talk their way along the trails of scoundrels—and then convince them to pay up! The debtors can lie, move and hide behind unlisted numbers, but the diligent skip tracers are right back at 'em. Rejection means nothing to these tough guys.

Bad debt buyers have it the roughest. What these folks do is pay cents on the dollar for court-awarded judgments that the creditors (astutely) consider uncollectible. What happens then, in theory, is that the new paper holders use their superior knowledge, techniques and persuasion to make these scoundrels cough up at last. What happens more often is that the debtors laugh loud and long, having now outsmarted two poor fools instead of just one. Guys who "buy paper" call me up all the time, claiming they make a living at this and asking we throw some asset work their way. Usually by the time I return their calls, they've quit the biz and gone into the heirfinder profession.

Investigative Jobs Normally Requiring Another License

Bounty hunters have developed the skill of finding out where a person is *right now*. Tracking a bail-skip requires that the investigator discover not necessarily an actual address, but which phone booth the MP (missing person) is standing in at that very moment.

Process servers are hired to hand over papers to some poor schmuck whose life is about to change. Often, however, the goose is already on the loose, and it is up to the sorry server to track him down. Step one: checking the contents of the mailbox to see if he's really gone or is just playing hide-and-seek; step two: canvassing the neighborhood for nosey snitches; and step three: checking with the U.S. Post Office for a change of address (*only* when a summons is to be served will the post office give out this information).

Repo persons are legalized car thieves. Ultimately, it is the auto that the finance company is paying them to find, not the driver, but of course, they often go together. Investigators start sorting out the erroneous information on the credit application. After that, it's a whole lot of gumshoeing.

Licensed Private Investigators

This is what the rest of us do when we don't have the years of training required for a government investigative job— or we have just retired from said government job and think now we can make the big bucks and we happened to have, in some way, qualified for the license.

What Kind of Person Becomes a PI?

Who makes up your local investigative population depends almost entirely upon your particular state's licensing requirements. In some, those who qualify might be restricted to retired police officers, folks who have toiled under another's license for three years and the like. In others, no experience at all is necessary for a would-be sleuth to hang out his shingle. In some states, an examination must be passed, the person must be at least 18 or 21 or 25 years of age, be a U.S. citizen or legal resident, have letters of personal recommendation, have a note from a psychiatrist, be "of good moral character," never have been arrested for a felony or certain misdemeanors, etc. There are as many individual requirements as there are states. For the specifics, see Appendix A.

The entire fabric of the PI population differs according to these restrictions, but no matter how stringent the rules for qualifying, in each state there exist a good deal of excellent investigators and an equal amount not so much. Regardless, there are certain *types* attracted to this field—good and bad—and I've done my best to portray them justly.

Ex-Cops, Ex-FBI and Ex-CIA Types

These folks frequently become private eyes because they have already completed the experience some states require in order to qualify. Assuming their skills are easily transferable, copper types often find without their two main databases—DMV and National Criminal Information Center (NCIC)—their tootsies have been knocked out from under them. Some then limit their activities to "gumshoeing"—interviewing, surveillance, etc.—and pay some computer-savvy colleague to get the other stuff for them. Smart guys catch on quick and acquaint themselves with the myriad of online services they've been denied during their years on the job, usually from their superiors' lack of knowledge or surplus of stubbornness rather than legal limitations. *Really* smart guys do that *and* retain a pal on the inside to pull the confidential stuff.

Macho Cop Wanna-bes and Macho Criminal Wanna-bes

They don't have the discipline to become cops nor the guts to pull off a stickup. Their answer to participating in this crime-riddled netherworld, therefore, is the wonderful field of detectiving. What's important to them is that they get to carry a weapon—preferably *not* concealed—and get to shoot at somebody once in a while.

I once knew such a guy. This colleague, a disgraced sheriff's deputy, snuggled into a case of mine at the eleventh hour when he smelled national publicity. To make a niche for himself, he waltzed into the SFPD where a friend of his was the investigator on the case and sashayed out with a copy of the "chronological," the internal official written report of the case, complete with statements of all witnesses, some of them anonymous informants. He then attempted to register the stolen document with the Writer's Guild so that when the made-for-TV-movie guys came a-calling, he'd be the guy with the rights. When the Guild rejected the document because it didn't fit into any of its categories (it wasn't a treatment, a movie script, etc.), this fellow tried to sell it directly to tabloid television. When that failed, he endeavored to peddle the *complete rendering of the murder case* to the defense! To this day, this disgraceful wart insists this is what PIs do: get information any which way they can and sell it to the highest bidder.

This mentality is flagrant among Macho Cop Wanna-bes and their first cousins, Macho Criminal Wanna-bes.

Ex-Skip Tracers, Retail Investigators, Reporters

They make excellent investigators as they have already, essentially, been doing the work for years. There are no other careers that so closely parallels a PI's day-to-day experience, yet Macho Cop Wanna-bes and Macho Criminal Wanna-bes (see above) lobby the state, sometimes successfully, to keep these folks from taking the licensing exam. Their contention is that the skip tracers' experience has done nothing to qualify them for investigative work or, if that doesn't fly, that every hour they've worked should only count for fifteen minutes.

Since I come from this category, I find this mentality—and it's subsequent reality—particularly appalling. There are so many specialties in the PI trade that one must ask, Why is it that ex-cops who specialized in criminal work should qualify when ex-skip tracers who concentrated on finding people shouldn't? Especially when finding missing persons is the most common denominator in all investigative work, criminal or otherwise?

Luckily, I was certified before such stringencies took place, as were a lot of other competent licensed investigators. But I suspect this category will be weeded out as time goes on, and we will be left with, simply, more of the above. Sadly, this category is a huge supplier of women working in the field today, so I expect a lot of them to disappear as well.

Investigators Trained Under Another's License

This is one of the largest categories to turn out licensed investigators. In California, it takes six thousand hours (about three years) of working under another's license to qualify for taking the private investigator's licensing exam. Since so many

PI services are one-man operations, such jobs are difficult to come by, and additionally, it takes a rare animal to stick it out for so long—especially if the fledgling operative happens to be assigned to suburban surveillance for that full amount of time. These factors keep licensed private investigators at a minimum, which is exactly why existing PIs lobbied to instigate such restrictions. Make it through this system and one has really paid his dues.

Midlife, Second Career Seekers

One fellow wrote that after his "friend" charged $1,200 on his Visa card, moved out of his apartment overnight, changed jobs and left no forwarding address, he gave a private investigator $700 to track down the guy. He provided the fellow's Social Security *and* driver's license numbers, and eventually his new address, employer and phone number as well. What the PI basically ended up doing was serving the court papers. After realizing how much of the work he'd done himself, this man then decided he had the makings of a good detective. Further, he had enrolled in a school that promised him an investigator's license upon completion. He asked for tips on advancing his career.

Oh, where to begin.

First, I figured his wife already covered the part about his ability in sizing up people—that embarrassing $1,200 mistake—so I segued right into how paying a private investigator $700 to serve a summons was roughly 900 percent over the going rate. Providing a Social Security number should have put this man's search somewhere in the $50 range. There can be extenuating circumstances, of course, but for 700 balloons, I'd be tempted to go out to Wrigley Field and dig up Jimmy Hoffa. To assume all PIs get $700 for laying paper is downright silly. Only the bad ones get that. The good ones get a lot less.

Also, a primary quality of a good investigator is knowing where to get *accurate* information as close to the source as possible. Had this man done that, I wouldn't have been the first to tell him one cannot obtain a California private investigator's license by attending an institute found advertised on the inside of a matchbook cover. Any legitimate school would have made it crystal clear that in that state, one needs six thousand hours working under another investigator's license, or in some other qualifying trade, in order to take the exam.

And, of course, one doesn't need to attend a school to get a job with a PI. Should one be "lucky" enough for that (a little PI humor) he should expect to be assigned a coffee thermos and regulated to the front seat of his car for the full three years. Forget working on a fascinating case; those puppies are snapped up by the guy with the credentials.

Once licensed, a PI's day is usually no more exciting than an insurance agent's. For this, the wages hover just below "slave," since if a PI were to charge what he thinks he's worth, 98.6 percent of his clients would run screaming from the room.

Specialties of Private Investigators

One reason I think requiring an aspiring PI to pass an examination is silly is because most firms are so specialized that their entrants could conceivably answer only a fraction of the questions.

Take me, for example. At the time I took my exam, I was considered an authority in the collection of court judgments, even though most of my endeavors had been successfully thwarted by "collection-proof" scoundrels. Armed with that limited know-how and the documentation supplied by the Department of Consumer Affairs regarding licensing requirements, I drove to Sacramento to take the test: one hundred questions, multiple choice, regarding rigor mortis and whatnot. Never in my judgment-collecting experience had I encountered rigor mortis, and if my career went as planned, I never would. I also had no knowledge of how to determine the cause of a fire nor the number of people necessary for riot conditions. That I passed, I owe largely to *Rockford Files* reruns.

My point is, there are really a lot of specialties.

Arson Investigators

These fellows can sort through a burned-out structure and come up with the very spot in which a fire started. Hopefully, this skill was learned via some previous fire-fighting experience, not some self-taught tendency. The investigation undoubtedly encompasses a lot of canvassing for witnesses, following up on physical descriptions, spotted cars, etc. The client is usually an insurance company and the goal determining *how* the fire started, as well as tracking down the offender.

Asset Locators

I began my private investigator's career by specializing in the collection of court-ordered judgments. Once I had thoroughly acquainted myself with the process, I wrote a book detailing how one could, in theory, use public access sources to discover another's whereabouts and assets.

As I continued writing, I found I could not shake this vague shame that I was penning a thoroughly dishonest book. Yes, I was expounding upon court-sanctioned procedures, but in reality—between America's red tape-tangled judicial system and its misguided adoration of privacy laws—a person cannot, in most cases, collect that money that is *legally owed to him.*

Embarrassingly, even though I am considered an expert in this field, our agency has garnished pitifully paltry sums and therefore no longer takes asset cases. While technically "asset locating" is a specialty, in truth, there are few PIs working in this field, and there won't be many more until it becomes a job that is doable.

The MPs sought after are obviously of the scoundrel variety, and it doesn't much matter if they're found or not because they have no intention of paying.

Bugging, Unbugging and High-Tech Surveillance Specialists

These people are having *waaaayyyy* too much fun to look for MPs. Still, they might have to do that once in a while if their debugging of a telephone divulges an unknown harasser. In states where Caller ID is unavailable, they might then work with the phone company to legally trace the calls. Or they might just hire someone a little less scrupulous to do it.

Child "Snatchers"

These investigators specialize in grabbing back a kid when the noncustodial parent takes off with him. First they must find the duo, often through the location of relatives or even by scamming school officials to open their records. Then comes the meat of the job: the real-life kidnap. Although this activity is technically legal, it is fraught with danger—both physical and legal. If the parent does not have 100 percent legal custody with no appeals pending, the investigator could be sued. Many, therefore, choose to *find* the child only and leave it up to Mom or Dad to snatch him.

Civil Suit Investigators

Finding and interviewing witnesses is a nice, simple, sane job. Or is supposed to be. Locating the bystander is just the preamble to what the investigator is *really* paid to do: getting the eyewitness to spill the beans. If the case is a car accident, the PI usually starts with the bare essentials—a name, old address and phone number taken down by the driver in the confusion of the moment—and his job becomes, simply, following the witness forward through time. If the litigation is a sexual harassment suit or some such, it might take developing a list of witnesses from the witnesses already found.

Criminal Work

Working for the defense. When I considered the PI trade, naively I thought I would be out there working hand in hand with the good guys to rid the world of scoundrels. Quickly I learned PIs almost *never* work with the prosecution, as district attorney's investigators must come up through the ranks of the police department. A good many are excellent, some are not, but almost all of them know how to pick up a glass without smearing the fingerprints.

Alas, that reduces private investigators to working for the defense, as defense attorneys are free to hire anyone they choose. Now, I'm not saying that every single person accused of a crime did the deed, but having seen what cops must go through before making an arrest, I can tell you right here and now, a great many of those who get as far as being indicted *did it.* This, of course, means that a PI who chooses to specialize in criminal work is going to spend most of his career trying to get scumbags off the hook.

Working for the prosecution. A woman once wrote suspecting her sister died at the hands of her husband of six months. She was convinced he had a violent past as well as a hefty life insurance policy on his new bride. Despite the fact that her former brother-in-law had threatened his wife with a gun and was now under a "5150" hold (whereby a "crazy person" is booked for their safety or the safety of others) at a mental health clinic, he had not been arrested. This was particularly disturbing since the possession of this weapon clearly put him in violation of an existing probation.

It is a sad state of affairs when an advice columnist has to address the issue of how to get one's friend's or relative's murder investigated by the authorities. Yet, increasingly, DAs are electing to not bring charges against people whom they know are guilty because the burden of proof is too great an obstacle to overcome, given their time and budget restraints. They simply have to pick and choose which bad boys they can afford to prosecute.

This unfortunate situation, fortunately, creates a business opportunity for the PI whose heart is set on criminal work. Citizens who can't get the cops' attention (when they have money) will hire a private investigator to put together a case just so the district attorney can see light at the end of the tunnel. Ironically, once a case is handed over to the authorities, the PI is often nudged out, as continuing his work is frequently construed as mucking around in an ongoing investigation.

Domestic and Child Custody

These cases involve a lot of surveillance and a little bit of identifying and locating. As often happens, the wayward spouse is suspected of witchcraft, drugs, philandering and/or pandering, and the poor PI is dispensed to sit out in front of the house and wait for the action to commence already. Once that occurs, the errant ex will hopefully meet up with a sidekick whose identity may or may not yet be determined. The car's license plate then becomes the "identifier" and the driver identified from that.

Insurance Claims Investigators

These are among the highest paid specialists in the business because they have steady customers and are actually paid for each hour they work. They might be inquiring into something as mundane as a workman's compensation claim, a torched or stolen auto or a vehicle involved in a staged accident. Or they might be looking for the suspect in a murder-for-profit scheme. In the case of the latter, the MP could be the assassin, the beneficiary or even the "corpse" who just happens to be someone else.

Missing Persons

This is what our agency does, the bread and butter of our everyday business, and probably the most common request of people in America today when it comes to investigative work. Still, maybe *once* in their lifetimes people feel the need to hire a private investigator: to find that first beau who's sounding pretty good right now; to locate a birth parent who left a hole in your heart; to track down that debtor you'd like to squish between your fingers like a bug. Because of this, even satisfied customers rarely return, which makes it pretty hard to build up a business.

Security Fellows

These folks stay up all night and watch the parking lot. Once in a while, boredom turns to terror, and then it's up to them to either grab the intruder or at least get a physical description and/or plate number. Somebody else actually finds the guy because if the security guard did it, he would have to leave the parking lot unattended, which most bosses would find unacceptable. In the case of the bodyguard, it would be optimum to grab the interloper *before* he becomes an MP.

Shoppers

They are paid to hang around department stores and make sure the money goes into the register (vs. all other options) and restaurants to make sure the bartender and servers are not making "cash or service violations." They *never* look for MPs, so there is no reason to further torture ourselves that they get to do this for a living and we don't.

Why Being Able to Find Missing People Is the Heart of Being a Private Investigator

Simply put, no matter what your PI's specialty, if he can't find people, he has no one to play with.

WHO ARE THESE MISSING PEOPLE AND WHO'S LOOKING FOR THEM?

By the time we got the case, the birth mother had already passed on. Like her mother and grandmother before her, she died of ovarian cancer, which could have been prevented if only it were detected early. Yet, none of these deaths had occurred, nor even been diagnosed, when this woman's child was adopted back in 1965. Which was exactly why her biological aunt was searching for her now. If only her nineteen-year-old niece were aware of her birth family's medical history, Auntie was sure this largely preventable disease could be halted before it claimed another victim.

Archaic adoption and privacy laws are just one of the reasons PIs are in business. People *need* to find other people, for a variety of reasons, and although the information is out there, increasingly, traffic on the information superhighway is moving so fast that most poor souls are just sitting on the shoulder waving at the passing busses. What they need is a taxi driver, someone who knows the curves in the road and can read the signposts, and that's where the PI comes in.

Who Is the Easiest Kind of Person to Find, and the Hardest?

The Easiest People to Find

- Men, because they do not change their names.
- People with unusual names, because then your PI doesn't have to wade through all the Richard Smiths in the world to find the one he's looking for.
- The recently missing, because it was just 1988 or so that computers came into wide use. When that happened, data began to be added, but hardly anybody went back and typed in any history.
- Property owners, business owners and other professionals, because the more paperwork someone creates, the better. For our side.
- People who don't stray far from their origins, because then one knows exactly where to look.

The Hardest People to Find

- Women, because many change their names when they marry.
- People with ordinary surnames like Smith and Thomas and common first names such as Mary and Thomas, because there are just too many possibilities to sort through.
- The long-gones, thirty-plus years, because the longer someone's been gone, the more time there's been to move, marry and disappear again.
- Scoundrels, because that's the way they want it.
- The homeless, because there is no place to find them.

The Two Categories of Missing Persons

Misplaced Persons

They aren't hiding; the clients just have no idea where they are.

- Women get married and change their names. When old beaux finally come to their senses, they have difficulty delivering the messages.

- Old friends get a(nother) life. Nobody says good-bye, certainly neither party realizes he might never see the other person again. It's just that one day one friend calls and the second friend isn't there anymore.

- Witnesses move away with no thought at all to the auto accident they observed years before.

- Heirs to unclaimed funds have no idea anyone's even looking for them.

- And yes, some people even go as far as to die.

None of these people are *necessarily* hiding, although they could be—from this situation or some other the client knows nothing about. For years we lowballed these cases, thinking they'd be simple. What we found is that nobody comes to a PI with a simple case, as today's savvy consumers have usually explored all economical options before calling in any professionals.

Missing Persons

These are a whole other story. These people don't want to be found or at least it must be assumed until there is evidence to the contrary.

- Adopted children often feel the need to find their roots before they can understand who they are. Sometimes the birth parents are thrilled, but in an equal amount of cases, they haven't told their new families of the "indiscretions."

- Birth parents may have been waiting for the child to grow up, or they may have long debated whether they had a right to look. Either way, just by virtue of the name change, these cases fall into the harder-to-find missing persons category.

- Family members may have lost contact through desertion or divorce. Siblings are often open to contact with fellow sibs since they rarely had a say-so in being pulled asunder, but as for the parent-child relationship, if contact was lost, then one party usually did so deliberately.

- "Scoundrel" is our in-house term for judgment-jumpers, deadbeat parents, con artists and killers. Because scoundrels' lifestyles demand they cut ties on a regular basis, these guys are experts at getting and staying lost. The result: a string of AKAs.

- Victims might desperately want to be found, but we're labeling them "missing" rather than "misplaced" because *someone else* is hiding them. Whether they're the casualty of foul play or the kids on the milk cartons, it's unlikely there'll be any sign of them in a computer database. To find them, the abductor must be found, and since these folks are high-level scoundrels, they're not easy to find either.

To begin the locating process, your detective should first determine if the person is missing or simply misplaced. If it isn't obvious from the client's story, then it shortly should be by analyzing the paper trail the MP has left along the way. Or conversely, hasn't.

Common Behavioral Patterns Show the Way

People don't change much. Even though they may move, their behavioral traits remain the same. They read the same magazines, live modestly or well, continue to get DUIs (Driving Under the Influence), evicted, married once for forever, many times or not at all. Most times, a PI can determine where someone's going by where he's been. And certainly, almost always, the PI can determine he's still on track by the pattern of the MP's paper trail.

For Example . . .

Take the case of Suki who was searching for her father who ran off with his dental assistant back in 1961. Rarely did the little girl see her increasingly secretive father after that, and the last time there was any communication at all was on a Quincy, Massachusetts, street corner when Papa told the teenager he was retiring and moving away. When he walked on down the street, Suki was crushed.

Now fifteen years later, all Suki knows of her dad is his approximate age and that his wife's name had been Marilyn.

Even though we could not identify the doc (more on that later; for now, all you need to know is that it requires a unique factor attached to the name, such as date of birth), we took the case. I don't know why. Maybe we needed the money.

Anyway, everywhere we looked, there were more Frederick Schmidts than we'd expected to find, many not distinguished by age or professional license. Seven 78 to 83 year olds were deceased nationwide, but without ordering their death certificates, there was no way of determining if the informant's name was Marilyn—the only thing that might have indicated this was *our* Dr. Frederick Schmidt. Had Marilyn preceded him, or if the marriage hadn't lasted, or if the death certificate was issued by a state where that record was not public access, we'd learn nothing from that costly experiment anyway.

There were thirty F. Schmidts in the nationwide phone disc, and sixteen others who owned property, none with a spouse named Marilyn. Without an exact DOB, our resources did not allow us to access driver's licensing records.

And so, without someplace to track Dr. S. from and no DOB, we were doomed to sift through every Frederick Schmidt we could find, eliminating all we could by age, income level and spouse—*when* that information was available by computer.

The most promising F. Schmidt proved to be a property owner in Florida, but this possibility was handicapped when we realized the address corresponded to a trailer park and disqualified altogether when he turned out to be a thirty-five-year-old gay antique dealer.

Finally we were reduced to phoning the remaining candidates and asking for Marilyn, reasoning only one Frederick would be married (past or present) to a woman by that name. Eventually, it worked, and a gravel-voiced, incoherent, loud-mouthed dowager who answered to Marilyn babbled something about how Frederick had been moved from the veterans hospital, but she couldn't remember exactly where to. No amount of coaxing, nor hint of financial reward, could make her sing.

As it turned out, Frederick had moved—immediately after his demise. Learning his date of death finally enabled us to identify him, alas two years too late for a reunion with Suki. But what allowed us to find him was eliminating all other Frederick Schmidts in the world by age, name of spouse and income level.

Finding Out About Someone Along the Way

When in Denver, staying with his Armenian-speaking mum in a tiny rented apartment, Joe was attentive and called Dolores daily. But when Joe went home to his Cincinnati mansion and his lucrative diamond business, he never put so much as a call in to the fortyish single welfare mom.

Joe referred to himself as widower, as his wife committed suicide leaving him with two teenage sons, now being raised by grandparents. He'd come a long way emotionally since finding her dead on the couch two years before. Now he had plans to move to Denver—ostensibly because of Dolores—and had even proposed marriage, although he'd never so much as kissed her.

Although Joe was very generous, there was this tiny voice inside Dolores telling her she was being scammed. Yet, if not love, what could a man with all this money possibly want from a single mom on welfare? she wondered.

And so, the assignment was to find Joe; not when he was in Denver, but wherever he lived in Cincinnati. Checking that town's real estate records, we found, of course, that the man did *not* own property there, nor did he have any corporations or Fictitious Business Names (FBNs) in that area.

Beginning again, this time in Denver, local courthouse records revealed a series of addresses that accounted for the last fifteen years of Joe's life. One previous residence was a mobile home still occupied by his ex-wife, very much alive and also looking for Joe—for reasons having to do with child support. Their 1979 marriage application listed Joe as a drywall contractor, and the two-year-old divorce decree claimed he had a monthly income of $1,200.

Voter's registration records indicated Joe was now living with a forty-six-year-old divorced manicurist. The Grantor/Grantee index showed she had recently mortgaged her $78,549 property for $49,000.

Obviously, Joe was not the catch of the century, but far more bothersome was the extent to which he'd lied. It seemed to me that the lying was clearly a precaution for some later date when someone would come looking for him—preferably in Ohio, rather than in Denver. But was that someone Dolores? Or, perhaps, an insurance investigator looking into the circumstances of their recently departed $100,000 insurance policy holder?

And so, by "finding" Joe, we found out far more. We found out what he was up to and perhaps even saved a life.

Gauging the Reception by the Paper Trail

Since the records one accesses in a search are tax liens, marriage license applications, lawsuits and other public documents, by the time your PI has finally caught up with the MP, the investigator will usually know quite a bit about the MP just by the litter of his paper trail.

Take Claire's case. She was searching for the pop who'd paid his child support for ten years, even though Mom had denied him court-ordered visitation.

When Claire was eighteen, she got up the courage to call her father's sister. The aunt told the girl her dad blamed her for not searching for him sooner and so would not want to see her now. The aunt said her brother's new wife didn't know about his first family and wouldn't want to. Being led to believe her father was in southern California, Claire ran personal ads there, searched through phone books and made countless calls to directory assistance—all to no avail. She even wrote her father, care of this aunt, asking her to forward the letter. The lack of response tore at Claire's heart for many years.

Was it true? Did Dad want no part of Claire, or was this just a judgment call on the part of her aunt?

Right away, the voluntary payment of child support, along with the ease of the search, indicated Dad might actually want to be found. In fact, Pops was in the phone book! No, not the California directories where Auntie had directed her, but in Texas, the state of his birth. Why would a man who was hiding from three grown children choose to have a listed phone number if he didn't want to be found?

But there was a negative factor here as well—and Auntie was her name. What possible motive would she have except protecting her brother?

And so, with some prodding, Claire did call and found a shocked and tearful father at the other end. No, he had not told his current wife, but he certainly would. And yes, he'd voiced his frustration to his sister, but that was all it was—frustration at having lost contact with his child. Now faced with the reality of his first daughter, telling his bride seemed like a small price to pay.

And so the indicators that gave conflicting signs as to Dad's feelings about a reunion ended up portraying them justly. Dad was ambivalent. Part of him wanted to be found, hence the phone book listing, and part of him continued to deny the painful breakup of his first family.

What You Don't Find Out Tells You a Lot

Ten years before, sixty-one-year-old Vera met Skip Danforth, an international banker who traveled the western states within the course of his work. Because he disliked flying, Skip drove his Cadillac convertible on his rounds. According to Vera, Skip was "distinguished, six feet tall, graying but bald at the top, well dressed, with light blue eyes, a gray moustache and a gold pinkie ring that spelled *love*." After two dates, Vera declared Skip "the one," and the divorced San Diego resident seemed devoted as well.

On their fourth date, Skip was supposed to come over and just "veg out." In the past, he had wined and dined Vera, and now she wanted to do something "homey" for him. Privately, she had even homier plans.

Until then, Vera never had occasion to call her suitor when he wasn't in Phoenix, but after his no-show, she realized she didn't even have his office number, let alone the name of his company. Now, after ten years to think, Vera considered that Skip might have still been married and had either been found out or had just started feeling guilty about it. Still, he could even have had a terrible accident; she just didn't know.

I wish I could say we found Skip and gave him a good tongue-lashing, but because we didn't—or rather couldn't—we did, in fact learn much about flyboy, by the lack of information that *should* have been there.

First, Skip did not then, nor did he ever, own a home in San Diego, something a majority of international banker types invariably do with their incredible wealth. Neither did he get divorced in San Diego County, not under the name of Skip, nor any other first name we could discern. He didn't vote there, nor did anyone of the Danforth clan recall any family member with a pinky *love* ring.

All this says Skip (how prophetic) lied about *something*—his name, his job, his marital status, that he was from San Diego or all of the above. Because we couldn't find a "hook" for Skip, it seems this dream robber made a clean getaway. And the con? I suspect it wasn't anything as sinister as Dolores's scoundrel had in mind. More likely, Skip just wanted a little company on the side, and when Vera looked serious, it was simply time to move on. The fact that he made himself unfindable from the very start spoke of his ultimate intentions.

He had none.

The Paper Trail Is Just the Skeleton of the Story

This is not to say that the paper trail can be relied on to tell the whole story, as there are many events that simply do not end up in the county courthouse.

Take the case of Adrienne's pop. Her parents had separated when she was a baby, and the kids went to live with him and his parents. They rented a house, were very happy and visited their mother every other weekend.

After a while some bad things happened (Adrienne wouldn't say or you know I'd tell), and the kids decided they didn't want to see their mother anymore. Regardless, she got custody, and none of the family ever heard from her father again.

Via his SSN, we quickly updated Pop's whereabouts, as of just four years prior, to a frightening east Oakland neighborhood noted for gangs, drugs and the absence of Rat Dog. Since nobody would answer his door and no one in our office would go over there at night, we segued into the letter-writing portion of the investigation. Alas, our correspondence to the building owner went unanswered even though we knew Pops had been property manager of this complex just before he dropped out of the computer databases.

We then attempted to locate the woman Pops left town with after that disappointing custody hearing in 1968. We found Carol had adopted his last name, indicating they'd married somewhere along the way. Her paper trail paralleled his, and when his came to a screeching halt in 1991, so did hers. Carol's death certificate from that year described her as a fifty-six-year-old housewife who'd succumbed to a stroke.

Finally, a year later, Ann Flaherty, my patron investigator of lost causes, came up with a Las Vegas address for Adrienne's father. Pops had no credit, the apartment manager told us he had no phone and a demographic database gave the neighborhood the lowest denominator on its rating scale. Still, Ann instructed Adrienne to write or even heroically fly out, cautioning her to be prepared for whatever shape her father was in.

I changed the names and wrote the story up for an "Ask Rat Dog" column, the point being how you could tell someone's present condition by his past paper trail. I would have gladly gone on believing that had I not heard from a San Jose dentist who recognized Adrienne's father by his circumstances.

"Jeff could have become a rich man, but he chose not to," he wrote. "Instead he has helped many people who could not help themselves, mostly folks he met while managing properties. He's lived with these people and understood their problems." The dentist told how Pops fought one slumlord for a new refrigerator for an elderly tenant and took another resident items from her apartment when she ended up in jail.

"Jeff mentioned his children frequently, always with that look only a parent can get. When Jeff called me last Friday from Las Vegas, I could tell he had been crying. Apparently, his daughter had taken your challenge and dropped by."

Adrienne then wrote to fill us in on the reunion.

"Who is it?" her father had called through the door.

"Adrienne."

Pops opened up and there his daughter stood, in her arms the same gift she used to bring him as a child, a man-sized box of facial tissues. Accompanying it was a picture of his very own parents.

He stared at them a long time before finally looking up. "What is your name?" he asked through tears, although Adrienne was sure he already knew.

And so, I was happily forced to change my perception of this man I'd never met. No, the paper trail did not lie, but neither did it tell the whole story.

T H R E E

PROFILE OF THE MISPLACED PERSON

Misplaced people are usually easier to find than scoundrels or victims because here you are dealing with just normal lifestyle changes and not conscious attempts to deceive on the part of ne'er-do-wells. At least in theory.

In reality, many people you'd think were just "misplaced" are gone because of some factor that either the client doesn't know about or simply has failed to mention, like the time Mom hired us to find her kid but neglected to disclose he was in the Witness Protection Program. People consider hiring a private investigator a pricey endeavor and so usually don't do so until they have exhausted many of the leads themselves. Because of that, our agency's Missing Person's Profile form contains a question asking what efforts have been made in the past, enabling us to determine what we're up against.

So who are these misplaced people, who's looking for them and what happens once they're found?

Old Boyfriend or Girlfriend

It seems a quite common occurrence to look back on that un-
complicated first love with a certain degree of reverence. Those
were simpler times, the only interval, in fact, in which many of
us threw ourselves into a relationship with utter abandonment.
From the pain of that early breakup, we learned to hold back a
bit the next time around, and the next time to hold back even a
bit more. What eventually happened, of course, was that eventually we were putting almost nothing into a relationship, and to
cope with that unhappy circumstance, the same was true of our
current mate. That being the case, why are we surprised when
our current relationship becomes nothing but a much watered-
down version of that magical first love?

Who's Looking

Two groups, really.

- Folks about to jump ship and looking for another ship on
  which to jump

- People whose first plans didn't turn out quite so hot, and
  now that they're alone, the ones they rejected, or who rejected them, are starting to seem like pretty viable Plan Bs

For Example . . .

Fifty-year-old Adam *really* wanted to find his high school
sweetheart, Brooke, circa 1960 to 1961. It seems that while
Brooke was graduating from high school in Colorado Springs
and Adam was in the Marine Corps in California, their impend-
ing marriage plans were being thwarted by the young man's
disapproving parents. Adam buckled to the pressure, and all
contact with his sweetie ceased in the fall of 1961.

Now, thirty years later, Adam enclosed an eloquent love
letter I was to pass along to his ladylove. "Every morning I rise
and greet you. Each evening I bid you peace," it began. Adam's
letter further stated he'd regretted the split for thirty years, that
he'd questioned his sanity for agreeing to the breakup and that
his life had become a vat of perpetual emptiness.

I loved this letter. I wanted someone to write me this letter.
I longed to see the hotshot who left me corsageless on prom
night suffer for three decades and grovel at my feet, begging

for forgiveness. And so, of course, I took the case.

As is often the case with clients, Adam had already done quite a bit of searching on his own. Every time he traveled back to his hometown on business, he inquired about Brooke. On one trip, he discovered her mother had passed away and learned her married name as of a few years ago. On another, he attended her school reunion.

Adam even visited the dime store where Brooke had worked and then contacted its corporate headquarters, asking for her Social Security number. After being turned down, he requested someone forward a letter to her last address. This guy had it bad.

My initial plan was to get Brooke's DOB off her marriage application and then run voter's registration records, DMV, etc., to determine where she was now and if a hubby resided at that same address. Instead, I learned Brooke did not tie the noose in Colorado Springs nor any of the surrounding counties. Other local documents revealed Brooke was the lady's middle name and that her first—the one used in all legal documents—was Kimberly. That break led me to Brooke's daughter, living in what Metronet, our demographics database, labeled an "E" neighborhood, the lowest denominator on their fiscal and aesthetic scale. Alas, she too had disappeared.

Now, usually, once a PI picks up a paper trail, he's home free. In this case, the address Brooke had given the DMV turned out to be a city park, and the library where she supposedly worked transferred me to the reference desk, but then the librarian cut me off and abruptly hung up.

Brooke was in hiding, I was sure of it. And certainly not from Adam because he'd never gotten close enough to spook her. I cautioned my client this might not be the same sweet girl, but our love-struck guppy had gotten a whiff of his object d'amour and wasn't about to back off. The romantic part of me said maybe this was one of those damsel-in-distress things, and the practical side said the client was still paying, so shut up and search. And so, I did.

The manager of the apartment complex across from the park claimed not to know Brooke, but she too melted when she read Adam's suck-up letter and took my number—just in case.

Well, call Brooke did, and I put her in touch with Adam who was winging his way to Colorado faster than you could say, "Fasten your seat belts. This is gonna be a bumpy ride."

Adam later phoned to say he'd presented the newly divorced Brooke with thirty-one roses representing their years apart, dined with her at a romantic candlelit dinner and then followed it up with a carriage ride in the snow. He'd even proposed marriage, an event that could take place just as soon as he dumped his present wife.

Hmmm.

Brooke's story was that she'd recently broken up with her employer and he was stalking her. That her boss would know very well where she worked was lost on Adam; he'd waited way too long to be off-put by a few major inconsistencies in his true love's tale.

A few months later, Adam phoned to say he and Brooke had broken it off completely. Apparently, the chaos evident from her paper trail permeated their short reunion, each episode always accompanied by some inadequate explanation from his ladylove. Heartbroken, he'd said good-bye to his high school sweetie and remained with his wife.

What was really going on with Brooke I never discovered, but I suspect she was just a scoundrel with a string of creditors after her. That happens a lot.

What You Seek Isn't Always What You Get

Adam's marital status should not have been a shock to me. As a woman, I know what it means when a guy gives you only a work number. Why did I think it would be any different for a detective assigned to find a man's lost love?

As for his seeking out of Brooke at this unhappy time of his marital life, that, as we've discussed, also was to be expected.

But as Adam found, returning to your first love doesn't reverse the jading of the human spirit. When he finally located Brooke, he couldn't help but notice that in the thirty-one years since they last met, she had become as damaged as he.

What You Do Get

A few years ago, I got weary of vicarious reunions and pledged to look up everyone—both male and female—who had been special to me at some point in my life. Now I'm best friends again with my best friend from college and my best friend from when I was four years old. (The childhood chum hasn't changed at all. It's as if someone put an air hose in her ear and blew her up.)

Although my current boyfriend nixed my schemes to find my ex-boyfriend, and my ex-ex-boyfriend and my ex-ex-ex-boyfriend, I've done plenty of this kind of thing for clients. If there's one thing I found to be overwhelmingly true, it's that the person you find is exactly the same person you lost however many years ago.

Duh.

What I mean is, what people liked about their old loves, they can still expect to like. If they were soul mates then, they'll be soul mates still. If he thought she was funny, he's going to still think she's funny. If she loved his thick head of hair . . . well, never mind.

But the reverse is also true. Whatever wrenched them asunder is probably going to break them up again. Look at Liz and Dick. Nuts for each other. Got married twice, and divorced, hit for hit. Never did get over each other, yet their second union lasted just a fraction of their first.

The truth is people have much less tolerance the second time around. And when some forgotten behavior results in déjà vu, the "I'm-outta-here" comes quicker in the latter go-around.

Lost Friends

What's the usual reception? Good. Much less is required of an old friend than an old lover. It's OK if he got married. It's OK—in fact, even preferable—if he now outweighs you. And he isn't required to look into your eyes, say how marvelously you've been preserved and offer to leave his wife to be your friend.

In the rare instance when friends don't want to see friends, it is because of situations like the story below. The lost one had embarked upon a journey difficult to explain, and he feels it best to let things just lie.

No Hope for Charity

We once had a client who seemed to have unlimited funds with which to locate a number of his old high school chums. Hope Charity Faith was his first endeavor, the "bad girl" from his junior year, the one who made mothers all over Chicago cringe and ground their teenage boys until they were forty.

In 1948, Hope dropped out and joined the Air Force. In 1955, she married a guy she met at basic training—she said— but since the ingenue was as much of a pathological liar as she was fetching in a poodle skirt, our client wasn't altogether sure the marriage had actually taken place. Regardless, he suspected the lady had had a slew of unions in her lifetime, which, of course, would result in several name-changes along the way. In the mid-1960s, Len learned Hope's father had moved to Los Angeles with her much older sister, Esther. Years later, Len checked out that address, but there was no sign of any of them.

Hope fell into one of the hardest categories of people to find: a woman who has had 3,141 counties and four decades in which to change her name. Frequently, when attempting to locate such a troublemaker, we look for, instead, a male family member, therefore eliminating the name-changing portion of our search altogether.

Hope was brotherless, but we were able to pinpoint her pop's passing in 1967 in Los Angeles County. His death certificate listed her still unwed fifty-year-old sister as informant. Citing a national magazine's research whereby a woman is more likely to be winged by a flying meteorite than to marry postmenopause, we ricocheted our search to the now eighty-year-old Esther.

Social Security's Master Death Index contained no record of her, neither under her unusual maiden name nor when we ran the first name of Esther along with her DOB. (Hey, meteorites happen.) Neighbors of the Los Angeles property claimed ignorance of the family even though it had been a mere thirty years since anyone had seen them out mowing the lawn. A national computer check on Esther brought more of nothing.

So where would this octogenarian be savoring her golden years? Recognizing that Westerners stay in the West and old folks go home or go south, we veered our search from southern

California into Arizona, and sure enough, there we found a 1980 voter's registration for Esther. A call to neighbors brought news of the lady's passing.

And what of her next of kin, we inquired. The Utah-based sister apparently whisked in and out without much to-do, claimed one fellow. In this chap's words, "She came. She liquidated. She left."

Now, although many states have determined dead guys have no right of privacy, Arizona still chooses not to show you anyone's death certificate but your own. Instead of my usual eloquent lecture, including the flourishing finish where I'm arrested for disturbing the peace, I chose instead to quietly study Esther's probate file the next time I visited Phoenix.

Esther's 1976 will left $10,000 to "my only sister, Kay, who is now married but whose name I do not know." Luckily, this multimonikered missy made amends posthumously when she swept into town, somehow finagled her sister's executorship away from a friend and claimed right to the entire paltry estate. To accomplish this, the mysterious lady gave up but one thing: Her name and address were finally recorded on a public document.

From 1988, we easily traced "Kay," and although neighbors confirmed her residence, she declined to answer our correspondence regardless of how we addressed her. And many ways we addressed her never made it onto the envelope.

All this confirms our motto. You can find 'em, but you can't make 'em write.

Witnesses to Auto Accidents, Civil Cases, etc.

These people casually gave out their names and then have the gall to go south. Years later, when an attorney requires their testimony, he can't find them, usually because whoever took down the information in the first place simply didn't get enough of it. Normally, just an inexpensive "address update" search will work, but many times a PI will find that folks who hang out on street corners are not the easiest people to find.

But then, finding a witness is how I got into this little game to begin with (see the Introduction).

Heirs to Small Fortunes

In every state, there exists an Unclaimed Funds Index consisting of folks due money from one source or another: a relative who died intestate, a forgotten bank account, a HUD loan benefit, whatever. Routinely, enterprising "investigators" scour these lists, and then—on their own time and at their own expense— present the heirs with contracts, promising to deliver the money for a percentage of the take.

Most times, heirfinders are forced to compete, each hurry- ing to find the missing beneficiary first. Arrive too late and they get nothing. Arrive in a dead heat and they are forced into negotiating with the heir, lowering their percentages to beat the competition. It's a gumshoe-eat-gumshoe world bearing little resemblance to the easy money they were promised in the pre- viously mentioned best-seller, *How to Make $100,000 in Fifteen Minutes Without Even Sitting Upright in Bed.*

My Own Personal List

Early cases, you might ask?

Well, shortly after going into business, I came across a recently defunct corporation that, after losing money for thirty years, had just sold its building and now had two million dollars to be divided amongst its stockholders. Trouble was, nobody knew where they were anymore.

And so I went to work on finding them, beginning, of course, with the chap owed the most money. Because I was still somewhat of an amateur, I simply went to the library and commenced scouring the mountain of southern California phone books until I found this fellow's distinctive name.

I called him up and gave him my pitch: I know about some money that you don't know about, and I'm holding it hostage until you promise to give me a big fat finder's fee. (Probably not my exact words, although they might well have been.) How much was he owed? $120,000. How much did I want? A mere 20 percent: $24,000.

Oh yeah, right, said the savvy stockholder. Is this about that old ship chandlery stock?

So much for leverage.

In the end we settled on $12,000, which I thought generous given he could have gone around me completely and I would have gotten nothing. All in all, not bad for an afternoon's work.

After that first big coup, I went to work on the rest of the lost stockholders, eventually finding all but two of the thirty, who, incidentally, weren't owed enough to make it worth my while to look. In this particular circumstance, I found the heirs belong to one of two categories.

- The old folks were very trusting, never questioning the hitherto unheard-of inheritance, signing most anything put before them and promptly forwarding a check to me upon receipt of their funds.

- A small minority of stockholders didn't question the windfall but resented me trying to make a buck off of it. (Guess they thought I should have found them for free.) They refused to sign the agreement and undoubtedly spent much time attempting to locate the source of the funds themselves. Since the stock was held by deceased relatives, their luck was not good. It has now been over seven years, and the money, by law, has gone onto the unclaimed funds list, ironically resulting in hoards of heirfinders beating down their doors, all armed with contracts, all happily informing them of their good fortune.

People Who Have Passed Away

So you're probably wondering how Hope Charity Faith's sister, Esther, managed to keep herself off that terrifically complete death index of Social Security's when clearly she was no longer walking around upright.

Compiled in the mid-1960s, the index contains about 85 percent of all deaths that have occurred since then. Who doesn't it mention? John and Jane Does, for one, since nobody knows who they are. In Esther's case, what's more likely is that she never collected benefits, perhaps because she received a teacher's or civil servant's pension instead, or she'd been longtime institutionalized or, simply, she never worked a day in her life.

So oftentimes, locating dead people is a whole lot harder than just accessing Social Security's Master Death Index. As with the finding of live persons, each case's circumstances are unique and, therefore, so is each solution.

Five Ways to Find a Dead Person

1. Social Security's Master Death Index is always the first place to look. There will be more on interpreting what you find—and don't find—in chapter eleven on public records.

2. Statewide death indexes contain everyone identifiable who dies within that state's borders. Trouble is, not all death logs are public record. For a complete list, see Appendix C.

3. Obits, coroner and news sources. Once your detective has identified the county where the person died, he can then call local funeral parlors, the coroner, even regional newspapers to see if the event was covered in a news story or obituary.

4. Veterans die, sometimes long after the battle is over, and when they do, often they are buried in national cemeteries. Calling (800) 697-6947 will determine if this is the case.

5. Another possible solution is to run the SSN or last address through an address update database. If the chap is deceased, the file should either indicate that or show who is now paying off the bills acquired during his lifetime, for example, relatives.

Finding Out About the Dead Through a Funeral Parlor

Sharon's grandfather was born in 1885, named Aaron and called Asa. In 1925, Asa married Sharon's Canadian grandmother and snuck her across the border in the middle of the night with the headlights off. When Sharon's father was six, the little boy's mom told dad to hit the road. She placed her two boys in a Sioux City orphanage, went to work and visited whenever she could. Charles, Sharon's father, recalls when he was ten, his father appeared at the orphanage with his new wife and tried for custody, saying he wanted to take the boys to his "new farm." Ultimately, he was refused.

Another time, Charles's mother took both boys to a park across from the orphanage and a man with a cart came by selling Yankee Ice Cream Bars. He sold them a couple of bars and kept walking. Later Mama told Charles that had been his father.

Several times during those years, Asa's wife put him in

prison for nonpayment of child support or alimony or whatever else he did wrong. Only when it became apparent his incarceration didn't help her cash flow any did she stop.

Until her death, Sharon's grandmother never waffled from her stonewalling of information about Charles's father. Now Sharon wanted to give her dad the details of his family history.

For once, something worked out just the way it was supposed to. Quickly, we located Asa in Social Security's Master Death Index, under his given name, Aaron, born on July 18, 1886, and passing away in December of 1968 in Fontana, California. We could have requested the death certificate from the county, but that would have taken a week and cost $8, so instead, our cost-conscious chief investigator, Ann Flaherty, whipped out a CD-ROM cross directory of residential and business listings and sorted the entries by funeral parlors in Fontana, California. On the second call, she sent a little lady scurrying into the basement in search of Asa's contact sheet. Arrangements had been handled by the public administrator, which of course, meant there was no relative nor spouse to manage the chore of Asa's passing. Final papers were signed by his niece, Thelma, of Sioux City, although his immediate next of kin was listed as his sons, Raymond and Charles, whereabouts unknown.

Now, thirty years later, Thelma had passed as well, but we did find her husband still living in the same house they'd shared in 1968.

John described Asa as a "rawboned" man, who, although likable, had no "stick-to-itive-ness." Likeable he must have been, for at least six wives (that he knew about) found him irresistible, and a few lady friends betwixt and between. As for a profession, Asa aspired to none, instead traversing the country taking odd jobs along the way. He visited Sioux City a year before he died, and Thelma and John heard nothing until the public administrator called with the news of his demise. Asa died as he had lived: broke and with his last lady friend by his side. He was cremated at state expense.

Of course, Charles knew better than to hope his father was still alive, but at last he was able to discern how he lived the rest of his life. And that was accomplished through the liaison with the funeral parlor.

The Coroner Tells All

In 1956, Alan and Irene were just beginning to fall in love. One night, after listening to records, talking and smooching a while, Alan ended the evening by announcing he was moving to Tucson. Irene was crushed, sitting several hours in a stupor after his departure. When she got up to go to bed, she noted it was 2:20 A.M.

Irene never saw Alan again, but in 1969, a mutual friend told her he'd been killed in an automobile accident. Then, in 1981, she was at a ski ranch and saw someone watching her from a distance. She looked up and was startled to see Alan smiling at her! Irene's first thought was, "He's supposed to be dead," and without saying anything, she hurriedly rushed away.

Obviously disturbed, Irene made a phone call to Alan's parents. His father repeated the story of the accident and said his son's body had been brought home for burial. When Irene asked what year, Pops called out, "What year was it Alan died?" and his wife yelled back "1968 or '69."

It seemed to Irene that if a couple's only child died, the year would be permanently engraved in their memories. Now she wondered, could Alan have feigned his own death because he was in some kind of trouble? When she knew him, he wasn't into drugs, although he did drink too much at times. She also recalled that once he had an accident on his way home from her place. Could someone have been killed and Alan fled manslaughter charges?

Irene was embarrassed about her need to know what happened to an old boyfriend from so long ago, but years afterward, she still woke up at that time, as if from a nightmare. She felt if she could make sense of his departure—and what happened later—she could put this tragic story behind her.

We first attempted to locate Alan via Social Security's Death Master File (always our first move in finding someone we suspect has taken a dirt nap) and found no record—not surprising since in the years from 1965 to 1969, only 25 percent of decedents under forty-five had benefits sufficient to make it onto the system.

Because Arizona's records are released only to family members, obtaining a death certificate was not an option, so instead, we called the Pima County coroner's office and found Alan's life had, indeed, been reduced to a $3'' \times 5''$ card.

"Death by natural causes. Alcohol level .46."

Sometimes, in investigation, as much can be deduced by what you don't find as what you do. There was no mention of an automobile accident, for example, meaning there was none. That story I'd chalk up to the parents' official explanation of their only son's less than honorable demise.

Still, I found "death by natural causes" a curious diagnosis, given the alcohol level in Alan's system. Fatality normally occurs around .35, at which time the body "passes out" and the imbiber simply stops breathing. "Forgetting to breathe" is not an uncommon condition; however, when it occurs in normal slumber, the body "snorts" and awakens itself. Dozing in a sitting position, which drinkers tend to do, creates constriction of the windpipe, which can be lethal. That Alan could actually have stayed conscious long enough to reach .46 can only mean his tolerance had been built up by years of excessive libation. It seems Alan's youthful "too much at times" had become a lifelong and fatal addiction.

Obviously, it was not a living, breathing Alan that Sharon encountered on the ski slope. Whether it was merely the glance of a chance admirer or some form of Alan come back to Earth, I'll leave to other experts. Sometimes our eyes tend to recreate what our minds cannot fathom.

PROFILE OF THE LOST FAMILY MEMBER

Family members lost through divorce, desertion or lack of contact make up a huge percentage of the MP business. No matter what the explanation of the disappearance, remaining family members—sons, daughters, siblings, moms and dads—find they can't let go until they can perform that act that has come to be known in our culture as closure.

When the Parent Is Looking

While in Vietnam, Al fell in love with and married Nguyen. The lady was not happy in Al's next post, Iran, so she took baby Sandy and went to live with her husband's brother in America. In 1977, the marriage finally went kaput, and she remarried and moved on. When Al returned to the states, Nguyen's mother-in-law would not disclose her whereabouts.

Because we had Nguyen's Social Security number, we

were able to ignore whatever name changes might have occurred throughout the years and cut right to her whereabouts. Quickly, we found her living with her fourth husband in Texas, and twenty-two-year-old Sandy residing there as well.

Fearing Nguyen might have spoken ill of him, Al, now working at Stanford, wrote his daughter a letter explaining how he'd come to lose contact with her and what he'd done to find her these fifteen years. He even went so far as to offer to pay her way through the university that was his employer (of course it helped that Stanford provided the siblings of its employees reduced tuition). Sending such a letter was scary, of course, since if there came no reply, Al would never know if his daughter received the correspondence and chose not to answer or never received the letter at all.

Almost as soon as the letter was in the box, Al's wife stepped in and made the call, handing the phone over to her husband. A shocked Sandy had time only to say she'd been told her father was dead and ask if he'd remarried and if she had any half-siblings before her stepfather took away the phone. He told Al that Sandy had no wish for a relationship and that he should not contact her again. When told of the Stanford offer, he declined *for* her, saying he'd already paid for the girl's college education. Faced with this hostile brush-off, a flustered Al agreed to let her go.

I cautioned Al to reconsider his hastily made promise. Sandy had had no time to assimilate the news of his aliveness, let alone all the other lies that might have been told about him. It would take some time to find the courage to defy the people she'd always trusted. Expecting this to happen during the course of a phone call was unrealistic.

It was also worth considering that anyone capable of telling a child her parent was dead might also be capable of lying about the extent of that child's education. And even if Sandy had already attended college, wasn't it up to her to determine if she wanted to pursue graduate studies at one of the finest universities in the country?

Al is still patiently sending Christmas and birthday cards, waiting for the day when Sandy will feel free to respond to his offer.

Will Sandy Come Around?

Our unofficial research says yes. While, oftentimes, a parent can dismiss the concept of bonding, a child's craving to know he was loved by the parents who bore him can not as easily be ignored. More often than not, he simply *must* know the circumstances of his genesis and find some explanation of his parents' absence, whether it be because of adoption, divorce or desertion.

At twenty-two, Sandy is still awfully young to have to deal with such a dysfunctional stepdad, but in time, I believe she will. Until then, her biological father's job is to remain findable so he'll be there whenever she is able to work her way out of this stupor.

When the Offspring Is Looking

Three years before, Ginger's forty-year-old mother had "literally vanished into thin air." None of Marianne's close friends had heard from her, and Ginger just couldn't fathom she would walk away from the four-year-old grandchild she adored. Now that the young woman was engaged to be married, she wanted her mother to meet her fiancé.

The DMV showed Marianne had a current Michigan chauffeur's license with no accidents for the past five years. Was she merely a safe driver or did she no longer drive at all? We had to wonder. Voter's registration records yielded only that Marianne wasn't civic-minded of late; and her credit header revealed nothing but familiar past addresses and a partial one Ginger did not recognize.

Checking back with our client, Ginger now admitted Mom had had some past trouble with the law. Nothing serious, but she was afraid if she told us, we wouldn't have taken the case.

Well, she was right. Just as writers specialize, perhaps in copywriting, penning novels or covering the news, so do the finders of missing persons. Because our databases consist of public records, they work best when finding people who own property or corporations, vote and the like. And since misdeeds can also end up on record, DUIs, lawsuits and evictions can lead to a low-grade scoundrel as well. Not so for a victim of foul play or an AKA-laden criminal, as we were now learning was Ginger's mom.

But these were the days before we put the big disclaimer on the Missing Person's Profile form that stated that if the clients lied to us, we were keeping the deposit and telling them to get lost. And so, we continued on.

Contacting the Michigan State Police, we learned that in 1979, Marianne had been found guilty of a nonsexual assault and fined $100. The docket also provided a physical description of her at that time: 5'2" and 245 pounds. We figured she'd couldn't be moving that fast.

We did a whole lot more, but what finally broke the case was recreating that partial credit header address via the post office's Zip Code Directory. That done, a marketing database indicated "Tillie" was the three-year occupant of that "E" inner-city Detroit, single-family dwelling.

And so we sent Ginger drudging on down there with instructions not to believe Tillie if she told her she'd never heard of her mother. They were having exactly that discussion when her 350-pound mama waddled up.

After a tearful reunion—tearful because Marianne wanted nothing to do with her daughter—Ginger departed. Dirty and on drugs, Mom insisted she liked the life she'd chosen and knew exactly where to find Ginger if she ever changed her mind.

Is This Case Typical?

Sadly, yes. Finding lost family members is never simple, and there is *always* more to it than the client will admit. Parents, kids, brothers and sisters do not just walk away. They escape from dysfunctional families, always mindful that someone will someday come searching. Or, like Ginger's mom, they have troubles of their own.

How Can Parents Just Disappear?

In my years of finding MPs, I've found there exists a bond between parent and child that, while often denied, can seldom be dismissed for an entire lifetime. Sooner or later, a person who finds himself on either side of this equation feels compelled to look for the missing link.

Now, since a child's life is fairly uncomplicated, this bond is extraordinarily clear. Unfortunately, life does not remain un-complicated for long, and so, consumed with an adult's world of disappointments, a parent can lose sight of what's working—that innocent bond he shares with his child.

When that happens, parents (most often, dads) frequently remove themselves from their unhappy unions. There are *so many* things wrong that no matter how he has thus far dealt with it, now his best option seems simply to remove himself from his environment. Sure, he'll miss the kid. But at least that will be his *only* problem.

In theory, this allows a person to start anew, in a world where life is again sane and simple. To justify abandoning a child, a parent must convince himself that because this works just great for him, it also works just great for his kid.

Often the runaway parent is right. Maybe if he stayed, he'd end up predestining that child to grow into the same tortured soul he is. But what parents who desert their youngsters discount is that children have not yet hardened into emotional stoics. In the kids' minds, what's crystal clear is that they belong with their mommies and daddies, and that gut-level wisdom doesn't go away just because it would hurt a whole lot less if it did.

What I Learned From Oprah

In 1994, I had the opportunity of appearing on *The Oprah Winfrey Show* and attempting to teach America at large how to locate long-lost loved ones. The point of this program was not only to tug at some heartstrings, but to demonstrate to folks how they could do this themselves, thus giving the show's producers a respite from the daily reunion requests they received.

In preparation for the program, I had counseled the produc-ers as to which requests to choose in order to obtain the maxi-mum number of reunions:

- MPs who might still reside in the county

- Old friends who had simply moved away

- Folks we had good identifying information on

- Nobody gone for more than two decades

- No criminals or ne'er-do-wells

As a detective, my objective was to find as many people as I could within the time constraints I was given.

The producers' objective, however, was to push the sweeps ratings through the roof, and that meant finding the most long-gone people imaginable and bringing 'em on home to Oprah. Good television, lousy week in Chicago.

Against all odds, between the producers, the participants and myself, we managed to facilitate almost twenty reunions. The added bonus for me was, for the first time, I got to witness firsthand those raw emotions that happen when the clients finally meet the people they've been searching for, sometimes all their lives. The show was indeed a tearjerker, and people who meet me still recall seeing it.

But there was another sensation I came away with, one I'd been formulating for some time and simply crystallized in this intense environment: that most of these happy reunions probably would not remain happy for long.

That the dads who'd deserted their kids had been booted out by moms tired of their drinking or clobbering and had spent much of the time since, settled on a bar stool, picking fights with the guys seated next to them. That the sister who'd moved away simply had no need for family ties, and given time, she'd probably wander off again. That the young traveler wrenched from his girlfriend's grasp when he was thrown in a French jail for smuggling drugs onto an airplane just might not have gone on to Harvard.

There on the *Oprah* show, the lights are as warm as the hostess. It's a wonderful place where happy endings do come true. The only trouble with the show is it only lasts an hour.

When a Sibling Is Looking

In 1932, Marjorie's twentysomething sister left her northern California family to find work in Long Beach. Enid was a divorced mother of two, a good mom who'd never have abandoned her children. She promised to write and, whenever possible, send money for the children's upkeep. After several months, the family received a letter with some cash in it. In it, Enid asked, "Did you get the other money? Why haven't you written?

Don't you want me to come see the children?" She failed to provide a return address. Because they were in the midst of the depression, Marjorie's folks had taken in two very shady boarders and she was sure they beat the family to the mailbox and "whoosh went the letters." Along with the money, of course.

Shortly afterward came the big Long Beach earthquake, and the family never heard from Enid again. Her name never appeared in the papers as being injured or killed, and although a police detective friend of the family spent months looking, he never found the lost sibling.

Enid fell into every category of persons most difficult to trace:

- A woman who had six decades to remarry and change her name

- Someone whose own family doesn't know her whereabouts

- A person who likely died before Social Security's Master Death Index was compiled

- Someone who possibly died as a Jane Doe in a natural disaster

We tried the obvious: the Master Death Index, the state's death index, marriage records from the 1930s and 1940s and Long Beach newspapers from that same era. Alas, it was just too long after the fact to do much.

It's Not Their Fault

No, really, I mean it. Parents have no excuse for not immediately searching for an offspring, no matter what that kid's age. Since they are usually claiming to the PI that there are no extenuating circumstances, the question must be asked, Why did they wait so long?

But with a sibling-to-sibling search, the searchers are absolved of that responsibility. They were just kids. How did they know how long was too long? If their moms and dads hadn't panicked, why should they? It's only when they get an adult's eye view of the situation that they realize that if they want to be reunited, it's up to them.

Adopted Children and Birth Parents

Sometimes they want to be found; often they don't. Now that the social taboo of bearing an illegitimate child is over, many women who gave up their kids are anxious to seek out their companionship and/or forgiveness.

Or not. Oftentimes, the biological mom or pop is convinced his life will be ruined if this young stranger comes to call. Sometimes he's so far into denial he's refused to consider the possibility. Whichever way it goes, every one of these reunions is sure to create a lot of emotion on somebody's part.

When the Birth Parent Is Looking

While still in the hospital, a nurse inadvertently told eighteen-year-old Betta her newborn's adoptive parents' names and address. Betta memorized it immediately, and every year she would look in the telephone directory to see if the family was still there, content just knowing where her daughter lived.

Then eight years later, a friend bought a house across from where the adoptive family resided. Whenever Betta visited, she would time it so she could watch Stacey walk home from school. The birth mom felt very lucky. She had two beautiful children under her own roof and could catch a glimpse of her first child from time to time.

When Stacey was twelve, Betta saw a television show about how difficult it is for adopted children to find their birth parents. On impulse, she called Stacey's adopted mother and told her where she was—just in case Stacey ever asked.

When the adoptive mom recovered from the shock, she asked Betta if she had asthma. That confirmed, the woman started screaming about how many times Stacey had been taken to the hospital and even accused Betta of keeping her baby's hereditary condition a secret. She then told Betta that if Stacey ever so much as asked about her, it would be the child's walking papers. Betta was devastated. For years she had fantasized that her daughter had gone to a loving home, and had even bought into the myth that everyone who adopts a child does so because he will love that child unconditionally.

When Stacey was eighteen, unmarried and with a child of her own, her adoptive mother finally relented and revealed

Betta's maiden name. Stacey met her younger siblings, and everyone was one happy family until the day she told her biological mom she was pregnant for the second time. Because she was so young, unmarried and couldn't control the child she had, Betta suggested an abortion.

And that aborted this fledgling mother-daughter relationship. While Betta respected her child's privacy and let Stacey cool off, the girl quietly moved away and got an unlisted number. Although Betta had her DOB, California had already closed its DMV records to public searching, and so, although she desperately wanted to reestablish contact, she just didn't know how to go about it. Luckily, we were able to do that for her.

Stacey's reaction to her mother's suggestion was not altogether surprising, considering the circumstances. Her entire life she'd faced rejection—and the threat of rejection—from her adoptive mom, why would she expect her biological mom to be any different?

Many experts agree that adopted children live out their lives in an extremely fragile emotional state. These experts say bonding begins in the womb and that children cannot help but experience "separation syndrome" when taken from their birth mothers. Unbelievably, an extraordinary number of serial murderers were adopted as infants.

When the Adopted Child Is Looking

Angela's mother could never understand that her adopted daughter's need to know her birthright was not because she required another mother, but just to comprehend what made her tick. Even fifty years later, any mention of exploring her roots made the older woman crazy.

Angela wanted to search but had a lot to lose. Since she'd been adopted into an extremely wealthy and famous southern California family, if her birth mother was crazy or homeless or ill, she didn't want her disrupting her life or making demands on the family fortune. Angela was insistent that her adoptive mother not know anything until she could determine if the two families would mesh.

The first step in an adoption is always to write to the state for "nonidentifying information." Although the names of the parents are withheld, this data—their ages, ethnicity, professions, birth states, etc.—is released to the adopted child upon request. From Angela's data, we learned that at the time of her birth, her mother was a twenty-one-year-old office worker, born in California of Dutch-Irish descent. There were no details on Dad, except that he'd known Angela's mom just three months and was unaware of her predicament.

Through exhaustive matching of public records, we found Angela's mother's name to be Madeline Marie Benning. We found no Madeline M. Benning, nor "Baby Girl" Bennings, born in California during the right time frame, which indicated the clerk had either incorrectly written down the information or Madeline had flat-out lied on the fifty-year-old form.

With no choice but to continue believing in the accuracy of the other data, we researched California's marriage index from 1949 forward but found no Madeline Bennings of the proper age marrying within the state. Earlier marriages were searchable only by writing to Sacramento, but our diligence paid off: Madeline had married, in 1948, a John Harrison Sweet. This Madeline matched the nonidentifying data exactly, except she was born in Kansas. Quickly, we located her in Virginia, still married to the same guy.

At Angela's request, I flew east to check her out. Local courthouse indexes showed no judgments, lawsuits or other negative public filings, so I moved onto the ancient newspaper office and scoured its extensive newspaper "morgue." There I found Mrs. Sweet was quite active in the Republican Party, a society wife and active as a charity organizer for the local Heart Association. From all accounts, Madeline had integrated nicely into the life of southern belle and local community matriarch.

Three full days of surveillance indicated the couple was out of town and the proud owners of timer lights. After discreetly determining from one married son when Madeline would return, I broke out the tent and went camping in Appalachia.

In the mountain quiet, it was impossible not to ponder the magnitude of the news I was about to deliver. Did Madeline's husband of over forty years know of the child she gave up for adoption? Would my phone call be the scandal of this small town? Or would it be the call Madeline had been waiting for all her life?

"Mrs. Sweet? May I have a moment of your time?"

"No."

"You don't have just a minute?"

"What are you selling? MCI?"

"I'm not selling anything. I'm a private investigator, and I have a client who has hired me to find you."

Madeline showed very little, in fact, *waaay* too little—interest in my client. She simply said she didn't know any Elizabeth Ann (Angela's birth name), told me I had the wrong Madeline Sweet and hung up.

Frankly, I was shaken. I'd traveled three thousand miles on the client's dime to investigate the wrong woman! In a panic, I called Kate Burke, our world-class adoption expert, who calmed me down and pointed out that what Madeline *didn't* say was more telling than what she had. Did she ask Elizabeth Ann's last name? Wasn't she curious about why I'd told her the younger woman's DOB? Did she inquire where she might have known this person from?

Kate insists such denials are not uncommon among the "ambushed," especially when approached by an intermediary. She reviewed the paper trail and assured me that I conclusively proved Madeline was indeed the birth mom.

It took almost a year—and contacting every other member of Madeline's family, aside from her husband and children—before the naughty mommy would concede she'd given birth back in the 1940s. By then, Angela had established relationships with most of her aunts and uncles, not one of which—despite their sister's vehement denial—ever doubted Angela was their family member. The relationship Angela enjoys with her new family is priceless to her, but she and Madeline have still not spoken. And Angela doubts they ever will.

Family Myths

Many times a PI is presented with stories of heritage that have been told for so long there is no doubt in the teller's mind that these tales are true. They are presented as fact for the PI to investigate, as is, and no proof to the contrary is welcome or acceptable.

Why this phenomenon? Two reasons, really. One is the clients trying to make sense of why they are "how they are." The second, the need to believe they are more unique and special than their ordinary lives would indicate.

Space Bubble Syndrome

When Frank was born, his father came rushing home, all night by train, arriving just in time to see his newborn taken from the delivery room. When Mom came to, she asked Dad what the baby looked like, and Pops said, "It's a boy. He's a big baby with gobs of dark hair and looks just like his sister." However, when they brought the baby to her, Mother saw that not only was his hair light, he barely had any at all. Additionally, Frank was small and looked nothing like his sister. That Frank was switched at birth has become the family joke, told throughout the years.

Now Frank's wife had come to believe this was true. Correctly she noted that all Frank's family were tall, dark-haired, big-boned people, and he was shorter, blond and slim. They were workaholic, executive, type-A personalities, and Frank was a photographer with no aptitude for finances. While his family was busy chipping balls at the country club, her husband sat pondering environmental and social issues. Frank was self-reflective, almost self-absorbed, and the rest of his family found deeper matters uncomfortable.

Faced with these conflicting family traits, Mellie began to realize that her husband struggled with the same concerns that plagued adoptees, issues like belonging and abandonment. Frank frequently described himself as "being out in space, in my own little bubble, watching the spacecraft disappear" and had been in and out of therapy, for no apparent reason, ever since he was a teenager. Now Mellie wanted to find her husband's "real" parents.

Of course, the ultimate answer would have been DNA testing, but we could think of no good way to get tissue samples from Mellie's in-laws without them noticing. Our next best plan was to have Frank request his hospital medical records, in person, something he could do and we couldn't. While he was there, he was able to peruse the hospital log, a register of infants born on that date, along with their parents' names. He found the only other child born that day to be a baby girl.

Even though Mellie was wrong, she was also right. Adopted children routinely experience a deep sense of loss, which is neither avoided nor eliminated just because the child believes the people he lives with are his biological parents. Still, it was unlikely her theory would prove to be true since, statistically speaking, there are simply a lot more people experiencing "space bubble syndrome" for no apparent reason than there are children who are switched at birth.

Like Something Out of a Fairy Tale

The third twin story is the talk show idea from hell. The scenario: there are two seven-year-old twins who are happily futzing around the playground. Across the yard they see a little girl who looks exactly like them. Before they can go play with her, she is whisked away by her mommy. Very suspicious!

Later they learn that when they were born, the doctor heard a third heartbeat. Mom went under, the preemies came out, and when everybody awoke, there were only two kids and Dad wearing a strange smirk on his face. The twins, now grown, insist that their cash-strapped alcoholic pop sold the third child because he couldn't afford her care.

Oh, what a segment! Every reunion season, Thanksgiving to Valentine's Day, one luckless producer tries to get me to locate this missing triplet. It matters not that the twins were fraternal, so the little girl who looked "exactly like them" didn't look *exactly* like them at all. It also doesn't matter that for Pops to have done this, he would have had to line up an instant conspiracy team involving the entire hospital, including a handy baby buyer who just happened to be waiting in the lounge. It didn't even matter that the twin's birth certificates clearly stated, under Multiple Births, 2 not 3.

Yet, this is the kind of story that pops up when people recount the circumstances of how they came to be. All people want to feel they're special, and if they have accomplished nothing to distinguish themselves, they often refer back to their very famous and/or rich relatives or to some magical birthing incidents that, right from the get-go, set them apart from the rest of us. The actual stories are always unique and entertaining, but rarely are they true. What is true is that the tale-tellers are just as ordinary as the rest of us.

F I V E

PROFILE OF THE SCOUNDREL

People who are missing on purpose are harder to find than the misplaced because that's the way they want it! To this end, they live their entire lives practicing deception and avoiding detection. Often they are proficient at such eluding tactics as altering the spelling of their first and/or last names, omitting or changing their middle initials, transposing their Social Security numbers and/or fudging on their dates of birth.

Whether the scoundrel qualifies as such because he has broken society's laws or because he's avoiding the payment of child support, the rogue still relies on the same methods of duplicity and the searcher still seeks him out in the same manner.

Thankfully, the rottener the crime, the less people out there committing it. There are less hardened criminals than deadbeat dads, for example, even though the former get a lot more press. And a typical PI's caseload is heavy on the judgment-jumpers, not so much on the serial killers.

So who belongs in this collective group of scoundrels, where did they come from, how do they operate, who's looking for them and what happens once they're found?

The Genesis of a Scoundrel

Way back in kindergarten, most of us learned the ugly truth: We weren't the smartest kid in class, nor even the most fetching. Luckily, we lived in credit-loving America, and that put most of us, more or less, on equal footing.

While still in high school, we got our first jobs, slinging hamburgers, loving it and making more money than we ever dreamed possible. By the time we graduated, we were on a first name basis with MasterCard.

We wrote them, they wrote back, and before you could say, "Charge it!" we were in business together. Suddenly that minimum wage job was just chump change; the really big stuff—the stereo, the rollerblades—we just put on plastic. Having a thousand dollar credit limit was like having a grand in the bank.

Then MasterCard got a little testy. The collectors actually started calling up instead of just sending out the bills. Now all they wanted to talk about was what they called "the outstanding balance." *Yeah, like they needed the money.*

Sure, if all of us had all the capital we required, we'd pay all our bills, but let's face it, we don't. Trouble is, we still want all the stuff. So what we do is we get the stuff, and then we tap dance on the telephone, paying everybody a little something so nobody gets too mad.

And that's how scoundrels get started, just like the rest of us. It's a stage many people go through, and if they're lucky, they learn to monitor their own behavior before somebody else does it for them. If not, then often they graduate into full-fledged scoundreldom.

Civil-Minded Scoundrels

I once had a partner—heck of a good sport she was—who, for a short time, slid us both into the lathery world of scoundreldom. We started a business that didn't quite fly. We paid our bills, just barely, but soon we found we couldn't pay every single bill every single month. Cindy's answer to this was to put all our outstanding invoices in a big pile and wait. Since I was busy with my own end of the business, I failed to notice.

Anyway, soon the bills weren't arriving in black ink anymore; they came in various colors, usually including some shade of red. Now, when a creditor called, Cindy's response was to ask indignantly, "Well, did you send us a *final* notice?"

After a while, Cindy had way too many red notices to be impressed by ink color any longer. From then on, she paid only those that came attached to a summons. When I went off to the Dominican Republic and left the balance of my MasterCard in her care, I was reminded of that fact for the entire four years it took the dun to disappear from my credit report.

Judgment-Jumpers

Some people's endeavors just seem slated for disaster: Their claims are inflated from the start, their deals destined to flop, their penny stocks not worth nearly that. Whether such "business opportunities" are thrust upon the unwary for purely fraudulent purposes or just because the presenter is inept or misguided, it hardly matters. Bottom line: Somebody gets taken, somebody else gets sued and, many times, the second somebody has taken off for parts unknown.

Since a ten-year court-ordered judgment can be renewed well past infinity, staying lost is a lifetime commitment for these folks on the lam. Of course that means anybody else who's looking for them—that prom queen from high school, Publisher's Clearing House's prize patrol, the son of a one-night-stand—is in for a tough search as well.

A True Story

I once had a client I'll call Robert Whalen (you know who you are) who bugged me until I agreed to follow his wife. That made me mad to begin with, since I personally think wives ought to be able to do whatever they want without their husbands following them around. (If that's a problem, then I'd suggest a marriage counselor, not a detective.)

Anyway, Whalen guilted me into doing this job by evoking our "friendship," which meant we had both once worked in the same building at the same time. I recommended another private investigator, but he demanded a retainer, so Whalen came back to me. Since Dolly was due to cheat the next day, there was no time to get me any money, claimed Whalen.

My first clue should have been that he never mentioned money to begin with. I mentioned it, of course. Said I wouldn't do this for my best friend, and in fact, my best friend wouldn't dare ask me to sit in a parked car all day long and watch a pretty ugly building. Whalen didn't get it. He wasn't a man for subtleties.

So I did it. And lo and behold, the guy she was "cheating with" spent his entire lunch hour in the backseat of his car with someone else.

That week, no money arrived, and the next Wednesday morning Robert Whalen called again. Oops! Forgot to mail the check. Well, he'd get me "something" this week. But I had to go out again *today*. Whalen was much too distraught to discuss money any further.

When Whalen called the next Wednesday at 6:30 A.M., he was frantic. He was sure his wife was going to cheat on him *that very day.* Only I could help him. He was getting ready to "make his move." And the money? Whalen promised he would get me "something" by the fifteenth.

Sorry, Whalen, if she really is an adulteress, then she'll be doing it again next Wednesday. You know next Wednesday, don't you? It's the Wednesday *after you pay your bill!*

Well, February 15 came and went, and then March 15 came and went, and so did the case in small claims court. Robert Whalen didn't show up, and after enduring a dirty look from the judge, who apparently didn't think Whalen's marital problems were any of my business either, I got a default judgment.

Only after attaching his wages did I hear from Robert Whalen. He really wanted to pay me, but he was being laid off and was declaring bankruptcy. The only reason he was holding off on finalizing the bankruptcy was so he could pay me off first.

Just after that, Whalen quit that job, and I was left again

to track down another place of employment. So far, I have spent three times as much time investigating my former client as I did tailing his faithful spouse.

Deadbeat Parents

These are rarely the target of a working PI. Those noncustodial parents who enjoy societies niceties—having a driver's license, using credit cards, owning property—must pay their child support to continue that lifestyle. Those who don't are the under-the-table folks who have reconciled themselves to existing in an underground economy in order to avoid this debt. In these cases, the custodial parents must rely upon the district attorney for whatever relief they can get as rarely do they have the money to track down their ex's unfindable funds. And no thinking PI would do it on contingency.

The Way Things Are

As of this writing, all states are in the process of compiling fully automated database systems, aggressively linking every state and federal agency imaginable, solely for the purpose of the collection of child support. When they have done so, there will exist a nationwide network that will make Big Brother look like Baby Huey. Since interest is accrued annually, the longer it takes a deadbeat parent to figure out he's *doomed*, the worse off for him. And no, there is no statute of limitations to outrun. Going on the lam will be a lifelong commitment.

Here's what will happen to anyone who chooses the life of a child-support scofflaw.

- If he has a driver's license, it will be revoked. If he applies for one, he will be refused.
- He will not be granted any state-issued credential, including a professional or commercial license.
- A lien will be placed on any property he now owns and the debt satisfied before he sees any of the proceeds.
- Since all three credit reporting agencies will be apprised of his debt, it's unlikely any bank or department store will welcome his credit trade. He may also have trouble renting an apartment, buying a car, even joining a health club.

- He will be unable to get a phone, water, gas, garbage or electricity in his own name since utility companies are now required to check their customer lists for child-support deadbeats.

- His wages will be attached. Since The Franchise Tax Board is routinely checked for assets and earnings, family support offices will eventually find out where he works. If he changes jobs, they'll know that too.

- He will be unable to maintain a bank account. He may even find his accounts frozen or cleaned out.

- If he wins the lottery, the entire debt will be automatically deducted from his winnings.

- He will never see a state or federal income tax refund.

- If he moves to another state, or even country, he will find— or soon find—that state has enacted reciprocal enforcement laws.

- He can be embarrassed. Not only are Most Wanted posters appearing regularly in public buildings, they are now also showing up on the Internet and even the *National Enquirer.*

- He may even be criminally extradited and prosecuted.

And if his solution is to live his life under someone else's name, then it's the suspense that will kill him, since there now exists the technology to find that out as well.

So Why Tell Us Anymore?

Because PIs still get calls from parents, hoping there is something we can do. Even with these new federal mandates, the district attoryney (DA) is busily collecting what he can, leaving the most needy to hang in the wind. In fairness, that's all he can do as just implementing the system above is a full-time job.

And sometimes there are things PIs *can* do. We have run a deadbeat's SSN and come up with a new address for Mom, who then turned it into the DA for collection. Why didn't the DA do that himself? Maybe he'd given up on the guy. Maybe he doesn't have the same databases we do. Maybe it was just on the bottom of the sixty thousand active cases on his desk.

Whatever the reason, since custodial parents still call, I'll still treat deadbeat parents as a category of missing persons.

What Is the Mental Makeup of the Parent Left Behind?

First and foremost, the custodial parents are oftentimes defeated in a way many of us, mercifully, will never know. For years, they've had to cope with an in-your-face deficit created because their significant ex-others waltzed away without a care. As a result, these sole supporters feel a powerlessness that infects the very core of their beings. To collect any debt, you have to think you can. These women (90 percent, anyway) have been conditioned to consider themselves "The Little Moms Who Couldn't."

What About the Parent Who Takes Off?

For the sake of argument, let's call them dads. Now, again, sometimes the roles are reversed and it is the woman who owes child support, but in the majority of cases, it is the fathers who scram. Right or wrong, they have reaped society's benefits of primary breadwinner status, and with that comes the financial responsibilities as well.

Deadbeat dads can come in a variety of flavors.

Some are merely selfish. They are finished with this life and anxious to get on with another. If they are left paying for their past mistakes, how can they possibly look forward to any kind of future for themselves? "It's just not fair, and I just won't do it" seems to be their attitude.

On the other hand, those payments really are high. The truth is, one man's salary can't support two households as lavishly as it did one. And since if his income does increase, his child support also rises, the time when a man is allowed to get on with his life is often eighteen years down the road. When the court expects a person to sacrifice a good portion of his income for a good part of his life, it is asking him to be a hero. And, sadly, most folks just are not.

The Biz-Op Opportunist

With a generic con job, the victim gets nothing for his money but the contempt of his family and friends. With a biz-op scam, he gets that plus an inferior product worth nowhere near the money he invested.

Everything I know about shady business dealings I learned from Loompanics Unlimited's *Biz Op; How to Get Rich With "Business Opportunity" Frauds and Scams.* Bruce Easley's frightfully honest, morally bankrupt and eerily entertaining memoir tells just how scoundrels go about hoodwinking "mooches," as he so delicately refers to the rest of us.

The Ingredients of a Biz-Op Scam

The bait. The majority of biz-ops are offered via the classifieds found in legitimate publications such as one's local newspaper or a familiar weekly tabloid. Folks assume since the periodical is trustworthy, so are its advertisers. Wrong! Many publications have no interest in policing their advertisers' claims since doing so would decrease their revenue and gain them nothing. And scoundrels learned long ago it was easier to pull an ad than to manage a midnight move to Tucumcari. A typical advertising cycle runs three weeks, just long enough for the victim to receive his shoddy merchandise and evoke his money-back guarantee. By then, the company has disconnected its 800 number and moved on.

The offer. Typically, biz-op scams are no-brainer turnkey operations offering a 30-plus percent profit for an under $10,000 investment. Added incentives are a work-at-home, flexible-hours and a be-your-own-boss environment. What's not to like?

Typical opportunities. They're classics, tried and true.

1. Charity boxes. The investor collects the loot and then sends some token amount to a "nonprofit" that's happy to get anything. In actuality, his take won't even cover the gas required to pick up the earnings.

2. Stuffing envelopes. Thirty-five bucks gets the investor instructions on how to place an ad identical to the one he answered.

3. At-home assembly. The investor pays $35 for $4.10 worth of stuff he cannot possibly assemble within the time constraints necessary to fulfill his contract.

4. Vending machines, pay phones, public fax machines. The investor is told the equipment is in and making money. Instead, he finds himself scouting locations and replacing candy bars for peanuts.

5. Greeting cards, cosmetics, doodads. The investor receives third-rate merchandise bought bulk at a government auction. Now the only way to unload the stuff is the same way the scammer did, sight unseen.

The guarantee. Sixty-day money-back refund. Yeah, if the investor can find 'em in sixty days.

The references. Those happy customers the investor spoke with were actually "singers," paid piecemeal for every call they took from a potential mooch.

The signs.

1. The 800 number. Dumping it takes minutes, and the mooch never even had an area code to pinpoint his tormentor.

2. The mail drop. Looks like an address, acts like a brick wall.

3. Cashiers check, COD only. Only companies with a storefront and a proven financial history can get a credit card swipe machine. A scammer has neither.

4. Materials come Federal Express. Mail fraud is punishable by death. Well, at least punishable.

Retribution. Sadly, the mooch often blames himself for the failed venture and doesn't even consider the offer was fraudulently represented. Were he to actually attempt civil litigation, he'd have to serve a defendant he could not find—across state lines—in hopes of collecting an investment of just a few thousand dollars. And then collect? It's something the scam artist doesn't spend much time worrying about.

Generic Scam Artists

These low-level career criminals confine their endeavors to nonviolent hustles. Although their actions exist only to defraud, they often are pursued civilly rather than criminally because of one or more of the following reasons:

- The DA won't take a case under a certain dollar amount.
- The DA won't touch nonviolent crime.
- The victim simply doesn't file a criminal complaint.

Since civil judgments are largely uncollectible, it means that in most cases, there simply are no consequences for a con man embarking upon this sort of nonviolent crime. And knowing this, many badboys are opting to trick a victim out of his hard-earned dough rather than to bop him over the head for it.

Gags fall into two categories: the long con, which takes a bit of time, both to set up and to execute; and the short con, the quick in-'n'-outer. As you will see by the first example, money is not always the prize they're after.

The Long Con

Lan was a fifty-three-year-old Asian divorcée, a mother and a high school science teacher. She came from decent, hard-working folk and had never encountered anyone like Ted, who was so secretive.

Lan called it a "relationship," although Ted had never given her his address, she'd never been to his home, never gone out on a date with him and never once talked to him on a week-end. As for his personal statistics, she knew only Ted's alma mater and that he'd been divorced for ten years. And, oh yeah, they met through the personal ads.

The couple had been together just half a dozen times, always at her house and when the boys were at school. Still, they were "sort of making plans to be together" when Ted was diagnosed with multiple sclerosis. Lan would have gladly nursed him, but Ted terminated their relationship and moved to New Jersey to take a job there. Lan hadn't heard a word since.

Now the lady was so distracted she found it difficult to carry on as a mother and teacher. She asked me to find Ted, thinking perhaps hearing the truth about his illness would awaken her from this stupor.

The first thing I discovered was that Ted had lied about the spelling of his name, a situation his alma mater graciously corrected. Next, I determined the phone number she'd been given was a voice mail, attached to no physical location. On that number, I left a sexy piece of bait, asking Ted to call me at an 800 number. When he did, his work number was recorded for posterity. That he left no message didn't save him in the least.

With this new information, I easily pinpointed Ted and wife Chelsey, not in New Jersey, but right there in Lan's own county. Tapping into medical files was outside my area of expertise, but I suspected the MS story was as phoney as the divorce.

A typical con man, Ted set this one up from the beginning. He told Lan what she wanted to hear because if his ad had read, "Married man into deceit, secrecy and bold-faced lies. Call phoney number as wife is as sweet and trusting as I hope you to be," he wouldn't have had near the response.

The Short Con

Grifters are impromptu actors, playing out their scams on unsuspecting bit players, many times senior citizens. Although the gags are short in duration, the results are invariably long term, sometimes affecting the rest of the victim's life.

At the end of every year, in the "Ask Rat Dog" column, I run my annual "Scams and Scoundrels Roundup: The Top Ten Rip-Offs of the Year." Here are the classics.

Shoulder Surfing. You're at the ATM machine. Behind you is parked a dark-windowed van with no particular agenda. What's going on? Inside the vehicle, a long-lens camera is capturing your pass code. Later the driver matches it up with the discarded receipt, and sometime after that, a third party manufactures a magnetic card, able to access your account.

Time Shares. Total strangers invite you for a resort weekend. "Great guns, of course I'll go!" is your response. To repay their benevolence, you suffer through a high-pressure sales pitch while other couples around you scream, "Take my money!" What's really going on? These properties are way overpriced and sell only to folks who don't comparison shop. And what of those other couples so eager to buy? They just might be "singers," employees of the company, who are paid to shout.

Paper Pirates. You receive an invoice and tear sheet—complete with the finger-walking logo—for your upcoming yellow pages advertisement. What's going on? What you may never discover is you've actually just paid for an ad in "In Your Dreams Yellow Pages," which appears, oh, let's see, *nowhere*. And the finger-walking logo? Not a trademark.

Credit Repair. They claim they can erase last year's bankruptcy, yet, still no one will give you a hamburger today for a promise to pay next Tuesday. What's really going on? *Nobody* can erase a bankruptcy before ten years or accomplish anything else you can't easily do yourself. Credit reporting agencies such as TRW used to remove troublesome items for thirty days while they were investigating the consumer's claim, and it was during that time your credit repairer flashed your cleaned-up credit report before your happy eyes. Then, suddenly, the item was back. And you'd never even know it until you tried to evoke your now-good credit.

Calling Card Fraud. Another "shoulder surfing" extravaganza, but this time the dark-windowed van loiters outside a phone booth, watching callers punch in their phone card numbers. Unless you meticulously checked your phone bill, how would you know?

Pigeon Drop. You're approached by a man who shows you a lottery ticket worth $1.7 million since the numbers match last night's winner. Since as an illegal immigrant, he cannot claim his jackpot, he's willing to sell you the ticket for $33,000 in cash. A second fellow approaches, anxious to buy, and suggests you pool your resources and split the winnings. Your new partner even phones the state lottery to verify the authenticity of the ticket and allows you to read the numbers to the "official" at the other end of the line. What's going on? They're in it together, along with the "official" at the other end of the phone. And the "winning" ticket? Purchased *after* the drawing, picking the numbers was kid's play.

Police Charities. It takes a courageous one, indeed, to hang up the phone on a cop with his hand out. What's really going on? The coppers probably don't even know the buffoon who's asking, and your donation won't even get you one Park Free on Park Place. These guys are just beggars with gall.

The Short Con That Became a Long Con

Our office neighbor strolled in with a problem. It seems a man had phoned his company claiming to represent an Arabian businessman anxious to invest in our neighbor's computer technology firm. When "Lee Marshall" inquired as to how much money he'd like, Eric, our neighbor, threw out the figure $250,000. Marshall suggested the entrepreneur ask Marshall's boss, "the Sheik," for at least a half million.

Eric was reluctant to accept the funds without checking out the legal and tax ramifications. Three days of meetings followed. Since Marshall knew nothing about computers, he brought along "Debbie," who sat in on the negotiations, but the technology was way above her as well. Our neighbor still had not met Marshall's boss, although he was a constant presence by phone.

The Sheik claimed he did not want to get any attorneys involved until after the money was wire transferred into the company account, as this is how things are done in Saudi Arabia. When Eric asked to think about it a while longer, the Sheik said this was not possible. In two days, he'd be winging his way back to oil land, and the offer would be rescinded. He then offered Eric an *entire* million for the foreign rights to his product.

Several hours after their last meeting, Eric got a call saying Marshall had left his Daytimer in Eric's office and to please meet him and Debbie so he could retrieve it. The next morning Debbie called, saying Marshall claimed the businessman had stolen his airline tickets, the whole company was made up of crooks and the deal was off. In the course of that conversation, Eric learned Marshall had met Debbie in a computer store just two days prior and promised her $1,500 to attend their meeting. And no, Marshall hadn't paid as promised.

Now, postdeadline, Marshall wasn't returning his calls, and all Eric was left with was an upcoming phone bill for the three days Marshall had camped out in his office. Was this a scam, he wondered, or had he just blown a million bucks?

Instantly, Ann Flaherty, my chief investigator, and myself pegged it for a long con. We didn't yet know what the "perps" were after, but the episode definitely contained the three key ingredients of a scam.

- The victim was (seemingly) getting something for nothing.

- Money was no object (since the confellows had no intention of parting with any).

- The offer came with a deadline (so the victim wouldn't have time to think, much less investigate).

One of my favorite fraud inspectors called this "a pigeon drop, all dressed up." Like any good scam, this one looks like the sucker will come out the winner. Grifters justify their actions claiming if the victims were not greedy, they wouldn't have fallen for the gags. It's their own fault, you see.

In this skit, all Marshall and the Sheik wanted out of this three-day "talk show" was our neighbor's bank account number. Had Eric capitulated, by Monday he'd have had a heap of computer-generated checks written against his account, each one just cents under Friday night's balance and each "guaranteed" by the bank had the recipient called to verify the funds. The promised wire transfer would have been as elusive as Marshall was after he decided to cut bait and run.

Not signing legal papers was to grifter Sheik's advantage, as well. Were he a bona fide rich guy, he wouldn't be for long if he kept pouring millions of bucks into other people's bank accounts on the basis of a handshake. Unfamiliar with the culture, our pals bought the Sheik story before they'd believe such behavior of a savvy American businessman.

We weren't asked to find these con artists. Since there was no victim, the cops said there was no crime. But had we been, that phone bill Marshall left behind would have been a heck of a paper trail.

Why Would Anyone Look for a Con Man?

Beats me. However, if you'd like a two-hour course on that subject, I'd suggest renting the most excellent video, *Six Degrees of Separation*, starring Will Smith and Stockard Channing. In it, a society family gets scammed by a "friend" of their son's, and they embark on an investigation of this person, even though they have nothing to gain except to make some sense of the matter. Although some consider such a premise ridiculous, as a PI, I found the movie to be quite realistic. People do become consumed with this uniquely irritating event, and they just don't let it go until they either get retribution or, at least, follow along that path as far as it will go.

Why Do We Fall for Such Charmers?

Realistically, as long as Publisher's Clearing House is out there surprising gray-haired grandmas on Superbowl Sunday, there will be people who will want to believe "It could happen to you!"

And it does happen, although rarely, and every time it does, the rest of us wonder when *we* will be the recipients of that lucky break. Because we deserve it! And we're special! And we *have* to believe in rags to riches because the alternative is to acquiesce to the unpalatable reality that we'll continue upon this pathetic financial course until the day we are mercifully laid to rest—probably at public expense.

Is There Any Point in Looking for These Villains?

Not much. Most times the sucker just *can't* get his money back. But if your protagonist does go looking, I suggest Florida. Not only is it a colorful backdrop for a story, but because of that state's laws, it's where most of these fly-by-nighters headquarter themselves.

Hardened Criminals

Our agency does not find hardened criminals. It's company policy. The first reason is hardly anybody wants one. Once the crook is gone, everybody just seems a whole lot happier. The second reason is because, deep down, we simply don't like tangling with these folks. Still, every once in a while, we start out searching for a son or dad or lover and end up looking for a nasty boy.

Who's Looking and Why

Family. Yes, hardened criminals have moms. Probably not the kind of moms you and I have, but moms, nonetheless. And being moms, they like knowing where their kids are.

Kids. Usually they never knew this parent at all but when they decide to find their dad or mom, they don't have much choice about who they turn out to be.

Ex-lover. It happens. Some chick gets smacked around, and once it's over, she realizes she'd prefer to have something happening to her than to have nothing happening to her.

Other cons. Many times, I get letters from prisoners who'd rather be clients, and oftentimes it's their fellow cons they want to find. This makes sense, since, after all, this is their circle of friends.

Birds of a Feather

Now, being in my line of work, I get lied to a lot. Scoundrels do it, of course, a parcel of clients, even a couple of old boyfriends, if the truth be told. But visiting an inmate on death row was a chance to look a wise guy in the eye and know I was hearing a whopper *while I was hearing it.* I thought maybe I could learn something.

Killer was incarcerated solely because he set his mom on fire a few years back, and the only reason I even knew that was because I accessed CompuServe's NewsFile and read about my nasty little would-be client and his family discord. Not that the torching much mattered. Mom was dead anyway.

Before I went, the administration told me not to wear blue because that's what the prisoners wore, so I wore green, and when I got there the guard said I shouldn't have worn green because that's the color the guards dress up in. Hey, I knew that. I figured if they divided into teams for some reason—volleyball, a prison break, whatever—I wanted everybody to know I was on the side of the guards. I didn't want anybody yelling, "Who wants the girl in the red?"

Past a sunny courtyard with a drop-dead view of the city was a long hall and, finally, a row of windows with telephones beside them. Just like you see in the movies. Through window #11 was a small square cage with a barred door at the back. Finally Killer arrived, wearing sunglasses, his hands cuffed behind him. He stepped into the room, and the guard clanged the bar door shut behind. Killer backed up, and the guard undid his cuffs through the bars. They looked like they'd done this before.

Then Killer sat, took off his sunglasses and picked up the phone. He smiled and so did I, but it wasn't a sincere smile, and I hoped he knew it.

It was then he told me how it was this other guy who offed his mom and not him. He described Lonnie Sandvich as a nice enough fellow, who, if only he knew the pickle Killer was in, would surely take the rap. I was to find Lonnie and convince him he would get immunity if he testified at the upcoming appeal hearing. Anyway, Killer would get out, Lonnie wouldn't go to jail—because he had immunity—and Killer could live to see light again.

Besides, said Killer, leaning in for an intimate tête-à-tête, it would be the best thing for Lonnie. Lonnie has AIDS, you see, and even if he went to prison, he'd get better medical care than he could ever afford on the outside.

I asked how it was that if Lonnie committed the murder, it was *him*, not Lonnie, the cops found cowering in Dad's garage, attempting to dismantle the murder weapon. Killer assured me that wasn't important. What was important was that I find Lonnie Sandvich and outline the state's medical plan to him. Perhaps I could pick up some brochures in the prison library.

That was pretty much it. He thanked me for coming and said next time to request a little room and bring some money so I could buy him a soda. His eyes crinkled and it almost took my breath away. Elvis didn't look so good in *Jailhouse Rock*. I knew instantly Killer had conned a few women in his time, but I knew for a fact he wasn't conning me.

Another thing I know for sure. Any guy who wants you to buy him a soda isn't going to pay you $95 an hour. You can count on it.

The Vanished

By far, the dramatic instances of scoundrels-in-flight are the ones who stage their own deaths or simply walk away, never to be heard of again.

Who among us has not had this fantasy? My particular one involves throwing a big birthday party for myself and then, with all my friends in attendance, going into the bathroom, crawling out the window well and hightailing it to Goa in time for Christmas. Sometimes, late at night, I work out the details.

And there are a lot of details to work out. How do I get out of the window well? Where can I dispose of the four-story ladder that particular feat would require without carting it all the way to India? What about transportation to the airport? Won't they ask for a passport when I request a one-way ticket to Asia?

And then there's the stuff I'd have to leave behind: my favorite Lazy Boy recliner, the hand-blown nativity scene I brought back from Venice, the only VCR I ever learned to operate.

I can't take my purse, of course; that would negate the "kidnapped by aliens while on the can" theory completely. That means relinquishing my credit cards, any money in my checking account and all my current identification.

The fantasy for most of us falls apart somewhere in the window well, listening to all our friends happily devouring the last of the shrimp balls. The rest of us, those who still want the fantasy to be real, fall in the category of having more to gain than to lose by disappearing; people consumed by debt, folks about to be indicted for embezzlement, ex-spouses about to be fleeced.

The vanished are not, in fact, an entire entity unique unto their own, but are one of the above type of scoundrels and have been or are about to be caught and see this as a viable option to dealing with their comeuppance.

How do they pull off an entire new identity? We'll talk about that in chapter eight, "How and Why People Hide Their Whereabouts."

Knowing a Scoundrel When You See One

Hard as they try, scoundrels are not all that unique. They all possess certain personality traits that, if your PI is astute—and I see no reason why he should not be—should clue him in to these less than sterling characters.

- Scoundrels deal in cash. For tax and expense account purposes, most of us like to pay by check or credit card. Anyone who deals *solely* in cash is usually hiding his money from the IRS or his creditors.

- Scoundrels are new in town, have no long-term friends and, by default, you're their new best friend. Most of us have moms, dads, siblings, even pals from our rowdy college days. When people arrive on the scene with no support system and immediately latch onto someone else's, you can bet it's because they've ticked off everyone who actually knows them.

- "Trouble" is their middle name. OK, stuff happens. But when a person is constantly complaining of schizophrenic ex-wives, card-eating automatic teller machines, stupid bank tellers, greedy landlords and unreasonable SWAT teams, it's not a good thing. When everybody is mad at somebody, usually everybody is right.

- They're secretive. Now, I know there are some folks you can sit next to for an entire five-hour flight and never even find out if they cheat on their wives. That's OK. What's not OK is when your new "best friend" won't give you his address. It's not OK when he answers the telephone in an Indian accent and he's not from India. It's also not OK when he's suspiciously evasive about his own life but thinks nothing of asking to borrow your birth certificate for the afternoon.

- Scoundrels try to create a sense of intimacy before one would naturally occur in a relationship. It starts with speaking in a low conspiratorial tone, a technique used extensively by many criminal defense attorneys when addressing a jury. Scoundrels like to intimate that only a "decent/kind/beautiful/sexy/caring person such as yourself" can help them with their troubles. The target comes to feel he's the last chance on the humanity train for this misunderstood fellow, and because the soon-to-be victim is such a gosh-darn wonderful guy, how can he not respond? After all, what would God say if he didn't?

PROFILE OF THE VICTIM

The last category of missing persons is the out-and-out victim: kidnapped kids, either by a stranger or by a parent; people who are hiding from a stalker; casualties of foul play; the homeless. However they came to be gone, finding them isn't just a matter of running a couple of computer checks.

Children Kidnapped by Strangers

Since databases are made up of property records, voting registrations, driver's licenses and the like, anyone under eighteen usually doesn't make the cut. In reality, nobody ends up here until he hits his mid- to late twenties. To search for a child, therefore, it is most expedient to look instead for the abductor than for the child. If your PI doesn't know the identity of the kidnapper, he's almost reduced to going the milk carton route.

Why would a PI be asked to do this, rather than the police?

Almost always, the case goes to the cops first, but when the leads peter out, or the authorities come to believe the kid is a runaway, the boys in blue are onto cases they can solve, and the parent is left dissolved in his own frustration and despair. It is only then the PI gets a crack at it, and then, only by families with bucks.

What happens, many times, is that kids aren't findable at all. The children are too young to help in their own releases or to even take notice that their names have been changed. It isn't until they are adults that they can make their way home again.

The Little Girl Who'd Never Have Been Found

When Regina was three and her father was in the service, her mother left the little girl with her paternal grandparents and split. John and Edna Garner, whom Regina always believed were the next-door neighbors, somehow ended up with the girl.

An album Regina retained through adulthood showed the Garners moved around during that time and gave her their last name. Vaguely, she recalls seeing a letter saying, "Tell Gina, Daddy will be home soon and that I love her." Edna never had any other children, the Garners were abusive and Regina was afraid of them until the day they died.

Now, fortyish and married to a disabled Vietnam vet, Regina's worst fear was that her dad was somewhere crying over her the way she cried for him all these years. She didn't want him to pass away with the pain of missing her and not knowing she was all right. Every time she saw a reunion show, she cried, but she knew she would never be able to pay for an investigation, nor could she afford to travel to these shows. So, who did that leave? Rat Dog.

Many people who can't afford to actually hire us write, hoping their letters will be chosen for a column and their cases accomplished for free. Many stories just are not interesting enough; others are too complicated to subsidize. Regina's fell into the latter category, but as it turned out, the *Rolanda* show was producing a reunion show right about then and asked for our help.

We, in turn, quizzed Regina as to whether she'd like to make a televised plea to her father. What she didn't know, of course, was that her dad was waiting backstage to meet her for the first time in forty-odd years. He had desperately searched for his daughter all his life; all his subsequent children knew of her existence, and they even celebrated her birthday every year.

On the show, Dad explained how he'd been in the service and thought all was well until the day he came home and his little girl and her mother were gone. His parents related how his wife had left with another man and then sent some friends (the Garners) to pick up the child.

After the show, the reunited family made some calls to Regina's mother's family. Now they heard what had been withheld earlier: Her mother had sold Regina to the Garners for drug money, and they'd given her their name so she couldn't be found.

Why Was Regina Unfindable?

When the Garners came for her, Regina's grandparents, thinking they were acting on their daughter-in-law's instructions, made no note of them. (No, they weren't neighbors.) Everyone thought Regina was with her mother, and it was her they'd looked for all these years. Without today's sophisticated databases, Dad's search for his vanished ex proved impossible.

Then Regina grew up and married, going from one unknown name to another. Poor Dad was doomed.

Why How It Happened Was the Only Way It Could Have Happened

Regina's dad remaining in the same state and retaining a listed phone number was his guiding light to his child. We found his very common name off-putting, as apparently had Regina, but producers with a TV show to tape two days hence apparently think nothing of such obstacles. They took our list of twenty possibles and called each one until they came up with a distant relative of Dad's.

Far too many children are abducted nowadays, and most are unfindable. Even those who survive the ordeal often live out strange existences with weird "parents" and never figure out what happened to them. And many times the only solution is when, as adults, they are able to make their way home again.

Parental Abduction

This is another messy situation, fraught with liability potholes. The first thing to consider when taking such a case is who has custody: the seeker or the runner? Why is he running? From abuse, perhaps? Unless the court documents back up the client's story, *your detective doesn't want this case.* Again, he won't find the kid in public records, so it is the parent who must be found.

One such case involved an operative who's still so jittery about the legal ramifications of her part in the snatch-back that seventeen years later, she doesn't want me to use her real name. We'll call her Morticia, since as it turns out, that's not anybody's real name.

Anyway, the client's ex had kidnapped his little girl and, as was the plan in many of these early parental abduction cases, had fled to another state, attempting to be the first to file custody. Because a court hearing would likely be scheduled within weeks, time was of the essence.

The destination of the father-child duo was easily determined: Lake Charles, Louisiana, the paternal grandma's hometown. And so, Morticia and her male counterpart posed as parents of their own eight-year-old child, bent on checking out all the second grade classrooms in the vicinity of Grandma's house. Unbelievably, their wish was granted, and there in one classroom sat the little girl.

Now for the snatch. For three days running, the child was observed boarding the school bus at 3:00 P.M. and departing into the arms of her beloved Nana. Never was the child left alone, even for a moment, so there was no place to accomplish their mission but the grade school parking lot, just as the little girl boarded the bus for home.

In a nondescript gray rental car sat Morticia, her client, the client's sugar daddy and financier of the snatch and Macho Male Operative, all in wigs and detachable facial hair. Macho grabbed the kid, shoved her into the backseat with Mom as masses of school yard kiddies began screaming along with their wailing pal.

Then Macho took off in the car, meandering through the after-class confusion. A female teacher, bent on heroics, jumped onto the hood of the car, but a quick side maneuver landed her on her butt in the parking lot.

Now for the getaway. An escape route had been set up in advance, a second car stashed along the way. The gang de-wigged en route, fled the first vehicle and piled into the second, leaving Morticia behind the wheel of the "hot" auto. Taking separate roads, both parties headed for Texas, where neither parent had custody. Morticia's car was dogged by helicopters the whole way. Luckily, the coppers were looking for an auto full of culprits sporting Dolly Parton wigs and Fu Manchu mustaches, so the newly shorn Morticia was neither stopped nor questioned.

Once safely in Texas, the convoy reconvened at a designated gas station and made its way to the Dallas-Fort Worth airport. There, amidst much walkie-talkie activity, the operatives boarded a plane for San Francisco and Mom, with her sugar daddy, and a very jubilant kid, headed for Sweden.

The teacher's butt, by the way, was not seriously injured.

People Being Stalked

Yes, sometimes we are asked to find people who are being stalked. Contacted by whom? Many times by the stalkers themselves.

Do we take these cases? Don't be ridiculous. How do we know when this is the situation? I hesitate to list the signs here, thinking some literary-minded stalker will read this and change his MO, but suffice it to say the bad boys call from a phone booth, attempt to pay by credit card and need the information *right now*. Then they phone back in two minutes, hoping you'll give them the goods before you run the card and find out it's stolen. The last time this situation arose, Ann supplied the "client" with the phone number of his local police precinct instead of the "friend" who had moved away. Another stalker thwarted.

We'll talk about the stalkers themselves in chapter ten, "Resource One: The Client," but as for the stalkees, I'd describe them as wary, nervous or scared spitless, depending upon how long this has been going on. These MPs are hard to find, as they well should be. Rule of thumb: When the client looks hinky (a bona fide insider industry word you can feel free to use) and the MP is as skittish as a big-horned deer in hunting season, it's time to bail.

Victims of Foul Play

Lisa had left her husband, moved in with her mother in Phoenix and started divorce proceedings. The last day anyone ever saw her, her husband, Paul, had taken her to buy a dresser, as was stipulated in their divorce agreement. When she didn't return from shopping by 9:30 P.M., Lisa's mother called the police. Paul's story was that they'd gotten into an argument and Lisa left with two friends she happened to see at the mall. His descriptions of them were vague, including the make of the car. Now, five years later, neither Lisa nor the kids' car seats, which Paul claimed she took with her, had ever been found.

Two days after the disappearance, Paul was picked up for driving erratically and was placed in the psychiatric ward, under suicide watch. The police noted several deep scratches on his neck, and finally he admitted that his last argument with his wife had gotten physical. When blood stains in the car proved to be Lisa's blood type, the authorities suspected homicide, but without a body, they couldn't prove Lisa was dead, let alone that Paul murdered her.

Lisa's mother took the children and moved away without telling Paul of their destination. Now, five years later, Lisa's best friend Julie was dissatisfied with Paul's nonarrest and asked us to look into it.

Since my mother lives in Phoenix, we sent her downtown to pick up the police report, which had become public record when the case went into an inactive state. The evidence against Paul was impressive but almost entirely circumstantial. Key points were:

- Finding Paul awake, dressed and nervous with a "faraway look in his eyes and a pale and clammy look to his face" when he was questioned at 4 A.M. the morning after Lisa's disappearance.
- Finding blood in his car that later tested positive for Lisa's blood type.

- Determining those blood stains had been doused with gasoline—widely known as a cleaning fluid—and noting Paul's gray pants also smelled strongly of gasoline.

- Observing deep scratches on Paul's face, neck and hand, which he later admitted occurred when he tried to "make love" to Lisa, against her will, in the parking lot of the mall where she disappeared.

- Lisa's four-year-old daughter's statement that Daddy told her he was taking "Mommy to his house and she would never see her again."

- His statement to a subsequent girlfriend that "I'm going to show you where I buried my wife." (Paul later claimed, "I told her that to get her goat.")

- Inconsistencies in his story, such as how Lisa and he moved to the backseat for their tryst when there were two child seats back there, per the baby-sitter's earlier testimony.

This seemed to be another case where, although the circumstantial evidence pointed exclusively toward Paul, the district attorney felt he could not eliminate "reasonable doubt" in the minds of the jury. He couldn't, in fact, even prove she was dead.

Unfortunately, like many potential clients, Julie and her friends could not financially support such an investigation. And, yes, it would have been expensive, since what the DA required was a body, and Phoenix, in case you are unaware, is built on top of a pretty big desert.

How Would a PI Go About Solving This?

The first thing we did was to run Lisa's name through our extensive database system, just to make sure she didn't take off for an extended skiing vacation in St. Moritz. Aside from a recent credit inquiry, giving her address as the very apartment building where she first met Paul, we found nothing. Since that was a curious instance, we sent our fearless Phoenix operative, Gray Tail, to check it out. Unfortunately, our little bum-legged grandma could learn nothing.

Without a budget, we could do nothing further, but we did receive word back from the Phoenix PD inquiring as to why we had requested the file. (Nice they notice stuff like that.) The detective working cold cases had a plan to lure Paul back to the burial site to check on his handiwork. Some of Julie's amateur sleuth friends had already tried *that*, but their keystone cop antics had done more harm than good. We trust the PPD to do better, but this one probably won't be solved until Lisa's body shows up.

The Homeless

Of course, one cannot, via the information superhighway, find a person who has no address. Although these folks *are* in public assistance databases, undoubtedly receiving Social Security, welfare or food stamps, those resources are unavailable to private eyes and must be gotten through a "confidential source," if at all. (Good fodder for a scam.) Unbelievably, even shelters aren't all that cooperative, as they are instructed to protect the privacy of their patrons.

So how do you find the homeless? By old-fashioned gumshoeing, much of the time. And even then, it's a matter of luck.

One of our most frustrating cases involved searching for a wayward brother, Jerry, who, since 1992, had declined to phone home. The last the family knew, Jerry was single and selling life insurance in Las Vegas. They freely admitted little bro had troubles, especially with drugs, and were worried he might even be in the hospital. They'd also heard he'd been in prison but were unclear on the details. Although they had Jerry's DOB, SSN and last address, they still hadn't been able to find him.

And neither could we. A thorough database search produced no entries in the last year. We were able to locate an old girlfriend, but she claimed no contact since the year before, at which time Jerry was living on the streets.

Eventually, we had nothing left to try but to send our chief investigator, Ann Flaherty, off to Las Vegas—poor thing. We armed her with a modest budget and permission to use whatever was left over on the slot machines. We never expected to hear from her again either.

To her credit, however, Ann did not begin with the slots. Instead, she scoured public records and found nothing but an old drug conviction and a new AKA for Jerry. A visit to his last address required a bulletproof rent-a-car, something we'd not budgeted for. Sojourns to neighborhood shelters ruined her happy mood, and flashing Jerry's picture on the streets where he'd lived brought only suggestions of new career opportunities for our fair-haired maiden.

Having nothing else to go on, our intrepid gumshoe then called the coroner, inquiring after the outstanding "John Does." The top gun personally displayed the photo lineup: a guy who'd succumbed in the desert leaving nothing behind but a skeleton and an afro and another fellow who'd been run over, not once but thrice. The ID found in the latter's pocket bore a striking resemblance to brother Jerry, but, thankfully, what was left of his fingerprints didn't match up.

After that fun-filled interlude, Ann officially gave up and proceeded to the gimlet-and-gambling portion of the junket.

Then, weeks later, came the client's phone call, stating that somebody's husband was going to Vegas on business and would try his hand at finding the black sheep brother. I must admit, we snickered, but still we sent off the information Ann had gathered on her own visit to Toon Town.

Well, la-de-da! A week after that, Jerry was back in the family fold. Seems the amateur sleuth had bypassed the public records, circumvented the snapshots of road kill and headed straight for the nearest T-shirt vendor outside his fancy hotel on The Strip. Who happened to know wayward brother. Who directed elated superslueth to a homeless shelter whose head honcho knew Jerry as well and the corner he was prone to hanging on. And yes, OK, there he was. Right in plain sight. Where any fool could find him.

The Client

(The phone rang twice. I always let it ring twice . . .)

Where Do Clients and Cases Come From?

We here at Rat Dog determined some time ago that what we ended up doing in a day depended upon who called and if what they wanted was legal, cost effective and feasible. There were several scary days, early on, when the phone didn't ring at all.

It was then we realized that although we had an Amtrak full of happy clients, nobody ever came back for more. Just how many true loves is one possessed to find in a lifetime? How many birth parents can you possibly locate for the same client? How often is a customer going to admit he fell for ye ol' gypsy sweetheart scam, *again*, and can you please find Peaches Yonko yet another time?

Because of the nature of the business, PIs who expect to be around at the end of the fiscal year need a plan.

Marketing Sources

- Many PIs rely on the yellow pages. I find, however, that advertising here brings mostly a lot of nutcases who have seen way too many *Moonlighting* episodes. Whenever life becomes unbearable for these folks, their first thought is not "Hey, I need to be institutionalized," but "A good PI can fix all this." They let their fingers do the walking, and frequently those digits come to rest on some obscure little agency with a name that has a domestic animal in it. That's why, not only do we *not* advertise, we're thinking of getting an unlisted number.

- Ads in legal newspapers are a far better idea. Since a large portion of attorneys are fairly normal, most have already weeded out the nut cases themselves and arrive with wholesome clients in need of honest investigations in tow. Sometimes, they even eventually return with another. Once a PI suspends the deadbeats from toying with him further, he can begin to build a client base to be proud of.

- Radio and TV show publicity works well for us—but only in the long run. My "Ask Rat Dog" column was created to take advantage of free (actually, paying) newspaper space on an ongoing basis, but that plan sort of backfired. Readers tend to see our services as an extension of the periodical, willing to solve any old mystery for the sake of a story, even when the writer requests we don't print the results of our investigation. Building a thriving business through public appearances takes years to accomplish, but a single radio or TV appearance can bring in a case or two.

Referrals

As with most businesses, word of mouth is the best way of getting clients. Of course, the people a PI is counting on to talk up his services are often the same ones whose investigations demand top secrecy, so he shouldn't expect a whole lot from them at cocktail parties. Still, despite client confidentiality, lawyers talk, and when they do, you get more of the same kind of cases you did for them in the past. Do the same thing a couple of times and you've got yourself a specialty.

For example, our agency started out specializing in the

collection of bad debts. Once we learned this could not be done, I did a radio show on finding lost loves, and, subsequently, locating missing persons (rather than their money) became our trademark. Then the very same attorney who gave me my first asset-collection case assigned me a fraud case against a gypsy who had hoodwinked an old woman out of her property. After that, we were off and running on gypsy cons.

Building a Loyal Client Base

Eventually, this is what it all boils down to. If you're good, they'll call you again. Eventually.

- Most attorneys only require an investigator once every couple of years. Some larger firms do use PIs on a regular basis, but frequently they keep one on retainer or simply fill that slot with an in-house paid employee.

- Insurance agencies are a good source of disability fraud cases, boring but well paying. How wearisome are they? Does sitting all day in your car waiting for someone to come out and start raking his yard sound like fun? Does making $95 per hour make the challenge a bit more palatable? Such is the dilemma of the PI specializing in this sort of work.

- The public defender is an ongoing end user of private investigators. Protagonists who routinely choose to help spring their usually naughty clients must be complete innocents, optimists or sociopaths themselves. If yours is hell-bent on criminal work—and what best-selling sleuth isn't—he must find that rare wrongly accused martyr, or at least have a rich client who convinces him this is the case.

Linguistics

Where would your protagonist and client meet in order to discuss a potential investigation? Since many PIs now work out of their cluttered, mortgage-riddled homes, more and more cases are initiated over the phone, paid for by credit card and concluded by typing a proper name into a computer.

You going to write a book about a case like this? Well,

that's up to you. You going to sell it? I don't think so. How much more interesting for your colorful client to suddenly emerge in the office doorway, shrouded in fog, Maltese falcon in hand—or, better still, have your protagonist scurry on out to meet the eccentric millionaire on his authentic Chinese junk that just happens to be floating in some nearby picturesque body of water.

Do that, of course. Make the meeting engaging, that's what fiction is all about. Just be sure to include some passing reference that shows you know that actually eyeballing the client—and the MP—is not the norm.

Signs of a Client Your Detective Might Not Want

Here we have a dilemma. The sanest clients obviously provide the most straightforward investigations. They come in or call, state their business, pay their money, say thank you very much and go away. We like these people. We live for these cases. The only problem with them is they usually are not fodder for award-winning literature.

Now, since one of a case's major ingredients is the person instigating the search, it's important for a writer to create a client with his own agenda. Why would a savvy PI take a case from someone like this? Not a clue. I can, however, provide you with some of the things I learned on my way to savvy.

Is the Client a Scoundrel?

This is our first-asked question about a potential client. Aside from all else, we like to avoid future litigation—and get paid—and that involves weeding out the blackguards. To that end, we use the same set of criteria previously mentioned in "Knowing a Scoundrel When You See One." Adapting that list to potential customers looks like this:

- Do they insinuate certain information is none of your PI's business?
- Do they have very little data on the people they're looking for?
- Are they requesting movie stars' home addresses?

- Do they use a mail drop? Must your PI call them only at work or only leave a message on voice mail? Are they calling from a phone booth?

- Are they in a hurry? Does your PI have to find the people before he has a chance to check out the clients' stories—and cash his check?

- Do they emphasize confidentiality and try to make your detective sign stuff saying he'll never ever tell—even if subpoenaed?

- Do they provide your gumshoe with names of people who know where the MPs are, yet they've never bothered to ask those people for the MPs whereabouts?

- Do their stories lack details—no explanation as to why they want to find these people?

- Are they obviously obsessed?

Such signs are *very* important, and ignoring said omens will surely result in a case that will cause a real PI to quit and become a tolltaker at the nearest suspension bridge. Fictionally exploring such a situation, however, might make one heck of a book, perhaps even a series if the protagonist can refrain from catapulting himself off that inviting span.

Does the Client Have Unrealistic Expectations?

Isaac was twenty-two and engaged to Ruth, his childhood sweetheart, when along came Janet who introduced him to slow dancing, champagne and a dazzling sex life. Now, fifteen years after marrying the temptress, Isaac referred to her as "an obsessive, paranoid hag who's an embarrassment on our rare occasions out."

Wow.

And now, of course, he longed for Ruth—her sweet quiet nature, her trusting manner and her trim figure, qualities he said he once took for granted. Now that he'd made it financially, why couldn't he have this one last thing? he mused.

Isaac was desperate to find out if Ruth ever married, preferably without her knowing he was trying to find this out. If she was, he swore he'd take his lumps; but if she wasn't, he considered it the incentive he needed to extract himself from his "horrendous" situation. Money was no object, he claimed.

Easily, we found Ruth in the State Index of Vital Statistics, a handy little microfiche that lists everyone married in the state between 1960 and 1986. Ruthie did the deed thrice, and checking the divorce records in the county where she last wed, we found decrees to match every blissless union.

Upon relaying this information to our client, Isaac promptly informed Janet he had a meeting in Omaha and made off instead for a secret rendezvous with his sweet baboo in Florida. This we know because his wife found his airplane ticket in a drawer and our phone number on their telephone bill and called the office assuming I was the other woman.

I think not.

We didn't hear from Isaac after that, although Janet still called occasionally, screaming obscenities and hanging up. When I say we haven't heard from him, I'm referring, of course, to his final bill of $175.

When finally we caught up with him, Isaac claimed he wasn't going to pay because he was dissatisfied with the results of our search. It seems Ruth had gained about thirty pounds, and that cute little beauty mark she had in college now had a long black hair growing out of it.

Well, sorry Isaac, but clearly it's not part of our service to make sure Ruthie does her jumping jacks for several decades, preparing for the likes of you to come riding up on your great white horse. Once again, a client had confused our service with that of Richard Simmons's.

Is the Client Calling From Jail?

Every once in a while, boredom overtakes me and I accept a collect call. My usual answer to the operator is, "Sorry, I don't know any Diane," but when Diane shouted out, "I'm a client!" I thought it best to see what she wanted.

Diane considered herself a client because three months before she'd paid $25 for a search that she was told *sometimes* provides employment information. In her case, of course, it hadn't. Although she'd been advised of the odds early on, Diane was now unhappy with our service. How much was it going to cost, she wanted to know, to finally get the information she'd already paid for?

At the highest telephone rates known to mankind, I began explaining to Diane that the only other way to find out her ex's latest career opportunity was to do surveillance—a costly endeavor at $95 per hour. If she couldn't afford this phone call, how did she expect to pay for us tailing the guy?

Diane could afford the phone call, she assured me. Some companies don't mind if their customers call collect.

We mind, I assured her.

Some companies have 800 numbers, she countered.

We don't, I informed her.

I offered to call her back, but Diane said she was in a phone booth that didn't accept incoming calls. To get her off the line, I proposed sending her some information on other searches, at which time she gave me a post office box in Yuma, Arizona.

Yuma!

Yes, I'd done it again—accepted a collect call from Yuma. (Now I'm just sure there is some obscure retention facility in that town, in whose library rests a copy of my book. Possibly an entire shelf of my books, if the number of collect callers from Yuma is any indication.)

Diane took great umbrage to my inquiry as to whether she was phoning from the slammer, as I suppose any client would. She then informed me there hadn't been a territorial prison in that part of the world for many years and that I had some nerve.

Of course, I had some nerve. I was paying $8 per minute to talk to a $25 client. I was running out of money. The only thing I had left was nerve.

Is the Client Looking for a Celebrity?

One fellow wrote saying he was a big fan of "a very exciting young lady" named Dian Parkinson, formerly a model of *The Price Is Right*. He had been trying for some time to get hold of her, both through the show itself and through the station that aired the program. Already he'd written to the production company. Nobody wrote him back.

All Sammy was asking for was the opportunity to

correspond with Dian and maybe ask her out on a date or two. Could I just, please, let her know he was dying to meet her for the sole purpose of getting to know her? Sammy included his address and phone number, along with the best times to call. He assured me if Dian said no, he'd abide by her decision with no questions asked.

Sammy fell into our "no-client/no-way/no-how" category. Company policy says we don't bother folks who aren't really missing but just happen to be lousy letter writers. Being one of those folks, I've declared they have the right.

Not that I wasn't sympathetic with Sammy's plight. I, also, had spotted my perfect mate and knew *for sure* the only reason Gene Kelly and I didn't end up together was simply because the grand tapper didn't know me from Cyd Charisse on a bad hair day. I freely admit fantasizing about how to "accidentally" meet the guy, having dismissed the traditional approaches. (Writing seemed ineffectual; stalking, a bit too much.) That Brigitte Nielsen met Sylvester Stallone through a fan letter gave me hope for a while, but then I realized she did it by including naked photos of herself. In my case, not an option.

In not taking this case, I tried to explain to Sammy what it was like to be on the other side of the admiration coin. Once, after appearing on *Larry King Live*, thirty strangers wrote asking me for dates. I thought this very weird since guys I knew didn't even ask me out on dates. The letters were of the true "fan" variety, including one 8″ × 10″ glossy and several love poems. Every time I got one of these letters, I felt like I was reading Cher's mail. How could these fellows write goofy love things to a stranger, I wondered, and were any of them one of those dreaded stalker types? Still, being a polite person, I answered the letters posthaste, anxious to be done with them.

Then they wrote back! My good manners had suggested we were now going to be penpals! I realized quickly, if I didn't nip this in the bud, I was going to continue chitchatting with thirty fellows I had nothing in common with until Larry King found some other cute girl detective to be on his show. I waited six months to answer the second round of letters and any letters after that. Enough to be polite, not enough to be encouraging. That seemed to work.

What I finally realized was that although I didn't know these chaps at all, they, in an odd way, knew me. They had watched me yapping for an entire half hour, and it created for them a familiarity that I, having witnessed no yapping on their part, had not experienced.

Conclusion: It's very hard for a normal person to initiate an intimate personal relationship with a "celebrity." Rule of thumb: If he can't get a date in his own hometown, chances are Pamela Lee won't go out with him either.

Is the Client Crazier Than a Loon?

And then there was poor Larry who had a "very puzzling problem" that began in 1977 when he was a freshman at Western Illinois University and still continued, as evidenced by his $50,000 lawsuit against that institution.

Ongoing since college, it seems, people had been entering Larry's apartment and drugging, beating up and sexually assaulting the poor guy while he was sleeping.

The only reason Larry knew this was happening at all was because people were constantly saying either "See you later" or "Talk to you later" to him. In actuality, he'd never heard or seen or felt anything from the time he went to bed until morning, although he'd often awake with pain in his head, arms and privates and with a drugged feeling. Now Larry wanted to know if this was really happening or if it was a delusion, as four psychiatrists had suggested.

I had a simple solution to Larry's dilemma, and it cost the guy nothing. (The last thing I needed was another $25 investigation coming back to haunt me.) I advised the fellow that the next time he went to sleep, he should shut all the doors and windows and put several pieces of transparent tape across the jams. Next, he should nail the tape into the wall and sign it, just for good measure. Once done, it would be impossible for anyone to enter his room without ripping the tape, and likewise they couldn't replace it because of the signature. In the morning, if the tape was undisturbed, Larry could be sure his demons were coming from within and not from without.

Think Larry listened to me? Heck, no. Now that he had someone who took his delusions semiseriously, *we* were pen pals! The only way to get rid of Larry was the same way a savvy PI gets rid of all the unwanted would-be clients who stumble across his threshold: You just can't play with these people anymore.

Cases Even I Won't Take

Yes, it's true. Sometimes it's just not worth it. If we determine we're going to get stiffed, stuffed or scallywagged, sometimes we choose to pass.

Is the Client Proposing to Mess Up a Bunch of Innocent Lives?

On St. Patrick's day in 1987, Alice met Bobby at a bar called The Boiler Room. She was wearing a button that declared, "Irish Whiskey Makes Me Frisky," and, apparently, it did. A few shots of the stuff and Bobby had bought himself a little fling. He was eighteen. She was twenty-seven.

Soon afterward, Alice discovered she was pregnant. She wrote Bobby, who had since left town, but didn't tell him the baby was his because she didn't think it was. At the time, Alice was not doing well. She'd fallen under the spell of cocaine, broken up with her boyfriend, lost her apartment and moved in with a friend.

When former beau Harold found out about the upcoming bundle, he hightailed it on back. He and Alice revived their relationship in August, married in September, and the child was born the end of December.

But now the couple was kaput. "As it turned out, Harold was not the person I thought he was," stated the lady. She declared her ex a lousy husband and even worse father to her son. Admittedly, Harold paid child support, but aside from that, he hadn't much else to do with the boy aside from minimal visitation every other weekend, asserted Alice.

And so now the disillusioned mom proposed to locate Bobby a la Boiler Room and let him know he had a son! No, she hadn't checked into the legal ramifications but didn't want to stir up the pot until she'd found her replacement papa. "I think I have waited long enough," declared the princess. "I don't expect Bobby to rush right out here and pick up a relationship with me, but I do not want my son to suffer for my mistake. He is very smart, has a great sense of humor and is very sensitive, just like I remember Bobby."

Alice's real agenda, of course, was to remove her "macho, redneck wanna-be ex-husband" from their lives. She claimed the boy didn't especially like the person he called Daddy, even though the kid wouldn't admit to that.

One of the best things about being the boss is not having to do what you don't want to do, and succinctly put, I didn't want to find Bobby. That Little Whoever Jr. resembled someone a drunken reveler knew briefly ten years before was a very bleary judgment call on Mom's part and certainly not enough to warrant messing up all the lives she proposed destroying. If she was so certain, I challenged, then why not test her ex for paternity and/or stop accepting his child support? To string Harold along until she could determine if she could snare a more likeable chap into accepting financial and emotional responsibility for her son was in nobody's best interest except her own.

Does the Client Already Know?

Many times they do. But because they have been lied to again and again, they have come to doubt their perceptions to the degree that they are buying into their spouses' explanations of their feelings, that they are "crazy" or "paranoid" or simply imagining things.

Take the case of Elaine Haley and her husband, both forty-seven, married for twenty-four years with two grown children. For the last seven years of that marriage, Howie had been having an affair with a twenty-eight-year-old woman who used to live down the street from the couple. The alleged tart had moved to Maryland five years before, but that didn't end the affair. Elaine said that even though Howie claimed he was no longer seeing the trollop, every few weeks he'd disappear for several days with no explanation.

Then a few days before she contacted us, Elaine, while hanging up her husband's pants, noticed a beeper attached. She pushed the button and a phone number appeared that she did not recognize. Elaine dialed, and sure enough The Other Woman answered.

Thinking back, Elaine began to fill in the pieces. In March, Howie had told her he had to go to Syracuse on business. Since he'd been talking about the trip for weeks, she believed him and even packed his suitcase. A few months later she found a receipt from a Maryland department store for a queen size sheet set, dated during the time he was gone. Elaine already knew her husband had spent a ton of money on this woman, which they could ill afford. He'd bought her jewelry, a VCR, a refrigerator, and once, having found a charge on their Sears card for a new battery, Elaine ordered a copy of the bill and found The Other's license number on the slip.

What could we do about it? Aside from offering Elaine a job utilizing her investigative skills, not much. The only thing we could possibly add to her knowledge was the obvious fact that Howie *wanted* her to know of his infidelity! He was just way too indiscreet for there to be any other explanation.

Investigating the Client's Story

Some agendas are transparent; some take a little more work. When something feels hinky, here's how to flush out the story.

Reading Between the Lines

The signs are usually right there. If the detective can just *get over* the huge retainer he's sure to get, he will see that the case has already been solved and nothing he can discover is going to change the results or make the client happy with the ending. I personally think if an investigator knows he can't satisfy the client, he should decline the case and save himself a lot of grief.

Lilibeth was just such a client. She was desperate and had been since about 1943. It was then she met a fellow "I was so attracted to that I couldn't eat or sleep and was almost fired from work." For a guy to affect her like that made Lilibeth realize Stanley was the one. One night, they confessed their love, even privately reciting wedding vows.

When Stanley went to war, Lilibeth felt sick all over.

Especially in the stomach area and especially in the mornings. Soon afterward, she moved into a home for unwed mothers and waited for Stanley to be discharged.

Upon his return, Stanley told Lilibeth he was moving to San Francisco and would never see her or his child again. She remained single a long time. Then, having no reason to stay in Seattle, she moved to the Bay area. Stanley never offered support and never came looking for them.

By the time she wrote to me, Lilibeth had already pursued all the logical courses of action. She'd consulted a psychic who told her that Stanley's seven-year marriage hadn't worked out, but she personally didn't think he ever married as she requested a license search from Sacramento and none could be found. Lilibeth knew Stanley had two children—she even had their birth certificates—but she believed the unmarried mate took them with her when she split. She also "knew" Stanley lived like a hermit and ate only junk food, so Lilibeth called Meals on Wheels to go over there and fix him a little something. Stanley wasn't home "or maybe he just wouldn't answer his bell," and then later he called Wheels back and said he didn't want the service.

The psychic assured Lilibeth that Stanley still cared about her, but the lady wanted to read this in a letter written by him. Although she herself had been writing him for four years, her explanation for his not responding was that he had "a very shaky hand." When she asked the psychic why Stanley was playing this cat-and-mouse game, she said Stanley was afraid he would be put in jail by someone. "This certainly is not me," Lilibeth assured me, "as too much time has passed for me to cause him trouble."

Lilibeth thought something was very wrong and didn't know what. Why would a person in Stanley's condition turn down Meals on Wheels, she wanted to know.

A man in that condition wouldn't, I told her. A man who owned a thriving variety store on prime city property, however, most assuredly would. Which was what was going on here.

By rereading the letter, it became quite obvious that almost the entire extent of Lilibeth's knowledge of her beloved came from her psychic, a woman who, incidentally, had absolutely no talent in her chosen field. Just the teensiest bit of investigation bore out these facts: Stanley's wife of over thirty years didn't leave him voluntarily; she died in 1989. He still lived at the address Lilibeth had, with two of his five children, and could answer her letters if he chose. His shaky hand worked just fine when he was working his cash register, which is what he did daily. It was then I had to inform Lilibeth of something I learned as a high school senior: Not always do our past loves become recluses, waiting in darkened rooms, surrounded by empty pizza boxes, waiting for our returns.

Did Lilibeth give it up? Heck no. For years she kept writing and calling me, even after Stanley's death, at which time she inquired as to know how to apply for a chunk of his estate for her son.

Men on leave, take warning.

Is the Client Fooling Himself?

Another problem with clients is that they like to tell themselves what they want to hear. They portray their motives as pure when actually they are hoping for another agenda altogether. By not having to admit their goals, they save themselves the embarrassment if things don't work out, as well as preserving their immediate situations (in most cases, marriages) until they can determine their other options.

Take Royce, for example. While serving in Germany in 1977, this GI had an affair with a military wife we'll call Susan Jacobs. Since their Code of Justice declares adultery a punishable offense, Royce was sent to the Czech border and his mail intercepted and screened. Susan, her husband, Daniel, and their two children, Kevin and Tommy, were transferred back to the States—along, of course, with Kristy, Royce's daughter by Susan, born November of that year.

Royce had already done some looking by the time he got around to hiring us. Knowing Daniel and Susan would now be in their late thirties and from the Modesto, California, area, he checked with the Office of Vital Statistics and found the only Daniel and Susan Jacobs listed had married while the family he knew was in Germany. Desperate to locate his sixteen-year-old daughter, Royce contacted the Military Locator Service in St.

Louis, the German government and the U.S. passport office. He also spent over $8,000 on private investigators—with no luck.

As I will mention ad nauseam in a later chapter, the first step in finding someone is always to confirm his legal name. Since we found, as Royce had, no record of the Jacobs's marriage, and since the military locator could not identify a Daniel Jacobs who served in Germany in 1977, that first step seemed impossible. However, finding nothing where you expect to find it usually indicates something else has occurred; in this instance, Royce had one or both of the couple's legal names wrong.

Moving then to identifying a Kevin-Thomas sibling combo born to a Jacobs family in the early 1970s in the Modesto area, we located the duo by comparing mother's maiden names on the birth index. Ordering the certificates showed the father to be *James* Daniel Jacobs, and since California birth certificates from that era listed the parents' Social Security numbers as well, we knew right away we had Susan.

As quick as we could type in her name, we located Susan Bradford in Illinois, having obviously shed the first husband. Unhappily, Susan's phone had recently been disconnected, and she'd left no forwarding address with the post office. Regardless, now knowing her maiden name, we were able to locate her relatives and finally her—this time for real.

After a few weeks we heard back from our ecstatic client. Of course he was thrilled because his long quest was over but also saddened because he learned that when Kristy was young, she may have been abused by Daniel Jacobs, who, lucky for him, was already dead. Susan told Royce that Daniel's truck went off a cliff and whether it was an accident or suicide was still in doubt. After his death, Susan lost custody (because of a drug problem), and Kristy's grandfather had raised her. The girl still believed Daniel Jacobs to be her father.

"Susan is now single," wrote Royce, "and after talking for days, we've discovered we never stopped loving each other! My wife says she'll let me go, but this makes me feel terrible because I will always have feelings for her."

OK, I'll admit it. I hadn't even seen this one coming. Royce's concern had always been for the child, not the mother, and I got fooled, probably right along with the man himself.

But because we don't encourage homewrecking as a by-product of our service, I felt compelled to leave Royce with a little advice.

Lose this lady. Understandably, this is an extraordinarily emotional time, and he was obviously caught up in the passion that this long quest's end has wrought. But Susan is a woman with many troubles, most of which are her own making. A marital affair. A lost custody battle. Drug abuse. Spousal suicide. Even leaving no forwarding address suggested Susan might still be on the run from her problems.

I suspected that Royce, rather than becoming the lady's savior, would instead become engulfed in whatever proved to be her current conflict. Should this happen, I could only hope it occurred before he could do irreversible harm to the marriage he already had.

Checking the Papers

Sometimes the situation's so weird, it's pretty obvious it might have made the papers.

I once had a woman waltz into my office, costumed entirely in black plastic. Atop her polyester ensemble were perched several rings of ivory neck, a bloated white face and a helmet of black hair, adorned with a cheap chiffon scarf. She looked like Snow White after way too many dwarf years.

Her problem was quite unique. It seems the SPCA had come and taken away her twenty-seven pooches for absolutely no good reason. Now she wanted me to find said pups' new owners so she could sue them and get her animals back.

Hmmm. And I'll bet you can guess why she picked my company name out from all the others in the phone book. To make her point, Black Lady started lining $100 bills up on my desk, a practice, by the way, I do not discourage.

Now, I don't know much about doggy law, but I do know this: Were Black Lady's story on the level, her attorney would most assuredly advise suing the SPCA and then making the SPCA staff tell where the animals were. That she was bypassing the legal system embodied the word *hinky* in all its magnificent glory.

It didn't take much to solve the mystery of the no-how/

no-way client. The *Oakland Tribune* headline blared, "Many Dead Dogs Found in Hayward Kennel." Seems Black Lady collected the pets from all over town, kept them in her yard and neglected to feed them. When the neighbors spotted a couple of the poor malnutritioned mutts, they called the SPCA who came out and found several more, dead and stuffed in ten gallon drums out back. It was not a pretty sight.

Does History Support the Story?

One would-be client was attending a family funeral where her grandma told a story about how her own grandmother was to have inherited $2 million from Germany in 1932. The client even produced newspaper articles stating how Grandma Wilhelmina was the heiress to an estate left by her brother, Martin Ott, the mayor of Otisheim, Germany, in the 1910s, who, incidentally, left $35 million to the town as well. Unfortunately, Hitler never allowed the money to leave the country, and Grandma Wilhelmina died penniless, as did many of her descendants.

Also included in the packet was a letter from a genealogist in Otisheim whom the family had hired, stating there was never a mayor by the name of Ott, no news accounts of the event and no one who could recall the town ever receiving such a sum of money. What she did find out was that Great-Great-Grandad was the illegitimate son of a woman named Susan Ott, thereby concluding the inheritance was probably nothing more than a "beautiful tale."

Well, Grandma was downright indignant at the suggestion that her mother and the newspaper would concoct such a story, and the whole family wanted the mystery settled, once and for all. For my contribution to the cause, I was offered a nice percentage of the family fortune.

Intriguing as the tale was, I had to pass, given the German genealogist found:

- Not a single Ott ever held the office of mayor in Otisheim, Germany
- No 1932 newspaper mentioned the event
- No one in Otisheim had ever heard of a $35 million inheritance to the village

- No Martin Ott died in the early 1900s

Upon cursory inspection, I noted the article that "proved" the story was not from Germany at the time the alleged events occurred but from Great-Grandma's own Iowa newspaper, published sometime before her death in 1946. It was a simple human interest piece, in no way researched for the authenticity of the claim.

The genealogist's research showed the legend was based upon a false premise: that Martin Ott was, at one time, mayor of Otisheim. Knocking away that false foundation unfortunately took the wind right out of its windfall conclusion. I certainly did not think Great-Grandma concocted a "beautiful tale"; I think she simply told the paper a story she believed to be true, having heard it all her life. That the newspaper reported the tale gave it the respectability of truth.

Unbelievably, many clients arrive with such fanciful tales, and most turn out not to be true. How and why do such stories get started? *Why* is simple. Everyone wants to be special, and if there is nothing immediate to glom on to, royalty or money often rears its heady head. *How* is often more complicated. As with the case of Great-Great-Grandma Wilhelmina, consider this possible scenario.

Say around 1915, unmarried Susan Ott told her illegitimate son about his "daddy," the fictitious Martin Ott, dead hubby and big important guy in Otisheim. As the years passed, this hotshot job of Martin's took the form of mayor of the bucolic burg. Mayors make big bucks, of course, and since Susan Ott had none of them, she might have then claimed Martin's estate was tied up in messy legal proceedings. The kid bought the story because that's what kids do.

Two decades passed and still no money. In the meantime, Susan Ott dies, never having to explain Papa's missing loot. Sure, mused the boy, twenty years is a long time for probate to close, but he'd been buying the dead-daddy story for so long, he wasn't about to stop now. Through the years, the myth continued, fueled by descendants anxious to redeem the lost fortune and hazy on the ancestral lineage necessary to back their claim.

As much as I wanted to receive a big fat commission, I

just couldn't fit the square pegs in the round holes. If I could have, I'd have invented some rich relatives of my own.

When Should Your Protagonist Decline the Case, or at Least Be Forced Into Taking It Through Some Clever Plot Twist?

Just what are an investigator's moral responsibilities? What should one do when it becomes obvious the person he's hired to find doesn't want to be found? What about locating underage kids for a noncustodial parent? Should your hero gleefully pick up when potential clients call collect from prison? The answers to all these queries reflect what your protagonist—and you as the writer—consider to be your own personal code of ethics. Were I to suggest such mandates, everyone who reads this book would end up writing the very same story. And it would be my story. (I got off the hook nicely on that one, don't you think?)

Cases No Thinking PI Would Take

- Legal ramifications. If your PI is asked to find an old landlord so the past renter can press his nose into cement in front of Mann's Chinese Theater, anyone but a morally challenged PI might want to pass. If it takes a judgment call—finding an underage kid, for example, or a woman who appears to be in hiding—a better idea is to act as an intermediary and deliver a letter or phone call only.

- People you can't "identify." Which of the fourteen thousand Rick Smiths in the phone book is the one your client's stuck on? If your client can't supply a proper name, middle initial, DOB, SSN, where the MP lived or *something* and your protagonist actually *finds* the MP, then you'll impress everyone but the professionals.

- The client has no money. Beware of clients who call from a phone booth, insist you run the information while they wait and then try to pay with a stolen credit card.

- The story's hinky as heck. When the client clearly has a

hidden agenda, then, as interesting as that is, any PI worth his weight in gin bottles would ultimately pass.

- Personal safety. Some cases are simply over one's level of expertise. Would Nancy Drew really swipe that kid out of Libya?
- Another investigator has already exhausted all leads, and now the client wants a "quick fix." These clients are simply a pain in the rear porch swing, and I have absolutely no idea why anybody would want to read about one.

Given the proper budget, of course, all cases are ultimately do-able, especially if we're talking fiction. As for the clients themselves, I'm not saying any one of the irritants above should be hung up on if their presence will fuel a good story. Just be aware that your protagonist *shouldn't* be taking the case but is anyway.

How and Why People Hide Their Whereabouts

First let me say that the primary way to hide their whereabouts is to misrepresent their *identity*, not actually hide their physical bodies. Unless one is committed to sneaking in and out of his apartment with a bag over his head, someone is going to notice the place is occupied. So instead of using groucho glasses, scoundrels attempt to muddy their statistics—name, DOB, SSN—so their persuers simply cannot detect them in databases and public record, much the way you can't find a word in a dictionary if you are too far off in the spelling.

Why do scoundrels do it? So they can continue being scoundrels. Why do they *say* they do it?

The Secrecy . . . Er, Privacy Issue

People *looovvve* to talk about privacy. *It's nobody's business*, they are prone to say. But more often than not, this banner of "privacy" hides a myriad of "secrets." In 1989, O.J. Simpson told police, "Go away. This [beating up Nicole] is a family matter." O.J. Simpson wanted his *privacy*. And that night he was granted it—by the police and by the press at large. Later, of course, circumstances were too abundantly fascinating for any of us to grant him that courtesy any longer. And then, after that, many people changed their minds a little about privacy. Like that perhaps the word might also sometimes mean "unaccountability."

But then, O.J. was a celebrity. Let's talk about real people.

Nobody Cares

Once a man wrote saying he was interested in the *reverse* of our usual activity. Somewhere he recalled reading that people have a constitutional right to privacy. ("Life, liberty and the pursuit of . . ." Nah, it must be elsewhere.) Anyway, he informed he'd like some! This man assured me he wasn't running from the law, nor had he "stiffed" anyone. "But really," he protested, "questions asking my grandmother's bra size are too much."

In an incoherent and self-important manner, this man went on to tell how, after hearing his fellow prospective jurors being subjected to "intensive, embarrassing and personal questions," he asked the judge about his own "Miranda" rights. When assured he could decline to answer anything he deemed too personal, this fellow then refused to volunteer any information at all, even simple things like his age, birthplace and marital status. As you can imagine, the questioning was mercifully brief. "Unfortunately," complained the letter writer, "no one else followed my sterling example, leaving the pettifoggers free to continue." (I looked it up. It means "an unethical lawyer who handles trumped-up cases.")

This man claimed he wanted advice on how to avoid the "busy's," as he put it, but I suspected he just wanted to draw even more attention to himself than he already had, which, now that I think about it, is the *exact opposite* of privacy. Still, he insisted, "It gets tiresome telling people I charge $499 for my time and having them hang up before I get a billing address."

This dope was making the same mistake many more astute folks make regarding the privacy issue. They are under the impression that others are innately interested in them. Bright guy here was invited to participate in our judicial process and not because the lady who stuffed envelopes in the jury department thought him an engrossing chap and was too shy to ask if he was married. He was called there, instead, to help comprise a team to decide the fate of one or several individuals. To that end, this prospective juror was asked carefully thought-out questions designed to determine if he'd be a fair and suitable juror in the matter before the court. When he changed the focus from the upcoming trial to himself, the court got its answer. Thankfully, before it was too late.

Turning Over a New Leaf

And then there was Scott whose life began to fall apart the day he touched the dome light cover in his car and it cracked wide open. After his car's exhaust system fell off on the tollway, the turn signal came off in his hand. His braking system consisted of turning off the key and pulling the hand brake. Because of these misfortunes, Scott claimed he missed so much college that his dream of transferring into Michigan State University was gone.

Scott claimed to be a much different person today—and he wanted to be one, too! Could I tell him how to get a new identity? This, he assured me, might be the only way for him to get into MSU. An honorable goal, to be sure.

I suspected there was more to Scott's academic downfall than he let on. OK, bad stuff happens to bad cars, but you can't go around changing your identity every time your fan belt busts. For the record, whenever people want to do something they know they shouldn't be doing, they find a noble cause. Starting over. Protecting their privacy. Protecting their privacy so they can start over.

Anyway, for the sake of argument, let's say Scott were to acquire a new identity—the most common method being stealing one from a child who died too young to sully his own name in the "system." The new Scott would probably not have graduated from high school, which, as I understand it, is a prerequisite to most good universities. And even if somehow Scott were able to earn a degree under this new name, wouldn't he then be destined to use it when applying for whatever terrific job was dependent upon the degree? Would Scott then marry under this phoney moniker? And what epithet would he put on his child's birth certificate? In short, by changing his identity, Scott was signing on to live the rest of his life in the shadow of this whole other dead person.

So in the end, this attempt at "privacy" was not only creating a whole can of worms, it was entirely pointless. Which, again, makes me think Scott had more to hide than a cracked dome light.

How People Purposely Hide Their Whereabouts—Lite

The gambit of hiding from humanity can run from just not answering one's door to faking one's own death, but the majority of shy guys adopt just a few sly habits that can allow them to go on with their lives unbothered by their past boo-boos.

The Mail Drop

This is one of the most effective ways to hide one's whereabouts. With it, scoundrels can be assured, aside from some really hot-under-the-collar camper-outer at Mailboxes Etc., nobody will be able to confront them with their misdeeds. In all my years in the biz, I've yet to figure out how to crack a mail drop. One can confirm someone retains a slot there, but since the proprietors' entire business consists of giving patrons a place to anonymously accept mail, these guys give out *nothing*.

The Post Office Box

This one is a whole lot easier to crack. Although it performs the same service as a mail drop, this government-run counterpart *will* give out the address if you have a summons to serve. Unlike the mail drop box, the post office has confirmed all the information presented when the box was opened, including the validity of the address. Of course, that might have been several years ago, and scoundrels can and do move.

Letters Accepted and Sent On

As strange as it may seem, many scoundrels still maintain friends. Usually these are confellow compadres who are willing to help out in exchange for friendship, cuddling, goodwill or some other viable compensation. Using this send-on method, the conguy retains the benefits of a real address—receiving mail and looking legit—without the hassle of having to be accountable for his actions. But unlike the mail drop or post office box, which requires a lengthy stakeout to locate the person's true whereabouts, this accomplice knows *everything*. Lucky for us, *ve have vays of making them talk.*

Unlisted Phone and Address

In many cities, the directory assistance operator cannot see unlisted numbers on his screen, and so, when he says there is no listing, it would be erroneous to assume your scoundrel does not live in that town. Savvy protagonists *ask* the operator if he shows "nonpubs." (Savvy protagonists also call them "nonpubs.")

Staying Out of Public Record

The *only* way for an American to obtain complete public record anonymity is to never have rented an apartment, bought a home, gotten a driver's license, registered to vote, applied for credit, sued or gotten sued within our country's borders. Even so, once captured for motoring about without documentation, all one's hard-earned "invisibleness" would be kaput in the time it took the cop to write the traffic ticket.

Now, while I steadfastly maintain that public records, for the most part, protect the honest from the unscrupulous by recording the authenticity of certain transactions, I also think the average person has the right to keep his *physical address* confidential if he wants to do so.

I, for one, have this problem. Because I'm a business person, I need to be findable; yet, obviously, I'd prefer no gun-toting ex-con know exactly which grimy window is mine. To this end, I use a post office box for home and business and *never* give my physical address to anyone whose identity I cannot verify.

Public Records

Until recently, most public records were available only at the county level. Should an investigator know where to look, he became happy, well adjusted and could afford good art. If not, he was banished to gumshoe hell with the rest of the dumshoes. Today, databases like Lexis-Nexis make nationwide searching of these records a one-stop shopping extravaganza.

Property records. Recording of one's site address here is unavoidable since, obviously, that *is* the point. Trusting scoundrels list this valuable asset in someone else's name; or they forfeit their homeowner's exemption, thereby masquerading their home as a rental unit; or they have one of their many corporations acquire it and accept the appropriate tax ramifications.

Voter's registration. Once a skip tracer's treasure chest, these files are becoming much less available to nonelection aficionados such as the PI. A physical address is required on the form, although cops and politicians are awarded confidentiality. Serious scoundrels often keep their political yearnings to themselves.

Driving and vehicle records. Most states' rosters are accessed by either name and DOB or DL# or SSN. If an MP keeps those three bits of information out of *other* public records, there is a shot nobody can find him here either, since all the PI will have is his name. Still, the DMV is not the end-all as a locating resource since nobody, especially the scoundrel, rushes down to inform the DMV when he moves. Expect these addresses to be several years old and possibly in need of update.

Business ownership. Getting listed in the Fictitious Business Name Index or in corporate ownership can't be avoided if this is one's destiny. True scoundrels up to no good don't bother with FBNs; they just do business under any names they fancy and cash the checks at a check-cashing establishment. More sophisticated baddies muddy the waters by having their second corporations own their first, but any competent, patient and well-paid investigator can eventually untangle their handiwork.

Civil suits, judgments and tax liens. All can be avoided by settling these disputes out of court and paying all liabilities before deadline dates. Which is exactly what scoundrels *don't* do.

Private Databases

Credit information. Kept pretty darn hush by a little piece of legislation known as the Fair Credit Reporting Act, the $5,000 fine stops most PIs from accessing this system, even when they have the authority to do so. But the FCRA is applicable only when it comes to accessing *payment history*. PIs don't care a whit about that; it's the whereabouts of the creditor they're after. That limited information—name, age, AKA, address and SSN—is known in the industry as "credit header information," and I don't know of a PI anywhere who can't get it any time he wants. This despite all three credit reporting agencies steadfastly refusing to sell it to anyone in the gumshoe game.

The consumer desirous of plastic can still keep his address private simply by listing his newly acquired post office box when paying next month's bills. The physical residence will then be recorded as "former address" and each month slide farther into history. It's still there, of course, but it sure *looks* old.

Marketing databases. Once sold only to direct mailers, these databases are made up of listed telephone numbers, property records, magazine subscribers, census demographics, cross directory information and the like. Anyone who maintains an unlisted number and a post office box is unlikely to appear, since the base information is made up of the physical addresses and everything added into that. Once that address is established, however, every other bit of data corresponding to it—price of the house, median neighborhood income—finds a home, including sometimes even the names of the kids.

Creating a Whole New Identity

In 1975, Randy decided to take on another identity because he had ruined his own with drug convictions, jail time, bad credit, etc. He was twenty-five years old and used the "dead child method."

First, Randy paid a visit to his local county recorder's office and researched microfilm death certificates for a suitable "donor," a male child born in his birth year who had died in infancy. With that, he applied for and got a California driver's license. Randy was amazed at how easy it was, but reluctant to use his new credentials just then. He tucked them away for when the timing was right.

In 1984, it was. After the metamorphosis, there was no one in Randy's life who even knew he had a former identity. By creating a whole new persona from this child who had died before entering "the system," Randy's records were free of conflicting input from credit, employment and Social Security sources—all major spoilsports. Everything was going great. He was self-employed and drug free for ten years. Then, in 1994, Randy lost his "donor's" birth certificate, and he wanted to know if, since the time he acquired his credentials, there had been instigated some cross-matching of birth and death records, making it risky for him to attempt to obtain another copy. Should he gamble going back to the recorder's office? he wondered. Were these birth certificates still available to the public?

Yes, they are, and easily orderable, even by mail. As for a cross-referencing of birth and death records, Randy would not have a problem since there is no law against ordering the birth certificate of a dead child. If Randy's new identify had not caused him any problems by the time he wrote to me, he was probably home free, since he'd already established plenty of evidence that his new self was, in fact, alive and doing business at Gumps. In reality, he really didn't even need the birth certificate any more unless he was desirous of a passport.

Changing One's Name

Plenty of people change their names every day—women altering their marital status, kids getting adopted, people called Kristophos Yukabonkerzkapowpolis who'd rather not be—and nobody thinks much about it. There is likewise no law against going by any epithet you choose, otherwise Cary Grant, Mark Twain and Milli Vanilli would all be singing "Jailhouse Rock" in the pen name/stage name wing of Sing Sing. What *is* illegal is using a false identity to defraud a person or business, such as in obtaining credit cards under a new name when your old one gets inexplicably sullied. You can legally modify your moniker for any number of reasons, but if you want to scamper away from creditors, dodge a lawsuit or escape capture for a crime, mark that down as a *no can do.*

Changing a Name Through Usage. (Legal) The easiest (and most paper trail-free) method of swapping names is simply by using the chosen epithet *consistently* in all aspects of one's personal, social and business life. Surprisingly, this is perfectly legal as long as it is not done in order to defraud anyone and one stops using the former name as soon as he takes on the second. The upside to this, for scoundrels, is that it leaves no paper trail.

The downside, ironically, is the same. Lack of paperwork makes people who *like* paperwork very suspicious, and wary folk rarely give out things like disability checks, food stamps or credit cards.

To cope with these quirky nitpickers, smart name-changers fill out a Declaration of Legal Name Change, thereby creating some paperwork but eliminating more hassles. For one, this form gives a starting date, which is essential for the passport folks who insist a newly named person must have been using his current moniker a full five years before they'll recognize it under the usage method.

Petitioning the Court for a Name Change. (Legal) If you're an actress and you think perhaps you'll get meatier parts if your name is Meryl Streep, I wouldn't order those monogrammed sheets just yet. If you long to be called an unpronounceable symbol that has to be hand-drawn by a Tibetan calligrapher, you'll probably be turned down, too, unless your name is Prince, and then apparently you can do anything you want. You'll also find resistance in changing your moniker to a racial slur, a number, a question mark or a threatening or obscene word. So how about a 1960s throwback changing her name just because she likes being called Moonbeam? If her intent is not malicious, or if the court doesn't know it's malicious, Ms. Moonbeam probably will get her wish.

Petitioning the court can cost up to $400 and requires publishing a notice in a public newspaper. The steps are (1) fill out a Petition for Change of Name at the local county clerk's office; (2) obtain a court date and pay the filing fees; (3) publish the name change once a week for four consecutive weeks; (4) check with the court to see if a hearing is required; and (5) send a copy to the secretary of state.

Name Change Through Confusion. (Illegal) Eugene James Baskin was born September 12, 1962. He was a decent fellow, always paying his MasterCard on time. Still, Gene didn't get much respect because his nasty twin, James Eugene Baskin—same DOB, of course, and whose SSN was, no, not one digit off but forty—was doing the bad thing all over town.

No wonder poor Gene was in a tizzy! Imagine a mother calling one infant Eugene James and the other James Eugene? Wasn't the twin thing confusing enough without her naming each the other's middle name, followed by his first? What must she have been thinking?

Chas, the client who brought us into this little fantasyland, was a gay man with dubious emotional connections to the man claiming to be Eugene James. Still, Chas was sick and tired of bailing out the good twin because of the screwups of his evil other. (Gene claimed the awful one had ruined his ability to charge because the credit files got all mixed up.) Had Chas ever seen the boys together, we kindly asked. We were surprised to hear he had, but not nearly as astonished to learn they were fraternal, not identical, siblings.

Funny thing, though. Although we found no match at all on the bad twin, the good twin had a criminal record longer than the English Channel.

Changing One's Sex

Robby, or rather Cordella, was missing. The last Mom and Pop knew of him/her was after the sex change operation when he/she went into court and obtained a restraining order against them for sexual abuse. (Completely untrue, they claimed.) Now they wondered if he/she was alive and well or in some kind of trouble. They last knew Cordella to be living with Barry, but they don't know much about him either, except, presumedly, his sex. Mom and Pop had Robby's old SSN but worried it might be changed due to the fact that he was now a she.

Now, normally we won't take a case involving restraining orders, but in this instance, Mom and Dad seemed just fine, and Robby/Cordella seemed a bit on the wacky side. So, after agreeing only to pass on a letter but *not* reveal Cordella's whereabouts unless he/she OK'd it, we plugged Robby's old SSN into a database.

And voilá! Up popped Cordella still operating under the same old number. This search listed four different names for her: maiden name, "married" name, Barry's name and a combination of both their last names. But nowhere did we find a Robby.

According to Nolo Press's *How to Change Your Name*, in some states—including Colorado, Cordella's birth state—once sex-change surgery is complete, a new birth certificate can be obtained from Vital Records, indicating the subject was actually *born* of that gender. With that documentation, Cordella was able to register her new name with Social Security, as well as marry her sweetie, since they are no longer of the same sex.

Still, note that the Administration didn't issue Cordella a brand-spanking-new number to go with her brand-spanking-new name and other various body parts. That's because the whole purpose of an SSN is to *identify*, not to *confuse*.

Obtaining a New Birth Certificate

- Legitimately, brand new birth certificates are issued for a smattering of reasons, falling mostly under the headings of updates regarding paternity, adoption and, yes, even sex-change operations.

- Illegitimately, there's a whole other thing going on here. Many scoundrels are desirous of new birth certificates because they've not done such bang-up jobs on their first go-arounds in life.

For these folks, states with death indexes available for public view are the answer. In California, for example, at the time of this writing, anyone can obtain another's birth certificate just by knowing two bits of data: the birth name and the date birthed. To guard against blackguards, counties keep their birth indexes out of public view so, in theory at least, the asker won't be able to supply the essential information unless he has some legitimate connection to the person.

In reality, to pull off "the dead baby scam," one would work backward, finding the death certificate first and then ordering the birth record from the information found there. And no, the clerk won't cross-reference a birth request with the state-wide death index since there is no law against ordering the birth certificate of a dead child.

Aging one's documents is a common practice. Brand new copies of old credentials are often suspect. To guard against this faux pas, Trent Sands, author of Loompanics Unlimited's *Reborn in the U.S.A.*, suggests wearing your documents around in your shoe for a week. He also advises putting them into a sandwich bag before presenting them, thereby eliminating a whole other set of questions.

Obtaining Another Social Security Number

There are almost as many ways to get a new SSN as there are SSNs, and which method is chosen depends mostly upon how long one intends to use the number before spinning off into the night. The more care and duplicity used going in, the longer the end usage.

Acquiring a Brand-New Number. So how does a grown-up walk into the Administration and explain why he doesn't already have an SSN? One method is to bring along an obvi-ously mentally impaired adult—one's (alleged) brother, per-haps, who has never had need of an SSN until now, since his parents have died and it is up to you to get him on public assistance.

Another method is to alter a teenager's certificate and then send in a sixteen-year-old accomplice to hand it over to the clerk. Variations on this theme include utilizing the credentials of a dead child (as discussed above) or even using a live child's certificate as is, knowing full well it will create a duplicate record when the kid inevitably applies himself. (When that mess eventually becomes apparent, the Administration will probably issue the kid a *new* number, since his old one has been compro-mised. Ironic, eh?)

Requiring the most preparation and planning, obtaining a brand new SSN often yields a lifetime of worry-free masquerad-ing. Sure, it's a lot of bother and takes face-to-face lying to a public official to pull it off, but scoundrels don't seem to mind that sort of thing.

Using Somebody Else's Number. Household trash often yields such treasures as bank statements and the like, which contain personal information such as SSNs. Or if you're not into filth, the same document can be snatched out of the mailbox on the front end. Public records like tax liens and judgments are chockablock with nine-digiters, but who wants to apply for a Gold Card using the identity of a tax dodger? The upside of using someone else's number is that, if you choose right, that person's already established some pretty fine credit. The downside is that the method only has a thirty to sixty day lifespan, since that's the long and short end of a billing cycle. Scoundrels who choose this technique are mostly into credit card fraud.

Making Up a Number. Keep it to nine digits and it will probably work, at least for a while, and depending upon what it is used for. What the scoundrel won't know is if the number belongs to a live someone else, to a person who is obviously dead or to nobody at all. Applying for credit under this recently acquired random fabrication will surely cause disappointment since the name and address where the scoundrel wants the swing set sent is certainly not going to be the same one that pops up on the credit report. Equally upsetting, the scammer may discover the person he's randomly picked has worse credit than he does.

Obtaining a Driver's License

The whole identity package is built like a set of dominoes, and the crowning glory is the driver's license and the Neiman Marcus credit card. With those two crowd pleasers, new identity seekers can feel well dressed and poised to face the world.

But getting there is a process. Even sporting a new old-looking birth certificate, how does an adult, faced with a skeptical DMV clerk, explain not already having a driver's license from *some* state? Easy. He says he lost it.

This new identity seeker will, of course, have to provide some other form of identification, and that's where that new old-looking birth certificate comes in. Alternative credentials include a voter's registration card, obtained by flashing a library card, which was gotten by displaying a piece of mail sent to the new-person-in-progress at a local address. Once the ball gets rolling, institutions rely on the validity of the documents before it and trust their predecessors to have checked them out. What kind of world are they living in?

Establishing Credit

So there a person is, new identity in hand, and still no one will fork over a sandwich today for his promise to pay next Tuesday. What *is* the point?

A savvy scoundrel knows what is needed is a "trainer" card, some innocuous piece of plastic to practice on until the world begins to trust the new him. (Silly world.) But who will take that dubious step as the first creditor?

The scoundrel's bank, that's who. After all, this person trusted his life savings to the tellers, the least the depository can do in return is to issue him a MasterCard with a $300 limit. Especially since he's just gotten back from Belize where he's been studying for his doctorate in New Age Herbal Liposuction, which will surely change the world as we know it.

But what if the scoundrel has trusted his entire credit future to the SSN of a dead person? Will he be found out? OK, yes, there is a "Dead Guy Warning" (not the technical term) that appears frequently on credit records, but this happens only because TRW, CBI and TransUnion all feed Social Security's death data into their files. By utilizing the widely acclaimed "dead baby method," such embarrassments will unlikely occur.

THE FOUR-STEP FORMULA FOR FINDING SOMEONE

For the first several years I was plying my trade, my focus was to find the MP, no matter what I had to go through to get there. As you will see from chapter fifteen, "Building a Dossier Until It Includes a Current Address," I took cases I now label "undo-able," and I do'd 'em, simply because I had no idea dat I couldn't.

Then as my expertise matured, it became a matter of not *if* I could find a person, but how quickly—in how few steps— I could accomplish this feat. Without really thinking about it, I began to reduce the process to a series of shortcuts. I found, for example, I didn't really have to scour every transgression listed in the courthouse records. By pulling just one tax lien, I could glean an SSN, which, back at my trusty computer, would usually yield the person's whereabouts. My courtroom visits were now reduced to (1) pull a tax lien and (2) go home.

Then came the day I was asked to teach a class on finding

people. The asker: the producers at *The Oprah Winfrey Show*. The audience: the nation.

Gulp.

The pressure was on. How *did* I do this? Forced finally to analyze my methods, I realized I had reduced the process to four steps: (1) establishing the person's legal name; (2) finding some "identifier" that rendered him unique among his same-named counterparts; (3) creating a dossier on the MP until the information included his last address; and (4) verifying he was still at that residence.

The following is the essence of that nationwide reunion extravaganza that allowed members of the studio audience to find lost loved ones—some gone for up to forty years—in just a matter of days.

Step One: Establishing the Legal Name

Unbelievably, many people who take the bold step of hiring a private investigator have made the first fatal error of not having the proper legal names of the people they are looking for. As well as they seem to know these people, often this essential tidbit is overlooked.

The Last Name

Joan Rivers had been throwing out the name Conrad Behuzelhoff for years on air, hoping her long-lost college sweetie would get the hint and give her a jingle. Or a bauble. He'd moved on, I guess. So when this girl detective arrived on the scene for her one-hour talk show, Joan couldn't resist throwing me the challenge. When I asked her how to spell Behuzelhoff, we segued into a brief but entertaining "Give me a *B*" cheerleading routine and then danced around the issue of just exactly *when* Joan was in college. Still, at least I got the name of the institution out of her, if nothing more, and once home I accessed the nationwide phone disc for the widely touted Behuzelhoff clan. Seeing there were none in all of America, I sensed, astutely, that Joan had the wrong spelling of the last name.

A call to the university alumni committee changed all that, and once the proper spelling was established, Conrad was easily findable in that very same phone disc. And no, I was not invited to the wedding, if ever there was one.

The First Name

You won't find Dan Quayle by bothering any of the other umpteen Daniel Quayles out there because the ex-vp's handle is actually J. Danforth Quayle. Multitudes of folks are going by their middle names, and even their best friends don't know—which is exactly why their best friends can't find them.

The Middle Name or Initial

Essential in finding someone with a common name, the middle initial can set him apart from all the others. To determine this often indispensable ingredient, or the proper spelling of the first or last, it is often necessary to go back to the last "sighting" and find the name written in a phone book, on a real estate record or even in a high school yearbook. Skip step #1 and anyone looking for an MP will be forever sorry—and a little lonesome on the holidays.

Step Two: Establishing "Identifiers"

What are they? Those bitsy bits of data that, when coupled with a name serve to "uniquify" an individual. Since there are far too many Richard Smiths in the world (what can their mothers be thinking?) coupling that name with a middle initial reduces the possibilities enormously. Add a date of birth and you get the numbers down to a wheelbarrow full, and throw in the town where *your* Rick Smith was born, and you're talking about, hmmmm, pretty much one. Yes, unbelievably, only one Richard I. Smith was born in all of Chicago on April 12, 1976.

If that.

The Best Identifiers Don't Ever Change

- The SSN is the best identifier because, in theory, at least, only one is issued per citizen, and an SSN is never recycled, not even when the MP is no longer in need of the Administration's generous benefits.

- The date of birth is the second best identifier because it, like the SSN, lasts a lifetime and is the one bit of trivia that family members, what's-your-sign kind of friends and anybody else whose ever gotten an application from the person is likely to know.

Some Identifiers Do Change
but Still Have Longevity

- The spouse lasts a while. Usually. Some die, of course, divorce or run off with the Avon lady, but oftentimes, all you know about the Rick Smith you're looking for is that he was the one once married to lovely Lindy Lou.

- The address is often the only identifier presented by the client. "He lived over on Elm in the 1960s" means to a good PI, did he or his parents own that house on Elm? Who did they sell it to? What was the legal name on the property?

- The place of birth is an identifier. Even amongst all the Rick Smiths born April 12, 1976, exactly how many have SSNs issued out of Illinois?

What Are the Chances of Finding
Two Folks With the Same Identifiers?

Slim and none. In reality, a name, even a common one, coupled with a date and place of birth, forms an identifier as unique as a Social Security number.

Here's why. With the lottery, you know it takes just six numbers to win a gazillion dollars. The state can make that generous offer because the odds are 18,009,460 to 1 against you actually being able to pick the right six numbers.

A birth date *also* contains just six figures. True, the month has only twelve possibilities and the date just thirty-one, but unlike the lottery, the numbers have to be in order for there to be a match. Package a DOB with a name and place of birth, and you've got a dead-on identifier that drives a bulldozer through a pop's denial that he's not the same Rick Smith who fathered little Ricky back in 1953.

Where Do You Find Identifying Information?

Go back to the beginning. Mary Ferrand watched *The Oprah Winfrey Show* and in amongst blubbering along with everybody else over their long-lost loved ones, she suddenly got a hankering to see her old high school heartbeat from Lafayette, California. She called Rat Dog, as well she should have, and requested a search. Find my man was the mandate given.

Now normally, we would have labeled Bob No-middle-initial Davis, haven't-seen-in-forty-years, don't-know-where-he-lived-or-his-parents'-names a long lost cause. But since the flirt fest began in our own backyard, we knew we could access old records that might very well lead to him.

Step one, therefore, was to identify Bobby. All we knew was that he was the Bob Davis who attended Acalanes High School back in 1967. A search of the library's yearbooks showed his middle initial to be *G*, and the school's projection of his graduation date narrowed his YOB down to one of two.

Using the school district as a boundary, we next identified the old homestead once owned by the Davis clan. Unfortunately the house had been sold four times over since then, making it unlikely the present owners would know where the family had gone.

Working then with just the full name, Robert G. Davis, and the year of birth, we scanned all California real estate records and found several likely candidates, one of whom owned a bookstore in a small logging community, was coming out of a bad marriage and just happened to be our still crew-cut and newly available Bobby. Case closed.

Public record. In searching for our Bobby, above, another tact we originally attacked was to look for his mum and dad, as they were of paper-trail age when eighteen-year-old Bobby wasn't. In doing that, if you recall, we did locate the family home, thereby gleaning Mom's and Pop's true legal names. Unfortunately, Dad's moniker was also Robert Davis—no middle initial given—and we didn't even have a YOB on him, so we ended up knowing more about Bobby Jr. than Bobby Sr.

But you get the idea.

Identifying Someone Through His Business

Poor Dave and his good wife, Glennis, responded to a classified ad in their trusted newspaper explaining how they could make $35,000 per year by investing in fourteen strategically placed pay phones. "Statewide Bell" referred them to three satisfied customers *and* the Vendors Association of North America *and* the Better Business Bureau, all of whom either gave the company glowing recommendations and/or called them "a member in good standing."

It took several weeks for Dave to complete the paperwork; meanwhile, a second company was finding locations for the pay phones. Although Dave received programming instructions, Statewide advised him to wait until they had all the locations to begin that complicated procedure.

Then, you guessed it, Dave called the company's 800 number and found it "temporarily disconnected." He FedExed the company a letter—using its own account number—and Federal Express phoned back to say the company had moved, left no forwarding address and its account was "not billable at this time." This, if you are unfamiliar with the pay phone business, is not a good sign.

Now poor Dave realized he had nothing. Statewide Bell was obviously a freshly formed band of renegades, and the BBB's newest member simply hadn't been around long enough (under that name) to garnish any complaints. Dave wanted his money back. But to do that, he had to identify the brainpower behind Statewide Bell.

Using a nationwide cross-directory database, we contacted the still-irked building manager of Statewide's lavish corporate suites, who confirmed the company had indeed vanished in the night, taking with them several months' back rent still grasped in their greedy little fists. Gladly, he furnished Statewide's corporate president's name, as well as some of the other key figures in the scam-on-the-run.

From the postal inspector, we learned this company's crafty corporate hierarchy managed to sock away $2.5 million in pay phone sales in the six months just prior to its becoming Statewide Bell. The "satisfied customers" Dave chatted with were what the FBI called "singers," one of whom was the scoundrel mum of the company president.

I'm sure what Statewide considered a successful conclusion to this business venture was for Dave and others to simply give up or, worst case scenario, pursue them civilly. Should these irked clients actually have found someone to serve summons on, they'd never have collected their inevitable court judgments since this perfectly valid corporation would, by then, have had no assets. What happened instead was that Dave's name was added to a long list of fellow unfortunates, all of whom might someday be called upon to testify in a federal fraud trial. Meanwhile, Statewide Bell—under other names—continued to advertise in major newspapers, daily luring innocents into this financial holocaust. Tragically, the Feds didn't dare shut the company down until they had all the evidence they'd need for a successful prosecution.

Misdeeds That Go Undocumented Equal No Can Do

Since finding people consists largely of following a paper trail, it is reasonable to conclude that without a paper trail, a detective would have difficulty locating someone.

Take the case of Cindy who was looking for the father of her daughter, now a young adult. The first time she saw Robert, he said hi and would she like to go out, and she said no because she had a boyfriend.

After a few more chance meetings, Cindy agreed to have a drink with her admirer. That event apparently required headgear, so when her date asked her to come upstairs to get his hat, Cindy innocently tagged along. Robert then "raped me very fast, in about one second." Since the event didn't even require undressing, she figured her then boyfriend wouldn't be interested. When she got pregnant, he unknowingly took the rap.

Cindy's daughter, at twenty-two, was not light like her "father" but dark like Robert. We all know what that means. Since life with boyfriend/husband didn't turn out the way Cindy hoped, she was now looking to find Robert and introduce him to his dark-haired daughter. Unfortunately, all she knew was his very common name and that he was a truck driver from New Jersey.

Yes, you guessed it, mark this another no can do.

As we've patently discussed henceforth, in order to find someone you must "identify" him, which means putting together a full legal name with date and place of birth, Social Security number or even an old address. Robert's name was so common that finding him would be next to impossible unless the state of New Jersey would supply us with his birth date, an unlikely scenario, given the limited information we had.

What happened to Cindy is now called "date rape" and not taken nearly as casually as it was back in the Free Love 1970s. Had she reported Robert then, she might have gotten a reputation as an ungrateful spoilsport, but the cad would still have been positively identified when Dano booked his body parts into evidence, leaving a nice paper trail to follow up on when her daughter's surprise ethnicity later emerged.

Finding Someone You Can't ID
by Finding Someone You Can

Jeff's mother, Loraine, died in 1952 when the boy was eight. During their ten-year marriage, Loraine's husband, Miles, forbid her from corresponding with her family, and after her death, the hubby disappeared with the child. All Jeff's aunt, our client, knew is that they lived in Milwaukee during the 1950s and that Miles worked for a newspaper there. Now she wanted to know more, like if the blackguard was still alive and what happened to her now forty-nine-year-old nephew.

Finding no record of Jeff in our extensive databases, we next checked Social Security's Master Death Index and found Miles had expired in Denver in 1982 of cardiorespiratory arrest, which seems to get about everyone regardless of what originally ailed him. The death certificate listed Jeff as informant, and so, finding no probate in that county, we contacted the funeral parlor. There we learned Jeff had resided at his dad's apartment prior to the wake, where he had stayed just long enough to clean out his father's belongings. Because Jeff was never on the lease, the apartment manager had no other information. Denver public records showed no trace of him either.

We did, however, find a 1978 property grant deeded from Miles to a lady legally described as "a single woman." Helen claimed to remember nothing of the former owner and was more than a bit fuzzy on exactly how she acquired the house. When we uncovered a marriage and subsequent divorce between Miles and Helen, we called again but never were we able to hit her on a day when this aging lady could recall her former husband and stepson.

After an exhaustive search, we ultimately located Jeffery in another county in the Denver area, a city where we never would have looked had his father not died there.

Step Three: Creating a Dossier Until the Information Gathered Includes the MP's Current Address

First, note there are two methods used in locating someone: searching "globally," by exploring various nationwide databases and/or phone discs, or by tracking the person from his last "sighting" to where he is today. In most cases, of course, the PI uses a combination of the two. (Please note also that "global" does not refer to the entire globe but just that portion of it bordered by Mexico, Canada, the Atlantic and Pacific Oceans.)

Globally

There exists a phone disc, available at all fine software stores, that contains a nationwide reverse directory of all listed telephone numbers in the United States. Although 60 percent of all Americans now have unlisted numbers, this is still a nice roster of nonscoundrels, adopted moms anxious to be reunited and folks who get off on talking to life insurance salesman. If your MP does not possess one of these sterling characteristics, your protagonist needs to know more.

So then, starting with the phone disc, let's talk about how to find someone when you don't know where to start, which is exactly when you should employ the global search method.

Phone disc. Although obviously incomplete, this is a quick and cheap way of locating possible relatives, as well as verifying the most common spelling of the name and where most of the family resides. A good PI would have this standard tool right beside his trusty CD-ROM. A financially challenged PI, or an out-of-town PI, would head on down to the local library.

SS's Master Death Index. If you find your MP here, prepare yourself for the client not wanting to pay the full fee. Still, it is nice to know before you spend a bazooka and a half on database searches that your MP is likely to be among the upright. Again, a savvy PI would have this disc in-house or online. Out of town? Forgot your laptop? Time to tiptoe through the genealogy library.

Various and sundry databases. The most widely ranging of these, at this writing, is a service that allows the searcher to plug in a name and DOB or YOB and come up with likely possibilities. Unlike the phone disc, this service allows you to weed out those who do not fit the age criteria. Made up of driving and voting records, it's a doozy.

Modified Global

Because there are so many possibilities when it comes to public records, discs and databases, it is often helpful to narrow down the search in some way.

Geographically. If your investigator is a very lucky PI, the MP will have disappeared from his very own neighborhood. One of the best ways to begin then is always to have the luxury of perusing one's own county courthouse records for background information. Since he's got four lawsuits on file, an eviction and a hit-'n'-run, you can be relatively sure he is the Rick Smith for whom you are looking, if that is the sort of Rick Smith he is. Building that dossier then, you'd now most likely be able to add Rick's middle initial, last address and perhaps even SSN to your file.

Sometimes one begins on a geographical note, and sometimes one ends on one. After running the name through a nationwide database, for example, you may find "sightings" of your MP in Florida and then, shifting gears to focus on those records, at last come up with a current address.

By deeds or misdeeds. If your MP is the marrying sort, then concentrate your (modified) global search on the marriage—and divorce—index. In real estate? Try property records. Bad boy extraordinaire? Skip on down to the bankruptcy court. A doctor or lawyer? Call and inquire as to a professional license. Sure you're fishing, but you gotta do something for three hundred pages.

Tracking From Place to Place

Sometimes there simply is no other way to find a person than to physically go out and follow him around the world. You run the computer checks, of course, but since the MP has no credit, he operates someone else's car without a license and the only voting he does involves 900 numbers, sooner or later your detective has to actually get off his duff and go out into the real world and burn up some calories.

And that's what happened when my mom (Gray Tail) and I went out looking for seven-year-old Heather's dad. It happened because the little girl's mom had written to Santa Claus, and a postal worker had passed the letter on to the *Contra Costa Times* who had forwarded it to me.

> Dear Santa Claus,
>
> I'm a single mother trying to raise four children by myself. My littlest child has only seen her father once, and he has only once called her one time on the telephone. She is a very hurt child, and thinks it's her fault her father doesn't come to see her. I try to keep her busy instead of thinking about him.
>
> My Christmas Wish is that her father show up to see his only child, wherever he might be.

Gray Tail and I headed for Clearlake, a recreational area known for its abundance of trailer parks. The last info we had said Dad was in one of two places, but when we'd tried to reach both sets of neighbors by phone, both denied knowing him.

At the first site, no one recalled our young dad so Mom and I took pie at the local diner, quizzed the locals and drove on. At the second trailer park, an affable biker pointed us toward Pop's battered Airstream, even though he'd told my chief investigator he'd never heard of the man. We waited around, but Pops was a no-show. Finally we were forced to leave Santa's letter and our own admonishment to call, and we headed for home.

Christmas night, we finally heard from Heather's pop— full of excuses he was—and then he called his girl.

Using These Two Methods Together

Most searches, obviously, are a combination of global searching and tracking. Where the expertise comes in is knowing when to explore by computer and when to go out and knock on doors. For the extravaganza of all searches, employing both methods, read chapter fifteen on creating a dossier.

Step Four: Verifying Someone's There Without His Suspecting

Once your protagonist *thinks* he's located someone, he'll need to verify that address as being current. Often, this activity can be combined with serving a subpoena or punching the MP in the nose.

However, if the investigator is not yet ready to make his move, say, there is still a warrant to be issued, a paternity to be disclosed, a wife's existence to be determined, or 150 pages to fill, the verifying process should, obviously, stand on its own. Let's talk then about how to determine whether someone is at the location you've found, without his suspecting.

Verifying Someone's Current Address Via Telephone

If directory assistance is still giving out the number, the person's still there. Unlike a telephone book, whose data is compiled long before the directory hits the streets and whose contents are frozen in time, directory assistance ceases to dispense information *the moment* the chatterbox moves on.

Unlisted number, but your investigator's somehow got it? Say your PI is (still) looking for Rick Smith; he can call, ask for Rick and listen for the reaction. If he gets a, "Who wants to know?" he's found the laddie all right, or, minimally, he at least knows where he is. "Rick Snotdorf?" your PI then asks. "Is this the number for Rick Snotdorf?" "No, you imbecile," comes the reply, followed by a quick buzz in the ear. Smugly, your PI hangs up, thinking to himself, *Ha! Who's the imbecile?*

But is it the *right* Rick Smith? Our client, Kait, knew she had the right number for Howard Nelson; she just didn't know if it was the same Howard Nelson who had walked out on her mother when she was a little girl of three. When Kait was ten, somebody from the FBI came looking for him, an incident Kait's mother refused to discuss, along with her entire marital experience.

Now, thirty years later, Kait had found a Howard Nelson— with one of his several DOBs—in the Las Vegas area. Even more incriminating, this Howard Nelson was very secretive in his lifestyle and was not on any kind of database or public record that we could find. Kait had ascertained that Howard lived with a woman with a different name but could find nothing on her either.

Through "trickery, a twist of fate and a minor miracle," Kait had somehow acquired this man's unlisted telephone number. We didn't want to know. She was anxious to call but wasn't sure he'd admit to being her father, even if he was. Although he had no inkling his daughter was searching for him, unless Howard had changed his evil ways, there might still be plenty of other people from whom he was hiding. He might even think Kait was somebody else trying to trick him.

What to do!

Actually, Kait had two problems. Besides trying to verify that the Howard Nelson she had found was the Howard Nelson she was searching for, she was concerned that finding this volatile dad might somehow put her family in an explosive situation. So the challenge then was twofold: verifying Howard's paternity, as well as keeping her own identity—and whereabouts— a secret.

Step one was fairly simple. Daddy Nelson was born in Czechoslovakia, so if this man in Las Vegas had that accent, however faint, Kait would know for sure it was him. But to call him, Kait would be exposing herself to potential Caller ID and/ or Caller Return, in the days before you could block such things.

To circumvent such a happenstance, we instructed Kait to make the call from a pay phone, or simply use a telephone that was hooked up exclusively to a fax machine or computer modem. Such numbers are almost always unlisted and very unsatisfying when called.

Kait did call, Howard *did* have a Czechoslovakian accent, but he claimed not to be Dada. Just what are the chances of that?

Verifying the Address
by Computer or Public Record

- Credit header information, that top part of a credit report, consists solely of identifying information, the most helpful of which is often the address. By running this inquiry, either in-house or through someone who has legal access to this highly restricted search, it will show the last time bills were paid from that address, a pretty good indicator the person is still there.

- If your MP is a property owner, then unless there's a home-owner's exemption on the property, it's likely you'll find him there. Nomadic MPs can move in thirty days—or overnight if they so choose—but few land barons are willing to walk away from a viable property. Minimally, the house will contain a renter who will be well aware of where he mails his checks every month.

- Or, if database after database keeps coming up with the same data and it looks current, it's a safe bet you've found your MP as well.

Verifying the Address by Mail or Delivery

- One way to verify the MP's whereabouts is to send a package anonymously (a little stemware is always appreciated) via UPS and then call the company and ask who signed for it. We actually save big Norstrom boxes just for this purpose.

- Your detective can also send a letter and wait for a response. Of course this does give away his identity and location, but sometimes, that's OK. If it's not OK, you're going to need a book on chase scenes. I'd include one here, but I've never made that silly mistake so I've never needed one.

Your protagonist shouldn't make assumptions based upon receiving *no* response from his communique. For example, Nicholas had long been searching for his father, an Italian immigrant who deserted Nick's mother, sister and his two-year-old son just three years after the family's arrival in 1932. One family rumor was that Papa married again—without bothering to divorce Mama—

and raised a whole other family in Philadelphia.

One day, Nick read an article written by a priest with his same very unusual, very Italian last name. Noting that his residency was in Philadelphia and they were close in age, Nick wrote expressing there was a strong possibility that the priest and he were half brothers. The delivery of his certified letter was confirmed, yet no reply ever came from His Holiness. This deafening silence, according to Nick, could only mean the men indeed had the same father, for if it were not so, the courteous thing would have been for him to write, explaining his own family circumstances. Now Nick wanted me to implore the priest to finally respond to his letter.

I didn't do that, but then I rarely do what I'm told.

Instead, I made a cursory check of the nationwide phone disc and found there were at least 271 families nationwide with Nick's same last name, 10 percent of them in Philadelphia. If Nick's "Same Surname Equals Brother" theory held, then Pops was a pretty happening guy for a fellow who lived during what most people referred to as the Depression.

As for why the priest didn't respond, maybe he was just a really busy holy guy. A single call to the rectory confirmed the priest was actually from New York and was simply assigned to Philadelphia—which shot Nick's Father Brother theory all to purgatory.

The moral of this story? No news means *nothing*.

Verifying the Address in Person

The package method. Sometimes, an investigator just needs to get out of the office and stretch his legs. Other times, there is a physical description that needs confirmation or he simply hasn't thought out his next move. Whatever the reason, it behooves the detective to not yet tip his hand; he needs to make sure he's dealing with the right location but without the MP knowing he's figured that out.

So how does one approach a stranger's door, watch to see who answers and then quietly back off into the night? Courteous PIs take a gift, that's how.

What kind of a present works best? Again, stemware is nice. It doesn't have to be anything fancy, maybe even that last unbroken wine goblet your protagonist's sister-in-law sent over at Christmastime. Or a couple of rocks, nicely boxed, if your PI is on a budget. Actually, it's not the contents that are important, but the presentation, since in all likelihood your detective will be long gone by the time the actual gift can be scrutinized.

Asking the neighbors is another fine idea. If your detective is afraid of confrontations like I am, then the old, "Hi, I'm looking for the Neilsons, but I think I have the wrong address," usually gets him out of that pickle. Many people have a lot less difficulty pointing out their neighbors than they do admitting to their own identities.

Surveillance is always my last choice. Yes, your protagonist can sit around in a dark-windowed van waiting to see who comes out, but why would he want to? Although, creatively speaking, I'm sure there are lots of interesting things that could happen on a stakeout, in reality, none of them ever do. Take my advice: go with the package.

Skip Tracing Lite: How to Find Someone in Two Steps Using Identifiers

Four steps too many? One not enough? Now that you know the rules, let's talk about how to break them.

We'll discuss more about databases in chapter twelve, but suffice to say, at the time of this writing, the most powerful tool in locating people is the credit header search, available to any half-witted investigator and legally leased to none of them.

To initiate a credit header search, also called an address update, one needs only a name and last address from 1987 forward, or a Social Security number. About 85 percent of the time, it will pop pretty much anyone who is a normal bill-paying type of person.

So then, Skip Tracing Lite simply involves acquiring enough information to run this mighty search. Grab onto a tax lien or locate a judgment in the county courthouse and you've picked yourself up an SSN. Peruse the voter's registration records and there find an old address on your subject. Plug it into the computer your detective *simply must have* and, because you as an author are in perfect control of your environment, your MP will no longer be among the M.

And to think you read this whole book to find out this one little thing. Tsk. Tsk.

Tracking an MP Once He's Disappeared Again

Since address-update searches don't kick in until the MP pays—or doesn't pay—next month's bills, if your protagonist arrives only to find the subject has just recently flown the coop, what is his next step?

While in the Neighborhood

Ask the landlord. Of course he's likely to be looking for the MP as well, but if your PI's smart and the landlord's sufficiently ticked off, often an exchanging of information is appropriate for both searchers. Go for the credit ap; it's got all kinds of delicious information on it.

Ask the neighbors. Did a moving van come and go? Ah, a U-Haul! How long between trips? A couple of hours? A couple of days? The difference equals the distance traveled between loads.

Ask the mailman. Although he shouldn't disclose any personal info, he will often let an interested party know whatever he'd find out anyway, had he time to mail a letter to that address. Like if that communiqué would end up stuffed into an already full mailbox or be forwarded on down the road. And where down the road.

Oh, go ahead, while your PI's there, just have him stick his head in the mailbox. After all, it's only a minor federal offense. And isn't abandoned mail, once a certain timeframe has elapsed, considered trash anyway?

Speaking of trash . . . But more of that in chapter fourteen.

By Telephone

Now that your detective knows about the U-Haul, he can make that important call to that company requesting a copy of "his" bill—complete with mileage information—be faxed to "his" new residence.

The MP's last phone bill often has the information your protagonist is searching for, things like where the last bill should be sent and who were the last people called before the MP set out for parts unknown. The detective can use the direct route, pay an inside contact for the scoop, or ask the phone company to fax a copy of "his" last bill to that same busy fax phone. Acquiring an 800 number for these sorts of scams eliminates those embarrassing questions about how come the area code is in California when the MP said he was moving to Carolina.

Aha, a clue!

Finding Someone Who Is or Has Previously Been in the Military

Basically, this is so darn complicated that, if this is the main thrust of your story, you're going to need an entire book on this subject, and the book you're going to need is Lieutenant Colonel Richard S. Johnson's *How to Locate Anyone Who Is or Has Been in the Military* (see Appendix F). For those who require just the basics, see below.

Currently in the Military

As with any location, the first step is identifying the subject, as every military branch will require a full name, SSN or DOB, or military number. If that information is not available, the most your detective can do would be to contact the National Personnel Records Center in St. Louis, Missouri and request that a letter be forwarded. Of course, very few PIs would actually choose this method since, after all, how much could you possibly charge for such a service?

The preferred method would be to run an address update or Social Security computer search—for which one would need an old address about 1987 or later—to determine the MP's APO (Air Force Post Office) or FPO (Fleet Post Office) and then decipher that number, via Dick Johnson's book, perhaps, to determine the geographical region where the MP is stationed. Then, under the Freedom of Information Act, your PI could contact the locator service at the installation and request the MP's unit or ship assignment. It's likely they'd provide a work phone number, although not a home address or any personal information such as SSN.

No Longer in the Military

Again, the first step is to identify. Our most common scenario involves finding "an old army buddy," "my daddy" or "my kid's daddy . . . probably," and the only information is when and where the MP was stationed. Without so much as a full name, DOB, SSN or military ID number, we can't yet embark on a normal search. The way to rectify this is to order the unit rosters (Army and Air Force) or ship muster rolls (Navy) for everyone stationed in that unit at that time from the National Personnel Record Center in St. Louis and note the MP's full name, rank and service number.

With this data, your PI can call the local Veteran's Administration office and coax out a little additional information. Officially, the VA is required only to forward a letter, but unofficially, the friendly operator will often state whether the veteran is receiving benefits (which means he has a current address, even though the operator won't give it to you) or if he is, gulp, permanently missing. Often the VA staff has been known to spill the date and zip code where the death benefit was sent, using the DOB for confirmation.

Here you can find unit rosters for Army personnel who were listed prior to July 1969, Air Force personnel prior to July 1972 and Coast Guard personnel prior to October 1974, as well as muster rolls for Navy personnel from 1939 to 1966 (ships only).

Resource One: The Client

So now that you have a clearer understanding of who detectives are, who makes up their client base, what kind of people those seekers feel compelled to find and the four steps involved in that process, let's talk about the tools needed to do the job. There are as many places to glean information as there are MPs to bring on home to Mama, but in this chapter, I've attempted to gather the less esoteric of them under one of five groupings.

The first place your gumshoe will invariably gather information will be from the client himself. The rest of the resources, in no particular order, are

- Public records
- Private sources (phone directories, newspapers, confidential informants, etc.)
- Databases
- Original information developed by the gumshoe himself

Not always having the best grip on reality (see chapter seven, "The Client"), this first source of "intelligence" can be one of the least trustworthy. Unlike our merchantry-inclined counterparts, the working PI's motto often is *The client is not always right and often is not even sane.* This is not to say most clients aren't perfectly fine; it's just that nobody's going to write a book about them.

Why would clients mislead detectives when bad information invariably just ups the bills? Sometimes they don't mean to; they've just been fed incorrect data and are too stubborn to consider otherwise. Other times, they honestly believe their tales to be true, and thirdly, they often think that by pretending it's true, it will come to be so. Most often, there is more than one of these factors at work.

Denial: Mother Is Thy Name

Thirty-year-old Todd disappeared from Kennedy Airport in 1989 after being ordered back to New York to talk to an attorney "about a drug case." Since Todd's mother had his SSN, DOB and New York driver's license number, she assured us finding her son would be no problem.

We first found Todd's driver's license had been suspended that same year for various misdemeanor convictions. Although Mom herself had given us the number, she assured us this information could not possibly correlate to her son. Checking driving records nationwide, we then found Todd involved in an automobile accident in Miami, even though Mom insisted her son could not possibly have gotten a Florida driver's license without her knowing it.

Through Lexis-Nexis, we then found an $881 Schenectady County tax lien dated postdisappearance. Confidently, Mom assured us this tax evader was not her son.

Then there was the 1989 *New York Metro* article stating Toddy Boy was wanted in connection with a drug-related shooting, whereby he plugged his victim eight times while driving around in Mom's white Mercedes coupe. Angrily, Mom explained this was while Todd was working undercover for the

Drug Enforcement Agency; it was old information, unimportant and irrelevant to our search.

In the end, all we determined for sure was that Mom would never accept the only Todd we'd ever be able to deliver. The son she craved undoubtedly lived in Beaver Cleaver's house, was married to Donna Reed, had three kids named Princess, Bud and Kitten and a dog called Lassie. By not coming clean with us, and perhaps with herself as well, Mom succeeded only in wasting our time and her deposit.

Transference: The ''I'm Being Stalked by Someone I'm Attracted To'' Syndrome

Then there was fortysomething Bennie from Marin County. His problem was that the girl he had an incredible crush on in high school had taken to following him around in a Volkswagen Bug and either flirting with him or giving him the finger, whichever happened to take her fancy at the time. It didn't matter to Bennie that the color of her car changed at every sighting or that she had the ability to follow him while he was traveling in another direction; this girl was *obsessed* with the attractively-challenged, ex-unjock recluse.

Like so many (would-be) clients, Bennie had already done some legwork before coming into our office. He had, for example, called Obsessed Girl's mom and found out the girl had moved to Colorado ten years before. He'd even gone to see Obsessed Girl in that state, admitted his long-term crush and gotten her to agree to a date. On that occasion, Bennie decided to just "throw out" the stalking/vilifying episodes and see how Obsessed Girl reacted. Her immediate cooling convinced Bennie she had nothing whatsoever to do with the incidents. At first relieved, when she would not agree to a second date, Bennie then decided that this conversation with her actually put the idea into her head! No, she wasn't stalking him *before*, he declared knowledgeably, but she sure as heck was now.

What did Bennie want with us when he was obviously doing such a bang-up investigative job on his own? To find Obsessed Girl's new unlisted number and make a few threatening phone calls in hopes she would stop, that's what.

No, I don't make this stuff up.

Delusions of Grandeur: The "I'm Just So Special" Syndrome

And then there was Consuelo. A couple of years ago she wrote asking that I prove her heritage. Seems the little lady had, in 1970 or 1971, attended a teacher's conference at Governors State University where the speakers were Rock Hudson and Lyndon Baines Johnson. "Rock Hudson was very handsome and an excellent speaker, and LBJ had a conceited, even 'paranoid' way about him and was met with boos from the audience," she declared authoritatively.

After the speech, according to Consuelo, the late president, "seeked out my company with conversation." He asked the young woman if her grandfather was still alive and then proceeded to tell her how she had been conceived, disclosing she was actually LBJ's biological daughter. The last time he stopped looking for her, LBJ allegedly stated, was when his first legitimate daughter was born and he settled into legal fatherhood. According to Consuelo, LBJ even introduced her to Rock Hudson as LBJ's Hispanic offspring.

Consuelo stated that LBJ was a teacher at Whells Hansen Elementary School in Cotulla, Texas, in 1929 to 1933, and her mother was one of his Mexican students. Mom got hitched in November of 1928, and Consuelo, her second child, was born in May of 1933. Although Mom always denied the affair with the ex-prez, Consuelo remembers, as a toddler, accompanying her mother "down by the river," at which time LBJ informed Mamacita he was off to marry Lady Bird. She also has recollections of the school principal, Miss Mamie, coming by each morning to pick her up, even though as an Anglo woman, Miss Mamie was not allowed on the Spanish side of town.

As an incentive, Consuelo offered me 50 percent of her inheritance if I could prove her claim. I, in turn, ran a contest in the "Ask Rat Dog" column, offering a prize of two acres and a cow to anyone who could assist me in this endeavor— but only if Consuelo got the ranch. Given my clout as a columnist did not include the digging up or DNA testing of past presidents, I suggested we forget about solving this puzzle definitively, but instead examine the likelihood of the assertion, given where the key players were when the alleged events occurred. Johnson, being a public person, was eminently researchable, and as for Consuelo's mom, all I could offer was her wedding date, her own DOB and her daughter's. And that the family stayed in Cotulla until 1940 when they went off to California to pick grapes.

Here, along with my readers, are our findings, all based not on a toddler's recollections, but on historical fact and logical deduction. Sherlock would have been mighty proud.

- The Cotulla Chamber of Commerce lists September 1928 through June 1929 as the only term LBJ taught at Welhausen (not Whells Hansen) Elementary School. A class photo confirms Mamacita was, indeed, one of LBJ's twenty-nine fifth, sixth or seventh graders, but her November 17, 1928, marriage license shows she married her boyfriend just six weeks into his tutorage. No, LBJ was not that boyfriend.

- Given Mamacita's DOB, she would have been twelve years old on the day of her nuptials. By September of 1933, when Consuelo was conceived, LBJ was up in Washington, DC, doing his political thing. Although we can't account for every moment of his time, all ties with Cotulla seemed to be broken.

- Consuelo recalls, as a child, Johnson giving Mamacita the kiss-off "down by the river." Since Johnson wed Claudia Alta Taylor on November 17, 1934, if this riverfront rejection actually happened, Consuelo would have been eighteen months old at the time. Psychology books list "recall" beginning at about age three or four.

- Regarding the confession incident at Governors State University, how did LBJ know who Consuelo was? Or that she would be there? Why would he admit such a thing—to her and to Rock Hudson—given the scandal that such an admission might surely erupt? Alas, we never got these questions answered because we could not find a single person who could confirm this conference actually happened. Neither a biographer of Johnson's nor of Hudson's. Not past articles in the local paper, not the editor of that periodical today and certainly not the normally nice public affairs lady at Governors State who finally took to screaming, "This conference never happened! You people have been calling for a month, and I don't know how many more ways to say it!" As it turns out, Governors State was newly formed in 1969, with no students and only about twenty people planning the curriculum out of rented space in a shopping mall. LBJ, according to the nice public affairs lady, was not one of them.

- In Texas at that time, as one reader informed me, it was the Mexicans who were not allowed on the Anglo side of town, not vice versa.

- Another reader noted that Welhausen was located on the Spanish side of town, so there would have been no need for Miss Mamie to come pick Consuelo up at all.

- Yet another reader groused, "The problem with Consuelo's claim is that it detracts from those of us who have true tales of famous biological fathers. In 1945, President Roosevelt asked King George VI to undertake a secret visit to California. George VI, whose penchant for philandering was well known, impregnated a hotel maid in San Francisco. My mother was that maid."

Are There Morals to These Long and Twisted Tales?

Yes, otherwise the editor would have zapped them out. The moral is: The client's input is just *one* resource to be considered during an investigation.

E L E V E N

RESOURCE TWO: PUBLIC RECORDS

Public records are accessible at the federal, state, county and city levels. Most can be had simply by walking into the appropriate office, tossing a microfiche into a machine, viewing the information, pulling the file—or not—and walking out. The MP will never know of your protagonist's interest because the equipment is put there for the public's use, and there is no recording of visits, aside from a disposable request form.

Why are records public? Close up assessor's records and it opens the door for every smooth-talking confellow who gets it into his head to sell his rental unit to as many potential condo buyers as can tromp through on a Sunday morning. Shut down voter's records and it leaves citizens to wonder how 110 percent of the registered voters ended up casting their ballots for the very same mayoral candidate. Secure criminal histories and you can never be sure that the sensible-shoed nanny you hired wasn't ever booked for child molestation.

Federal Sources

Below you'll find the federal offices who participate in some way in the finding of MPs, given you can supply them with a full name, DOB, SSN or some other pertinent identifying information. Please note that fees and procedures change periodically and never do these agencies alert me when that happens. So be forewarned. For the current scoop on federal, state and even county information, call the agency directly and ask. The numbers, at the time of this printing, are listed for your convenience.

Armed Service Locators

To unearth someone now on active duty, you'll need to contact the branch of duty directly. Each division makes its own rules and charges its own fees. Call U.S. Army: (317) 542-4211; U.S. Air Force: (210) 652-1110; U.S. Navy: (703) 614-3155; U.S. Marine Corps: (703) 640-3942; U.S. Coast Guard: (202) 267-6971.

The Federal Bureau of Investigation's Identification Division

It will, in theory, at least, supply an individual with *his own* anarchist activity file after receiving a Freedom of Information request, along with name, address, date and place of birth, $17 and a set of fingerprints. If your gumshoe happened to have all those things (and didn't mind committing a felony or two), it's conceivable he could fool the FBI and get the information on another. If it worked, a mere two years later, he'd then receive back a sanitized version of "his" life. Write to FBI, Identification Division, Attn: FOIA, Washington, DC 20537.

The Federal Bureau of Prison's Inmate Locator Service

This is a swell idea. It used to be you just picked up the phone and called; now you write and wait. What you ultimately find out is if the MP is currently incarcerated or when and where he was let go again on society. Call (212) 307-3126.

The Federal Aviation Administration

It will supply your searcher with the name, address, last exam date and license number of any pilot, as well as the owners, type, wing number and history of any airplane. Call (405) 954-3261.

The Federal Election Commission

This keeps the current stats on political candidates at this highest level. Expect to find name and address, campaign spending and loans, where the money went and a list of contributors. Since payment is required in advance, this is a write-and-wait kind of a thing; however, your investigator can set up a prepaid account if you, as the writer, thought to do that for him back in chapter one. Call (800) 424-9530.

The National Archives

Located in Washington, DC, this could occupy your PI for most of your chapters. It's more likely he'd visit one of the regional Federal Records Centers for genealogical information like census records, old immigration records, ships' passenger lists and rosters of military personnel. Since each records center contains its own unique collection of informational doodads, a call to your center of choice is imperative.

The National Cemetery Registry

This has a listing of everyone who has claimed one of their fine plots, so if your MP is a vet/six-feet-under combo, you might find him through this service. Write to Department of Veteran Affairs, Washington, DC 20420.

The National Personnel Records Center

What sounds like a good idea, in the hands of the federal government, simply isn't. To find military records on retired or discharged MPs, rather than calling and getting a straight answer, what your detective must do is to write the boys in St. Louis, supply them with a name, DOB, SSN or some other distinguishing data, wait eight weeks, get back some additional form to fill out, wait another eight weeks and then be told the information is confidential. A persistent investigator would then evoke the Freedom of Information Act and give it another whack—and another eight weeks. Quite frankly, unless you are writing a trilogy, I'd suggest an alternate plan. Keep in mind that a 1973 fire destroyed all Army records between 1912 and 1960 anyway, as well as those of everyone whose last name began with *H-Z* and served between 1947 and 1963—just another reason not to bother with this nonsense.

What they will actually do is forward a letter—if they happen to know where the MP is. It is up to him to respond, of course, and that does not exactly put your detective in a position of control. Call (314) 263-3901.

The Social Security Administration

It pretty much knows where everybody is and even what name everyone's operating under. Because of its omniscient powers, it doesn't need a Social Security number to identify. It can easily do so with the name the person was registered under, a DOB and that person's parents' names.

By Phone. Officially, the Social Security Administration (SSA) will spew forth nothing, but we've found benevolent clerks will often break for a good sob story, often telling if the MP is dead, making payments or withdrawals and sometimes even where that is happening. When calling, be aware that the reason the SSA provides a toll-free number is so there'll be a record of the caller's phone number. So, if your detective is a scam-pulling son of a gun, he just might want to have a series of phone booths staked out for his scamming pleasure. Call (800) 772-1213.

By CD-ROM. The death information is available on CD-ROM and discussed mightily in chapter thirteen.

By Letter. Clients tell me they've had varying luck with having their letters forwarded by the Administration. In a recent rejection letter of our own, the SSA kindly spelled out the rules: "We forward letters primarily for the benefit of the missing person rather than the requester. The service is available to inform a person about a matter of great importance of which he is unaware and would undoubtedly want to be informed, for example, a serious illness or death in the immediate family, or that he is due a sizable amount of money, such as an inheritance." Succinctly put, this means the Administration would pass on, "Mom died and you're getting a big inheritance," before, "I'm all alone in the world since Mama catapulted herself off Lover's Leap after Jimmy the Crook ran off with her huge zircon ring."

U.S. District Courts

These are plastered all over the country; there are four in California alone. Containing bankruptcy, naturalization, some civil and criminal records, a trip here could provide a wealth of information for your intuitive one. Our own most common inquiry involves bankruptcy records, since anyone whose ever taken that bold step has had to lay his whole life—including assets—at the public trough. Check your phone book for the office near you.

The U.S. Postal Service

This is yet another casualty of the privacy laws. Used to be, you paid your buck, you got your forwarding address. Then in the early 1990s, you paid your three bucks, you got your forwarding address. Within a year, due to pressure from privacy advocates, the laws changed again. Now you can virtually throw money at the clerks and all you get back is a bunch of stamps. What you still can get is a boxholder's address at the time the box was opened, but only if there is a subpoena to be served. You can get the same information on a business's boxholder without having paper in your pocket. All this at your local friendly and efficient branch.

The Veteran's Administration

Located in Chicago, it will also forward an unsealed, non-threatening letter, but, of course, it is up to the recipient to respond. We've had good luck with calling the local chapter, whimpering a bit and finding out if the MP is receiving benefits and the regional office where that occurs. Write to Veteran's Administration, 536 South Clark Street, Chicago, Illinois 60680.

State Sources

The names of these offices vary according to the state, so it is important to check the appropriate phone book in the area where your story takes place. Because procedures and fees vary by locale, it is impossible to provide definitive information regarding state, county and municipal agencies. Again, call for current data and note that all this information might not be "public access" in every state.

The Alcohol Beverage Control

This office keeps records on everyone licensed to sell adult beverages. Since these applications have been checked thoroughly, this information is assumed to be accurate at the time of issuance.

The Board of Equalization

It requires retail merchants to obtain a resale license or, alternatively, pay sales tax on the items they purchase for resale. This office will supply your investigator with the business owner's name, the business's location, type of company, starting date and permit number.

The Court of Appeals

Superior level civil and criminal proceedings are available to the public; however, in many instances, the only way to actually access the files is by a trip into the agency, since the courts are not prone to copy files for the public.

The Department of Consumer Affairs

It licenses professions such as accountant, architect, athletic commission, automotive repair, barber, behavioral scientist, cemetery board, chiropractic examiner, collection and investigative service, contractor, cosmetologist, dentist, electronic and appliance repair, funeral director and embalmer, geologist and geophysicist, guide dog for the blind, home furnishing, landscape architect, medical board, allied health commission, nursing home, optometrist, personnel service, pharmacist, private investigator, professional engineer and land surveyor, registered nurse, shorthand reporter, structural pest control, tax preparer, veterinary medicine, vocational nurse and psychiatric technician.

What information this office will part with depends on the state and the category, but it is safe to say your investigator will at least get the last known address of a current licensee. If he's looking for a California real estate broker, for example, and the Department of Consumer Affairs has no listing, it would certainly be appropriate to check the surrounding states where land purchases are still a viable option to living life out in a rented apartment.

The Department of Corrections

While individuals can't legally obtain a rap sheet (record of arrested person) from the FBI's NCIC computer, such information can often be obtained piecemeal, and this office provides one such source. Providing an MP's name and DOB or SSN will spring forth information on current inmates or parolees: their names, ages, birthplaces, residences, physical descriptions, health, sentencings and releases.

The Department of Insurance

It will tell you if someone has a broker's license.

The Department of Justice

It won't tell you much of anything. One thing it does share with the public is its files on nonprofits and charities, including these organizations' income tax returns. You can also find out who's running the show and how much of the take they're taking for themselves.

The Department of Motor Vehicles

This is another office that is, state by state, in danger of closing its doors to the public. California was the first to go, and now, unless your investigator has a subpoena to serve—and doesn't mind the DMV informing the soon-to-be-served of that—he'll get driving history only, not an address. Checking for current procedures with whatever state's DMV is involved in your story is a must.

- Driving history can be obtained by providing a name and DOB, or a license number, which in some states, is simply the SSN. What you get back is the person's exact name, driver's license number, DOB, AKAs, expiration date of the license and moving offenses. By decoding the court issuing the ticket, you can many times pull up the actual docket, which will supply you with a home address.

- Vehicle registration is accessed by plate or vehicle identification number (VIN). In California, this gives up the registered owner and legal owner of the car only. In most other states, they slip in those parties' addresses as well. Along with that, you get the car's make, model and dates of registration.

- Occupational licensing is also available through the DMV, as it pertains to auto manufacturers, dealers, sales personnel, junkyards, traffic and driving school owners and the like. Expect no more than confirmation of licensing, their site locations, disciplinary actions and bonding information.

The Department of Real Estate

It keeps records of brokers and sales personnel, including their work addresses.

The Highway Patrol

It never did much for me, mainly because it would not disclose information about any accident I was not directly involved in. Your detective would undoubtedly have the same bad luck unless he just happened to "be" the injured party.

The Secretary of State

It oversees the licensing of corporations, limited partnerships, notaries and holders of Uniform Commercial Code (UCC) liens. Its records can usually be accessed by owner's name.

- Corporate information can be had over the phone in most states. Usually accessed by business or owner's name (check!), depending upon the state, your detective might get back such goodies as owner's full name, other corporate entities owned, site and mailing address of the business, corporate status, directors and officers and agent for service.

- Limited partnerships are sometimes filed at the state level, sometimes at the county. Expect to find the same sort of information available for corporate filings.

- Notary publics are listed here as well, and getable information includes their names, addresses, DL#s and sometimes even thumbprints.

- Uniform Commercial Code is a fancy way of saying someone has borrowed money and offered a piece of equipment as collateral. A leased photocopying machine is a prime example. Most times, detectives don't necessarily care about the loan; it's just another list pertaining to business persons. This index can often yield an SSN or current location, as well as other UCC holdings.

The State Bar Association

This will spill forth any licensed attorney's full name, location, date and place of birth and admissions date, as well as standing, education and disciplinary actions.

The Office of Vital Statistics

This is one of the most privacy-sensitive agencies known to investigators. Check the county listings in this chapter (under Vital Statistics) for the kinds of data that are listed on birth, death and marriage records and Appendix C for a list of which states will dispense what information to which people—relatives, self or busybodies. California, ironically the first state to close its DMV records to the public, is quite relaxed in dispensing its vital statistic documents. In fact, this office actually sells its microfiche marriage, divorce and death indexes to the public, no questions asked. You just never know.

The Workman's Compensation Appeals Board

This keeps records on all those accidents that couldn't wait to happen. Although technically not available to anyone without just cause, in actuality, many investigators have claimed it's pretty easy to get in to view the files.

County Sources

The most comprehensive collection of hands-on public records can be found in the county courthouse complex. Just by running an MP's name through the various indexes found there, your detective would surely gather a pretty mean paper trail of marriages, evictions, lawsuits, property ownership, etc., whatever happened to be the MP's particular MO while residing in that county. Such fishing expeditions often lead to other folks who have a thing or two to say about the MP as well, not all of it flattering.

Because in reality, many cases are actually solved within the confines of the courthouse in just a couple of hours, how can your protagonist embark upon this necessary journey and not have your novel turn into a short story? Your detective just *must* hit the recorder's office—it would be illogical and unrealistic for him not to do so—and if he does, won't he surely see that Bubba Jones filed a mechanics lien against old Misses Dawlripple, which is quite obviously the reason Sergeant McAllister felt compelled to kill Barry The One-Eyed Butler in the drawing room with the candlestick?

Lucky for howdunit pundits, another real-life factor comes into play here as well. County offices close notoriously early and at varying times. While your detective is off scouring the assessor's records—and learning practically nothing—the clerks can be pulling the shades and sneaking out the back door of the recorder's office. Just like in real life.

Obviously, the architectural flavor of courthouse complexes differs greatly across our great nation. Some are housed in old monstrosities. If your protagonist means to visit a courthouse you're not familiar with, you'd do well to at least call over there and have someone describe the complex to you.

Actually, if you are going to write any kind of detective novel at all, even if your protagonist knows *exactly* where everyone is, you, as a writer, would do well to acquaint yourself with the workings of your own courthouse complex. Using this chapter as a guide, walk through the various offices, looking up your most hated enemy in all the microfiches you can find along the way. As you do this, you may notice an interesting phenomenon: If you live in a small rural county, some clerks will invariably tell you what you want to know is *not* public access, even though it is. They do this because, although they have no idea how ornery your most hated enemy is, for some reason they feel compelled to protect him from you.

I once requested a marriage license from Santa Cruz County, only to be told, "Unh-unh." Only after a thirty-minute discussion, a trip to the law library *and* a call to the supervisor did they acquiesce. Seems I'd said, "I'd like to look up this marriage license," rather than, "Will you look up this marriage license for me?" It wasn't that they were refusing me the information, I was assured, it's just that they thought I was asking to pull it myself, which as they had told me time and time again, I could not do.

Now let's talk about some of the offices your detective will encounter within the county courthouse complex.

Voter's Registration

These records yield a gob of personal information—name, address, date and state of birth, occupation, oftentimes even an unlisted phone number and other good citizens residing at that same address. The records are usually stored on microfiche or computer, and often the actual sign-up card can be pulled, which will divulge the MP's signature as well. That's the good news. The bad news is that many states are now closing their voting records from public view, forcing interested parties to demonstrate they have some legitimate "polling" type reason for the inquiry. This, of course, forces you as a writer to pen another scam scene into your novel.

The Assessor's Office

This keeps a register of all properties countywide and where the tax bills are sent for those properties. Although most often these taxpayers are, in fact, the same person as the property owner, it should be noted that lawyers and accountants can act as "straw parties" to accept bills for celebrities—and people who consider themselves celebrities—thus keeping their addresses out of public view. Expect property records to contain the site location, legal description, assessed value, structure summary and the name and mailing address of the taxpayer. Normally, this data can be accessed by the owner's name, the site address or the assessor's parcel number (APN). Most often listed on computer or microfiche, the two major tidbits your protagonist might be looking for here are if and where the MP owns property or, alternatively, who owns the structure where the MP now/used to reside. Obviously, the latter might have some idea of where the MP was going.

Also in the assessor's office is a listing of "unsecured" properties—airplanes, houseboats and the like. These items are also taxed, which is why they are listed there, but are not fastened to the earth, which is why they are unsecured.

The Recorder's Office

This office was created to keep a permanent record of documents affecting land transfers. The grantor/grantee index is the big draw here. Unlike the assessor's index, which lists only current ownership, this register will disclose if an MP ever did own property in that county or had any liens recorded against him. Here, your detective will find deeds—grant, trust and quit-claim—reconveyance, mechanics' and tax liens, powers of attorney, judgments and abstract judgments and even an occasional death certificate when accompanying a Death of a Joint Tenant filing.

The grantor/grantee index provides an excellent means of verifying a legal name, supplying a middle initial and/or determining who the spouse was at the time of the recorded incident. By isolating documents that your detective knows *for sure* pertain to his MP, he can be confident that the identifying information he's collecting is solid before moving into a national arena where there are so many more possibilities.

Your gumshoe will see, for example, that the Rick Smith who had the good sense to marry his client's best friend instead of her was Richard *J.* Smith because he owned a 1967 property with Olga K. Smith, which was the client's ex-best-friend's first name. Then, in the 1970s, Richard J. quitclaimed to Olga (a divorce is the most likely scenario) and a year later, hooked up with Tammy Faye, the two becoming quite the little land barons. In the 1980s, the Richard J.-Tammy Faye combo disappeared from the index, indicating they died some horrible duo death, or simply moved to another county. Luckily, before they did, they got themselves a couple of tax liens, a fine provider of SSNs. Now, armed with those powerful niners, your investigator can break for a nooner, return to the office and run both SSNs through his trusty computer, thus finding Tammy Faye passed just last year and widower Rick Smith quite ready for a second time around with his first wife, Olga's ex-best friend.

Most recorder's current records are now computerized, although documents predating installation day will undoubtedly be available only on microfiche. Clear-thinking recorders, when compiling these microfiches, combined grantees with grantors in one huge index spanning a good number of years so that busy searchers would have only one sheet to consult for an expansive search. Mean, ornery, shortsighted recorders segregated buyers from sellers, trustees from trustors, and then listed each year separately, immensely compounding the searcher's task. (If you are looking for a good plot involving justifiable homicide of a public official, this might be something worth considering.)

Vital Statistics

In some counties, this office has its own distinct location, in others it might be tucked into a corner of the recorder's office, or even the county clerk's. Keepers of birth, death and marriage records are the clerks most desperate to keep investigators at bay, even in states where these records are clearly public access. (See Appendix C for state restrictions.) Although most recent records may be accessed by computer, film or microfiche, older listings will almost always be found in large ledgers, the entries penned by a top-notch calligrapher at the time of the event.

It should be noted these records can be ordered at either the county or state level, as they originate at the former and are forwarded to the latter. I usually choose the county because the turnaround time is quicker, either when ordering by mail or going down in person to pick up the certificate, but your detective might prefer dealing with the state if he's trying to pull a fast one over on a restricted state, unsure of the county where the event occurred and/or has previously encountered a particularly snippety records clerk who has his number.

Birth Certificates list the child's name, date, time and place of birth, sex and whether it was a single or multiple delivery. Parental information consists of both birth names, ages, places of birth, occupations and, in some states, SSNs. These are the most restrictive of the three vital statistic documents, primarily because naughty folks routinely use them to create new identities after everyone starts to recognize their old ones. Even in states where anyone with a ten-spot can get another's birth credential, the indexes are usually kept out of public view so that patrons won't have enough information to pull that off.

Some states will provide a copy of a birth certificate only to the person named, but since the baby didn't sign at birth, there is no way of verifying this except to make sure the name on the enclosed money order matches that on the certificate. In the case of a baby girl, quite reasonably, she might well have married in the ensuing years since birth, and so a certificate requested for Kate Burke would be considered a "match" with a money order and a return envelope addressed to Kate Faron. Not that I've tried this personally. An extra bonus is that the mailman would have few qualms about delivering that mail since, after all, the silly vital records office at least got the first name right.

Before your gumshoe gets all darned excited about scamming the vital records people, he should note the information needed in order to request the document in a restricted state, namely, full name of child, date and place of birth and parents' birth names. If he has all that, he probably has no need of the certificate. If he doesn't, he probably can't get it anyway. Hey, they don't pay us the big bucks for nothing.

Marriage Licenses are, generally speaking, more getable. In a restricted state, the qualifications now may read "relative" rather than "self," and if your PI knows most of the information required to order, like the couple's names, but not the exact date of the event, that might do. What could happen, after waiting weeks to receive the document, is that your gumshoe receives back the minimalist "certificate," suitable for framing, rather than the data-laden "application" supplying the bride and groom's birth names, ages, addresses, occupations, years of education, number of prior marriages, signatures, birthplaces, parents' names and places of birth, along with naming two witnesses and the minister. In real life, that's known as a bummer; in a book, it could add thirty pages, a less direct but more entertaining Plan B and a few good dream sequences about where to hide the mulched-up body of a public servant.

Death Certificates provide the deceased's name, sex, race, SSN, DOB, birthplace, citizenship, military service, occupation, employer and number of years there, along with the parents' names and birthplaces and spouse. Everything your PI needed to know while the guy was still alive. In addition, there will be the name and address of the informant, the primary and contributing cause of death, if there was a coroner's inquiry and, of course, the date, time and place of the demise, as well as the final resting place.

Why do you need this, when Social Security's Master

Death Index is so much more convenient? Well for one, not everyone is on the index, as discussed in a later chapter. Secondly, since the index does not supply a middle initial or parents' names, often it is not until the actual death certificate is received that it can be determined that the MP found is the very same MP being sought; and thirdly, this is often the most direct route to finding the dead guy's relatives and determining how he led out his life.

It should also be noted that many times, the key to finding an MP lies in locating his dead spouse or relative. Take our aforementioned Rick Smith, who married Olga instead of our client, lo those many years ago. If the client happened to hear that Olga had taken a dirt nap and that's why she's now set her sights on lonely Ricky, your gumshoe might conceivably find *him* by searching for *her* in Social Security's Master Death Index. Alas, not finding Olga there, it looks like said client's happily-ever-after dream will be dashed and your book will have no ending, but then, because your gumshoe is smarter than many of his real-life counterparts, he will check his office copy of California's microfiche death indexes, which the state has so graciously sold him, and find Olga listed there. Why there and not on the Index? Because Olga was a school teacher, that's why, and therefore had her own pension plan and did not pay into or receive benefits from the Administration. Another case, swiftly solved and another best-seller coming on down the pike.

The County Clerk

This office is home to two helpful indexes: the Fictitious Business Name Index and Superior Court's Plaintiff/Defendant's Index. Kept on microfiche, computer or oversized computerized ledgers with green lines running through, a call to the specific office will insure accuracy as to how that state's records were in a specific year.

The Fictitious Business Names (FBN) Index is not, as one might hope, a legacy of scoundrels' AKAs. Instead, it is a countywide compilation of all sole proprietor and simple partnership companies whose owners have chosen to fill out this particular piece of paperwork, pay their fees and allow themselves to be listed in a legal newspaper.

Why would someone do this? For most, it's to lay claim to a particular FBN (Rick Smith d/b/a Launderland); for others, it's so they can open a bank account and therefore receive checks in the business name. For still others, it's because it's the right thing to do. Why would someone *not* register his FBN with the county? Usually so there is no paper trail between himself and his business activities. So how do these moppets cash their checks then? Malfeasants are infamous for frequenting check-cashing joints, or just endorsing the drafts over to themselves, or establishing FBNs in faraway, obscure counties and then using those documents to open bank accounts in their own neighborhoods.

FBN statements can normally be accessed by owner's name to determine enterprises owned or by business name to ascertain who owns that endeavor. In either case, the original application will spill forth info like the true names of the owners, their addresses, the name and locale of the business, the date and expiration date of the registration, as well as any partners and their signatures. (Corporations are registered at the state level, usually with the secretary of state.)

Superior Court's Plaintiff/Defendant's Index is the curator of civil cases over a specific dollar amount, probate, criminal and family court filings. Again, long ago The First Clerk chose how these records were indexed, that is, all categories lumped together in one index or segregated by plaintiff and defendant and/or by a span of years. Obviously, the former system speeds up the searching process considerably.

Civil files. These are slim to huge and, once located on the index, plucked from the stacks by helpful clerks and cheerfully handed over for your gumshoe's reading enjoyment. Typical cases would be divorces, money disputes over a certain dollar amount (say, $25,000), both domestic and nondomestic harassment charges, restraining orders, writs of mandates and appeals from both municipal and small claims courts. Amongst these legal innards, your detective will find the plaintiff's and defendant's names, their respective attorneys, the type of complaint, other interested parties and all of the legal actions that have occurred so far. If finding an MP is the purpose in perusing this file, then a helpful insert would be the Statement of Process of Service showing the actual address where the party was served. Other times, the best a PI can do is to contact the MP's attorney and hope he will get a message to his onetime client. Although it is useful to scan the file, seldom is it necessary to spend a lot of time dozing over its contents.

Divorce actions. Here is found a wealth of information, no matter how long ago the "disillusionment" took place. Since it benefits at least one party to list every asset of either, this is an excellent source of both real and unreal property. If a child is involved, expect to find each parent's income and wages, as well as their (and the children's) SSNs. Often there is a copy of a restraining order or some other dirt on one or both spouses.

Probate files. These files are indexed by the name of the deceased and contain a listing of assets and claimants, wills and the final reckoning. If the MP is, in fact, the deceased, that counts as a find, and the client has to pay. If the MP is *named* in the probate, your detective could not know that unless he had a lead or the deceased happened to have the same unusual surname.

Reciprocal Enforcement Support Law (RESL) file. This is a combined multicounty file concerning the nonsupport of a noncustodial parent. Expect to find names, addresses, wages and income, property and vehicles owned by each party, in addition to information about the children.

Criminal felonies. Included here are murder and manslaughter, obviously, but most crimes can be termed either "felonies," landing them in superior court, or "misdemeanors," which are heard in municipal court, dependent upon the dollar amount rather than the crime itself. As one clerk eloquently put it, "Big thief, go to big court; little thief, go to little court." Look for shoplifting, embezzlement, theft, burglary, assault, drug peddling or drug possession and bad check charges.

Municipal Court Clerk

Although actually city level, an index of these midsized money disputes and misdemeanor cases is normally available somewhere within the county courthouse complex. To view the file, your detective might have to travel to the actual city where the dispute took place.

- Muni civil files are made up of the same kind of money squabbles found in superior court, except under a certain dollar amount, usually around $25,000. Because of this money limit, most evictions or "unlawful detainers" land here rather than in the higher court. Search warrants are filed in muni court also, along with the supporting affidavit. Once signed, these documents, if unsealed, are public access, along with the "return" list, a rendering of what was confiscated.

- Small claims cases are those complaints under an even lower dollar amount, usually around $5,000, and designed to be heard without benefit of attorneys. There is a modest filing fee, and the results are Judge Wapner-like gavel bangs of justice—swift and no-nonsense. As in municipal court, only the defendant can appeal the decision, and then the case lands in superior court, where both parties would do well to turn up with a lawyer.

- The Muni Criminal Index is made up of misdemeanor crimes, those same shoplifting, theft, burglary, possession, etc., malfeasances where the equity is under $25,000, or whatever. DUI offenses are found here since that also is a misdemeanor.

City Sources

Certain public records are available at the city level but so few that most PIs rarely make the trip just for a fishing exposition.

Business Licenses

These are the foundation of the tax collector's annual hit list, but unlike the county's FBN Index (which exists for informational purposes only), many restaurants and shops are owned by corporations that are licensed but will not be found in the county listings. Since tax collectors have been known to go door-to-door, this often overlooked resource is certainly worth checking, especially when looking for a small company that is hiding behind a post office box.

Pet Licenses

These are normally accessed by owner's name or license number. An irate client of mine once actually identified the owner of a snarling German Shepherd by grabbing the beast and then memorizing its tag number. I would have just waited for the guy to get in his car, but then, hey, that's me.

Building Permits

These are kept at the city level, except for properties located in unincorporated areas of the county. Anytime anything is built, demolished, refurbished, plumbed or "electricized," the contractor *should* have signed up and paid for this inspection process. Permits are normally indexed by contractor's name, so looking for a property owner here might take a bit of time unless the clerk just happened to know his name. Expect to find the contractor's name, fees paid, work done, authorizing parties, etc. Your PI can even see the structure's plans, if that's something that interests him.

The City Elections Office

This keeps candidates' files for those running for municipal offices, including the school board.

Resource Three: Libraries, Private and Confidential Sources

Many companies, organizations and periodicals provide resources for the skip tracer, either knowingly or unknowingly, and are available at libraries, the businesses themselves or by tricking, paying or befriending someone in the know who doesn't have a clue what's going on.

The Public Library

You've seen it sitting on the street corner; you've read its books. But you may not be getting all you can out of your local public library.

Telephone Directories

In the days before modern technology, many was the hour I spent searching for some long-lost MP in the annals of these public listings. Now since online services and phone discs, a competent gumshoe has little excuse for spending his time thusly, no matter how cute the reference librarian is. It has made a trip to the library, for this purpose, pretty much obsolete.

Not so with looking for "old" information. Almost every library prides itself on keeping every directory compiled since its town was discovered by the Pilgrims and wallpapering one long corridor with it. This is a good thing since sometimes the only way to establish a legal name is to go back into those publications and look for some early sighting of the family. A "complete" rendering of this history of local residents is only available in the library of the actual town, so if your detective is looking for a Redwood City couple from 1910, he best not have his feet up in San Francisco's new main library forty miles to the north.

Reverse Directories

These consist of residential and business listings that are sorted by phone number in one section and by address in another so that the information can be accessed by those two fields rather than by name. This sounds like a right dandy idea until you realize that 60 percent of Americans today have unlisted telephone numbers. Still it is helpful for those nonscoundrel types as well as for compiling a list of neighbors to con out of further information.

The Polk directories were the first of these reverse directories, dating back to the 1870s. Earlier editions were not reverse, but simply a register of where folks lived in town. Along with their names and addresses appeared their occupations and places of employment, the color of their skin and names of other family members. Of course, no telephone numbers appeared since those volumes predated the widespread use of that invention. In the 1950s, a light green section appeared in the directories, the same residential information accessible by address rather than name. Advertising was added as well, preserving for posterity the flavor of the era. The Polk directories are still produced by the door-to-door gathering of information, but only in rare rural areas and only every two years.

Just for giggles, I looked myself up in San Francisco's last Polk directory, the volume marked 1981. At my old address, I found, first, the listing of Breezin' Faron, along with the occupation of sheepherder. After my best friend's came my name and trade, although I'd made it perfectly clear to the nice man at the door that I was the one responsible for bringing home the dog food. Even back in the early 1980s, it seems, women were getting second billing.

Nowadays there are eleven crisscross directory companies: Marc Publishing Company; Blythe Criss-Cross Directory, Inc.; Bresser's Cross-Index Directory Co.; City Publishing Company, Inc.; Cole Publications; Haines and Company; Stewart Directories, Inc.; Woodared Directory Company; Hill-Donnelly Corporation; Dickman Directories, Inc.; and Metropolitan Cross-Reference Directory Limited. These share the market, dividing the nation geographically among themselves. To determine which periodical covers the area where your story takes place, check the library in that area.

Company Information

There are several books that are good references on major corporations, all accessed by company name, with executives listed below that.

- The *Corporate Yellow Book* lists businesses, their addresses and phone numbers, along with major executives.

- The *Directory of American Firms Operating in Foreign Countries* lists the company, the U.S. address, phone, product or service and addresses of any foreign offices.

- Standard & Poor's *Register of Corporations* is a compilation of major corporations, addresses and phones, listings of chief executive officers, accounts, primary banks, primary law firms and numbers of employees.

- The *Million Dollar Directory* is Dun & Bradstreet's big fat book of 160,000 public and privately owned companies with over $25 million in gross sales, a net worth of a half a mil, and at least 250 worker bees. Accessible by company name, you'll find the corporation's address, phone number, sales volume, number of employees, founding date, main product or service, major accounts and the names of their top executives, along with their titles.

- Dun & Bradstreet's *Who Owns Whom* lists subsidiaries and associate companies as well as parent companies.

Executive Information

Dun & Bradstreet's *Million Dollar Disc* is a compilation of their *Reference Book of Corporate Management* and the *Million Dollar Directory*; it's available on CD-ROM. Unlike the books above, this disc is meant for researching executives rather than companies, which is best for our purposes. Accessible by an officer's name, find the firm's address and phone, the executive's title, his previous positions and education, year of birth and military history.

The Register of Officers

Speaking of military history, many libraries will contain an entire shelf of books, collectively called the *Register of Officers*. In it your detective will find a listing of anyone who was an Army officer from 1920 to 1972, a Navy officer from 1944 to 1984 and an officer in the Air Force from 1948 to 1974, along with their DOBs, military ID numbers and ranks.

Occupational Directories

These are put out by several publishers, and their contents differ dependent upon the industry. Expect to find a book on most every kind of licensed professional, from travel agents to private investigators, with their addresses, phone numbers and credentials.

Phone Discs

These are now available in many major public libraries. Their contents consist of "all" listed business and residential phone numbers nationwide and are accessible by name, number or location. Such discs can be purchased at software outlets for about $150 and should definitely be in the library of your gumshoe, unless he prides himself on being a real computer putz.

Who's Who

This is a nice fat book of folks who have made a name for themselves in the world—or have paid to make a name for themselves in the world. The result is a listing of whos and who wanna-bes in about any category you can think of.

Only fourteen of the proliferation of *Who's Who* books on the shelves are a Marquis or Reed Reference Publication, wherein a listing equals nomination and accomplishment rather than a couple hundred bucks changing hands. The prominent people profiled within their covers have accomplished some feat in their chosen fields and are legitimately honored for that.

All the rest, *Who's Who in the South and Southwest*, as well as all other geographical and occupational groupings are compiled by publishers selling space in their books and filled with folks who get a $200 hoot out of being in *Who's Who*. For your detective's purposes, it hardly matters since both *Who's Who* resources contain an awful lot of personal, professional and educational data on the individuals listed.

Genealogy Libraries

Either housed within the main library or occupying its own building, these nationwide curators of old phone books, reverse directories, marriage records, land deeds, etc., can be a wealth of information. And yes, one can actually find people by scouring these long-ago records.

Take the case of Glennis's Portuguese mother who left her Spanish count hubby for a life in Miami back in the 1950s. Esther hit the tarmac running and made it to the hospital just in time to have her fourth child. She left the little girl at the hospital orphanage and proceeded to raise her first three children in the wealthy community of Coral Gables.

A year later, my client, Glennis, was born—the offspring of an itinerant ladies' man. This child narrowly escaped being shipped back to Portugal and landed instead with her paternal grandparents in Los Angeles. Glennis saw her mother once, at thirteen, and after that had no contact at all with the count, her mother, her brother or her two older sisters.

All Glennis knew of the child left in the orphanage, she'd learned from three letters, dated 1959 and postmarked Miami, sent by a Mabel Maxwell who called the toddler Sylvia and appeared to be taking care of her. But had she adopted the little girl? Had someone else? Or did Sylvia still bear the name of her royal mum, or even her father, whoever that was? Or, no matter what that earlier scenario, had the child, now grown, gotten married and changed her name anyway? The answers lay in the genealogical library.

A 1959 Miami city directory labeled Mabel Maxwell a school teacher, and later editions referred to her as retired. Never was she living with a Sylvia or ever listed as a Mrs.

In 1979, Mabel disappeared from the directories as her neighborhood showed increasingly more "(c)" designations behind the names ("colored," according to the symbols translations). Did Mabel relocate to another community, did she "retire" from Florida to a colder climate, had she died or were unlisted numbers in vogue back then? And even if Mabel were still alive, would she know what happened to Sylvia these thirty-five years later?

Social Security's Master Death Index listed fourteen Mabel Maxwells, none succumbing in Miami and too many to order to see who was listed as next of kin. What I didn't know then was that schoolteachers have their own pension programs, don't pay or receive Social Security benefits and, therefore, are not on the index anyway. Searches for Sylvia Maxwell through Florida's DMV and marriage records proved just as fruitless.

Working backward then, I contacted the family who at the time owned Mabel Maxwell's last Miami home. Although city directories showed a six-year gap between Mabel's 1979 departure and their arrival, as it turned out, they had, in fact, bought the house from the Mabel Maxwell Estate, sending the check to the dead woman's niece in Iowa. It was she who told me that Sylvia moved around a lot but could always be reached through an old man named Milton who lived in Florida.

Milton got my message to Sylvia.

"This is Sylvia Ray," she said, taking the last name of Glennis's playboy father. Her words spilled out as if it were perfectly natural for her to be telling her life's story to a stranger.

A year after Sylvia was dumped at the orphanage, Miss Maxwell, a friend of Esther's, insisted the aristocratic mom deal with her baby. Dealing with her meant letting her go live with Mabel, then sixty-five years old.

When the child was twelve and Mabel was seventy-two,

the old woman decided it was time Sylvia lived with her mother. There she was treated like the poor relation—among other things, hidden in a closet when someone came to visit. That lasted nine weeks, until Sylvia confided to a neighborhood girl about her recent past. The scandal spread like a firestorm, and arrangements were made to ship Sylvia off to school in Switzerland. The little girl pleaded to go back to Miss Maxwell's and was put instead into a foster home.

In 1979, Mabel, too ill to live on her own, moved in with her niece in Iowa and died there several years later. By the time Sylvia was eighteen, she'd been in fourteen foster homes and twice divorced, had no family and no friends aside from Milton and worked as a house cleaner. What money Mabel had left her had been squandered years before.

Private Companies

Here we'll talk about those businesses and organizations whose favors don't need to be scammed. Newspaper curators are thrilled when someone thinks enough of their back issues to laboriously sort through them, for whatever reason. Likewise, the Mormon's Family History Center volunteers never ask questions of nonbelievers and are perfectly happy to help out an itinerant searcher, even when there's never any pretense of praying for the dead man's soul.

Newspaper Office Morgue

Local newspapers retain all their past editions for historical posterity. At the smaller periodical offices, old issues may be stacked on bookshelves in some dry dusty corner, but any major publication will have an index of names and even subject matter. Many times these same issues and/or indexes will be available at the public library.

Family History Centers

Maintained by the Mormon church, these genealogical centers either have a lot of information on hand or will help you order it from Salt Lake City. The thing to remember, of course, is that since their interest is in dead people not live ones, the information they keep there is old, old, old. If your detective is looking for a gunslinger who disappeared from the streets of Laredo in 1871, this would be a fine place for the PI to spend his time.

Illegal but Getable "Confidential" Information

Bottom line, as honorable as many PIs aspire to be, in some cases, it is impossible to do a thorough investigation without breaking some rules. Or, as some call them, laws. How far a gumshoe will go depends mainly upon his own morality, coupled with his qualms of getting caught and his fear of small dark spaces with exposed toilets. In this section, find those "confidential sources" that provide the link to anybody's business.

Law Enforcement

Every PI's got a cop in his pocket. At least every fictional PI. What have these law enforcement guys got that we don't? Most notably, access to the NCIC computer and a nationwide DMV database. Do they share? Law enforcement officers from the top on down have been known to help out an anxious citizen, PI or not, but every time one does, he leaves a "footprint" of his inquiry. Were he ever questioned, there could be a heck of a price to pay for this breach of confidence.

What do we have that they don't? Everything else. Many police and DA investigators simply do not have the computer resources that are legally available to anyone, and often their superiors are too stuck in their old ways to know what they're missing and way too macho to find out. To cover their butts, they cite budget restraints, which is, of course, silly, since one man with a computer can do the work of six—and one woman with a computer can do the work of twelve.

Still, many enforcement types recognize a little bending of the rules can benefit both parties and therefore ask—and grant—favors selectively. Once you develop a relationship with one of these guys, you'll find courtesies being granted back and forth. Especially in books.

• The NCIC computer has a compilation of criminal malfeasances, commonly called rap sheets. The database has two sections, automated and manual, and between them is every offense recorded by man. The automated section is a nationwide listing of repeat offenders whose records can be accessed by name and DOB and/or SSN with just a few keystrokes. The manual section contains all other records, and to use it, the officer must know where to look, going into a geographical area and even a specific court.

Obviously, this computer is a powerful tool, which is why the FBI keeps it out of the hands of the public. Although the rap sheet can only be accessed through this channel, your gumshoe can collect much of the same information by checking the county involved—if only he knows which county to check. For more, see the preceding chapter on public records.

- DMV records, nationwide, is the second exclusive database available to law enforcement and is accessible by name and DOB with just a few keystrokes. Luckily, privately owned companies are compiling this still largely public information into a giant treasure trove for the rest of us "unenforcement" types. At the time of this writing, twenty-three states can be searched at one whack, and more are being added every month.

The Phone Company

Having a contact within the phone company is essential, although not always possible in real life. There is no reason, however, that you shouldn't supply your fictional gumshoe with a willowy Uma Thurman type who just happens to have access to the billing records. Just remember, most operators, even at that level, can only access accounts by phone number, so asking Uma for a "nonpub" would, of course, be silly. It would be even sillier if Uma actually gave your detective the number. To be sure of the capabilities of your particular Uma, call the local company's public relations department, tell the person you're writing a mystery and ask. Then call me and tell me what was said.

Now imagine the kind of information one could glean from telephone records. Listed at the top is identifying data—name, address, DOB, SSN, etc, all data that was given when opening the account. Along with that are a "contact" number, that of a friend or family member who can be reached in case of emergency, any complaints regarding the service or billing, names of others who have called to inquire and, of course, all the toll numbers called from that phone or with any calling cards issued to that number.

These toll charges can provide a virtual diary of a subject's contacts, interests, income and financial data providing an obvious road map to an investigation.

And, of course, it is quite possible to find an MP by phoning someone who knows him—the mother perhaps—spinning her some crazy yarn, *knowing* she will pick up the phone and alert her bad boy. Then, after Uma forks over Mom's toll calls, your detective can easily pinpoint just where the little gray-haired accessory phoned during the moments after your detective's phone call to her.

Another thing to remember is that since the breakup of AT&T, long-distance charges do not appear on the local phone bill but are invoiced directly by MCI, Sprint or whoever. Therefore, these charges would not be something Uma would have access to, instead referring your detective to her friend Erma who specializes in retrieving these particular kinds of records (see " 'Borderline' Businesses," later in this chapter).

The Electric Company, Cable Company, Airlines, Bank, Etc.

All these private firms have within their files data helpful to seekers of MPs, details they're encouraged not to leak. Inside informants, of course, have already tackled that moral dilemma and, luckily for PIs everywhere, come up lacking. Still other clerks and operators have been scammed out of the information without even knowing what hit them.

To determine how to fool a particular agency, call customer service, inquire as to your own account and note what is queried of you in order to access your statement while insuring client confidentiality. Your cable company, for example, might require a phone number to pull up an account and then ask for an address in order to verify the person is who he says he is. If it's the address your PI is after, then supplying the addresss of an old residence just might trick the clerk to asking if the cable user is not still at 131 South Market Street.

"Borderline" Businesses

This is my own designation for firms specializing in providing their clients with confidential information on an as-needed basis. How do they do it? We don't ask; they don't tell. I'm sure some have developed "inside sources," but many more work via a colorful gag, developed and perfected with the help of someone who has been in the trade and knows the lingo.

What can they get? Phone tolls, credit card charges, bank accounts, stocks and bonds, health insurance—if it exists, somebody's figured out how to get it. When writing about one of these borderliners, you don't have to worry much about accuracy, since if you claimed to know a guy who specialized in X-raying safety-deposit boxes to determine their contents, some real-life PI would undoubtedly call you up and ask if you'd share your source.

How do PIs find such resources? They don't; the resources find them. Once a detective is licensed and firmly ensconced on various mailing lists, all kinds of offers start arriving in the mail, the peddling of confidential data among them. Why so open? Well, for one thing, information is an investigator's bread and butter, and finking on a potential resource is like shooting yourself in the foot after a fun night of line dancing.

Also, it's not the *having* of confidential information that is illegal, it is the getting of it. If a subject freely discloses to a telephone surveyor where he banks, then can the newly christened surveyor be prosecuted? For what? Crimes are victim driven, and collecting a court-appointed judgment is certainly no violation of any civil code I know of. And then, of course, there is the problem of identifying the caller, one of the key ingredients in prosecuting a civil or criminal case.

RESOURCE FOUR: DATABASES, MICROFICHE AND CD-ROMs

Every day we get callers saying, "He should be easy to find; he's on welfare." Or, "Just check the health insurance database," or, "I know you can find him, he filed taxes last year." The truth is, although all these databases undoubtedly exist, they don't exist as far as the private investigator is concerned.

And it's not just nincompoops who believe Big Brother has come to Toontown. Two of my favorite FBI agents, Knucklehead (AKA Knucks) and Mahmoud, as they are affectionately known to their cohorts, retired after twenty-five years of working on cases like the Unabomber and Polly Klaas and opened their own private investigation firm. While still setting up their resources and getting used to the "outside," they would occasionally call with questions. On one such call, Knucks wanted to know where he could get a listing of all blue Mustang convertibles registered in the state of California in 1962.

After giving him the old no can do, Knucks's perfectly

obvious response was, "So then this has to be hand-pulled in Sacramento?" After several such obscure requests, and long explanations of the hoops one had to jump through in order to compile whatever information he was seeking, I began to realize just how much these guys had been getting on the "inside." Yeah, OK, we got a lot of it anyway, but how much easier it would be if DMV, FBI, CIA, Interpol, welfare, etc., would just fess up in the first place!

Instead, nongovernment-sanctioned detectives such as ourselves must rely solely upon online services offered by credit raters, mail-order companies, public record holders and the like. While these databases were not originally compiled with the skip tracer in mind, searchers have declared them an essential resource in locating people and are subscribing en mass.

To tap into databaseland, your detective needs only a computer, modem, live telephone wire, enough money to pay the eventual bill and this chapter. From there, he simply:

1. Turns on the machine

2. Types in whatever is required at the prompt

3. Awaits the system's request for his user ID and password

4. Remembers that and manages to type it in correctly

5. Makes his request

6. Either gets the information right then or goes back in to pick it up later

The data he retrieves will either be current or a collection dating back to the mid-1980s when the first stuff was typed into the system. If your gumshoe requires something prior, he must then venture into the county courthouse or try to charm, by phone, a clerk at the appropriate facility.

CD-ROMs are also collections of specialized information—they could be phone discs, death indexes, street maps, etc.—frozen in time at the moment they were compiled and stored on thin, round, silver discs that fit into the CD-ROM drive of any computer so equipped. The upside, of course, is once purchased, a CD's usage is free, unlike a database where there is a charge for every minute online. The downside is that nobody comes in every day to update your disc, so the info just gets older and older and older. . . .

The third most popular method of storing information is via microfiche, a $4'' \times 5.75''$ piece of film plastered with data so tiny it can only be seen when magnified by a microfiche machine. Luckily, some states sell—or have sold—their marriage, death, divorce, voter's registration, property and professional licensing records to the public. Personally, we have collected as much of this data as is available and keep it beside our dandy microfiche machine, acquired at a San Francisco City and County Flea Market for $25, new in the box. Always, we decide whether to take a case based upon if we can identify the MP, and many times, we determine that based solely upon whether the MP exists in a statewide marriage fiche, knowing that ordering the application will yield enough identifying data to get the job done.

My (and Your) Responsibility to the Industry

There are plenty who will be angry at me for writing this book: privacy advocates, fellow PIs not anxious for their secrets to be told and, most notably, almost every database company we deal with. You'd think the companies would be grateful for the plug, but the truth is the modern world is so privacy prone that they're scared, and rightly so, that if the word gets out that this information is being used to find people, states will speed up their closing of public records.

Take Metromail's recent snafu as an example. One of this company's products is a mailing list of children whose parents might be interested in goods offered via direct mail. Well, the founder of a children's organization went berserk when he heard mention of this well-established and respectable firm, so certain was he that this particular list would be a resource for pedophiles. It seemed perfectly logical to him that a kidnapper would search out a direct-mail company, spend $270 on a list and then sift through it to arbitrarily pick out a victim. The fact that this had never happened did not deter him, nor did the factor that the procedure would prove so cumbersome that the usual method of just spotting a child on the street would undoubtedly win out in the end. Now, of course, I am 100 percent on the side of keeping our kids safe, I just don't see how curbing Metromail's ability to do business will in any meaningful way accomplish that.

And so, in the spirit of preserving our databases for what they are in most cases being used for, that is, bringing criminals to justice, the collection of child support, finding assets of judgment debtors, locating birth parents and adoptees alike and reuniting friends and lost loves, I am not naming companies but instead referring only to their searches.

Database Companies: Core and Gateway

There are essentially two kinds of firms selling online information: "core" companies, the originators of the databases, and "gateways," which offer a collection of databases under one easy-to-use software umbrella. To understand this rather complicated concept, picture the Internet (another complicated concept) as a gateway company and the Web sites as the searches they offer. Now, visualize the Internet standardizing the "look" of the sites and claiming them as its own. What this now resembles, of course, is one omniscient, omnipotent monster rather than the collection of individual, independent companies that it actually is.

Now, let's say your newly licensed, first-case-out-of-the-gate detective signs up for "InfoMegaNet" and is immediately smitten with his own sudden prowess as an investigator. OK, secretly he resents the $50 service fee/blood money that Info-MegaNet charges just for the privilege of doing business with them each month, but he keeps his mouth shut. The last thing he needs is to make God mad.

Then arrives the cavalry! InfoMegaNet-Two, InfoMega-Net-Too and InfoMegaNet-Me-Too all appear on the market-place, and their searches, although not known quantities like InfoMegaNet's "super-duper all-inclusive global address-update search extravaganza," look pretty damn good, from what the flyer reads. And no sign-up fees! So the next time InfoMega-Net fails to spew forth your detective's alleged scoundrel, the

PI gives InfoMegaNet-Too's "address update" a whirl. And then, being thorough—and having a client with a fairly decent portfolio—your intrepid hero runs all his inquiries through all four companies, just to be sure. What he doesn't realize, of course, is he's buying the same data four times over when he could have purchased it directly from the core company at a fraction of the cost.

Core Companies

These are the creators of the databases. They do not normally collect the data themselves but simply compile it into an online service. For example: Metronet (Metromail's sister company) took 1990 census data and combined it with listed telephone numbers and property records to create a dandy reverse directory that also spits out demographic information. No, they didn't go door-to-door to collect the data, but they still get the credit.

Gateway Companies

These also have a legitimate niche in the marketplace, and while they charge a markup on core company searches, they can save an investigator big bucks. Here's why.

The occasional search. Some core companies (and some gateways as well) impose a monthly surcharge or minimum fee. If a PI seldom requires a specific search, say, a real estate inquiry from the core company DataQuick, then it would obviously be more economical to pay $15 to a gateway company every couple of months than to incur DataQuick's $50 monthly minimum and get the search for, say, $4. Fiscally smart investigators utilize the core companies for searches they use extensively and a trusted gateway provider for obscure searches required only occasionally.

Ease of use. Since gateway companies have packaged all their searches in one (hopefully) user-friendly environment, in large offices, the boss may prefer to spend his money on searches rather than training a bunch of people who might not stick around after school starts in September.

Specialty doesn't require much database use. Some just don't. Arson investigators, workmen's compensation sleuths, shoppers—for their once-in-a-blue-moon needs, these PIs often prefer to have just one system to remember and one monthly fee to worry about. Life's hard enough.

How Does One Find These Databases?

Once licensed, PIs almost always land on various investigator-targeted mailing lists, which are sold and resold ad nauseam. By simply reading his junk mail, he's automatically in the loop. By comparing prices, he can buy closer and closer to the source until, at last, he's discovered the source itself. The lower the search cost, obviously, the more affordable it is to "play"—using what is learned from one search to run another—and the more efficient he becomes.

Also, PIs have been known to talk. We're part of a network of searchers—nonmacho types. We don't consider ourselves competitive, we keep in touch and we always share resources. We read the mailers, note new searches and watch for anybody selling the old standbys for less. Then we share information.

And no, we don't tell the macho types.

Nationwide ''Global'' Searches

Oh, come on, you remember "global": It means your detective hasn't a clue where to look, but he knows if he doesn't find Dr. Mortimer K. Plotkin by his son's graduation party on Saturday, Mrs. P.'s never going to be able to pay the caterers, let alone the hefty location fee. So the PI's first plan is to go "fishing," hoping Dr. Mort, as his beloved proctology patients called him, will leap out from one of the many databases, discs or other sundry sources comprising the information superhighway.

Credit Header

The Fair Credit Reporting Act prohibits the accessing of payment history without specific guidelines but has determined that header information—name, SSN, address, DOB, employment, etc., found at the top of the credit report—does not qualify under this classification. The upshot is although legally companies like TRW, CBI/Equafax and TransUnion can sell their headers to whomever they wish, each firm's own internal policy decrees they do not lease their service to private investigators.

Still, most every PI I know has access to headers, usually

through his own shell company or another firm that gets the data legitimately and then resells it. The credit reporting agencies make a concerted effort to close up shop on such enterprises, employing an ongoing cat-and-mouse game played out between detectives and this major resource.

Here's how header information is compiled:

Scenario one. When a consumer fills out an application, he's asked for his name, physical address and SSN, all of which is checked against an existing credit report to verify identity and determine payment history. That is pretty common knowledge among consumers. What is not is that simultaneously that person's credit file is being updated, alerting every other subscriber in the service of any changes in his physical whereabouts.

Scenario two. Being a fiscally responsible adult, the consumer fills out the change-of-address form that comes with his bills. Again, the surprise factor is that the info he's giving in confidence is being added to this giant database as well.

Scenario three. The consumer is a scoundrel, choosing not to let his credit-grantors know where he's gone off to. Having not filled out a change-of-address form, he considers himself scot-free. So free, in fact, that he shops for a new car. Or a better apartment. Or joins a health club. What he doesn't know is that all these organizations, potential credit grantors, share information, back and forth, with the credit reporting agencies.

Scenario four. The consumer knows all this but thinks he is smarter than the credit raters. Ha! He transposes his SSN, shaves a few years off his age and switches his first and middle names, thinking the computer will conclude he's some new consumer newly arrived in the marketplace. Well, excuse me, but the keeper of the credit files didn't just trot in from Missoula on a half-dead donkey. These guys know just how dyslexic scoundrels can be, so they've programmed their trusty databases to link files not just by Socials but additionally by a code created from the inputted name and address. Result: Scoundrels can transpose stats all they like, but their files will be linked up regardless, due to the double-checking capabilities built into the program.

CBI/Equafax's credit header information is the

"purest" of the three agencies' reports because it purges unconfirmed data, leaving the investigator with only the final rendering. CBI provides the most extensive header as well, literally the entire credit report minus payment history. What's left is plenty: full name, AKAs, SSN, DOB, last address and the date it was reported, previous addresses (with dates), employment, past employments, bankruptcy alert, opened and closed accounts and inquiries from potential credit grantors. The only information that tends to be outdated is employment, since people do not routinely alert their credit card companies when they change positions.

TRW header information has its strong points as well. Although this company provides less in the way of categories of information—just the name, AKAs, past and present addresses, SSN and YOB—TRW doesn't purge erroneous inputs, allowing the investigator to sort out the discrepancies himself. Such extraneous information has solved many a case since it shows if the MP is seeking to deceive and the names and addresses he is using to do so.

TransUnion's credit header looks very much like TRW's, but since this company is strongest in the eastern part of the United States, it tends to come up with more information on people living there rather than the West Coast. It also contains a "Hawk-Alert," a fraud alarm that checks for discrepancies in the SSN.

Credit header information is accessed in two ways: by SSN or by name and an address no earlier than the mid- to late 1980s. Because your detective (let's call him Dick) has Dr. Mort's SSN, the most direct route to finding him would be to see if the good doc informed his creditors when he moved on. Dick runs the social and sees that Dr. Plotkin appears to be still residing at his Livermore address. Being an astute fellow, Dick knows this is not true because Mrs. Plotkin hired him for a reason: She has to continue paying the bills, and until Dr. Mort informs his credit card companies of his new address—or makes one of the other fatal mistakes listed above—there will be no change in his header information or a cessation of the doctor's bills coming to Mrs. P's place.

EXAMPLE OF CBI/EQUAFAX CREDIT HEADER

05-23-1996 12:42:46 INQUIRY NUMBER: 585 OPERATOR: DD

DTEC457-42-8775

*PLOTKIN,MORTIMER,KENNETH SINCE 06/00/64 FAD 03/13/96

152121,FARNSWORTH,SAN LEANDRO,CA,94579,DAT RPTD 02/96

97838,TUTTLE,LANE,SAN LEANDRO,CA,94579,TAPE RPTD 04/95

BDS-02/27/49,SSS-527-42-8775

01 ES-,PHYSICIAN

02 EF-RESIDENT,UNIVERSITY OF PACIFIC,SF,CA,EMP 07/68,VER 12/86

TRADE LINE INFORMATION

ACCOUNT NUMBER	DATE RPTD	MEMBER NO.	FIRM NAME	TYP	TELEPHONE NO.	LAST ACTV
601194855350	05/96	155BB02747	DISCOVR CD	R	MAIL ONLY	05/96
542418024063	04/96	906BB90040	CITIBK-MC	R	MAIL ONLY	7/94
4816834010	04/96	132FM00124	FTB MTG	I	(214)484-5600	04/96

INQUIRY INFORMATION

MEMBER NO.	FIRM NAME	TELEPHONE NO.	DATE OF INQUIRY
136BB177	SECURITYBK	(503)267-5626	06/19/95

Phone Discs

These purport to list every name in every telephone directory nationwide. Available to anyone with $150 and a CD-ROM drive, to his credit, Dick qualifies. Dick begins his search here because now that he's purchased the product from his local software store, his access to it is forever free—and 112 million listings is a whole lot of listings for forever free. Unfortunately, Mortimer K. Plotkin has not chosen to go the listed telephone number route.

EXAMPLE OF PHONE DISC LISTINGS

PLOTKIN, MOISEY 22 S ADAMS ST DENVER, CO 80209 303-377-3536

PLOTKIN, MORRIS 7522 WHITLOCK AVE PLAYA DEL REY, CA 90293 310-822-6335

PLOTKIN, MORTON 1030 PRESIDENT AVE FALL RIVER, MA 02720-5928 401-247-1085

Business Discs

Dick has wisely nuked his bulky "smart yellow pages" collection and replaced it with this solo CD-ROM, which usually comes as part of the residential listing package. Dick hits F7 to access Type of Organization and chooses Physicians and Surgeons, but Mortimer, again, is not listed.

Next Dick curses himself for this wasted step. Since Dr. Mort disappeared but three months ago, he naturally was still listed at his San Francisco office, the correct address when the disc was compiled earlier that year.

EXAMPLE OF BUSINESS DISC LISTINGS

PLOTKIN, JACOB PA 847 RIDGEWOOD ST BROWNSVILLE, TX 78520-8645 210-541-1013

PLOTKIN, MORTIMER MD 381 BUSH ST SAN FRANCISCO, CA 94103-1234 415-555-9800

PLUMLEY, THOMAS F MD 3525 ENSIGN RD NE OLYMPIA, WA 98506 360-491-3980

Social Security's Master Death Index

Accessible either online or via CD-ROM, this is Social Security's own master list of deceased Americans whose survivors have received benefits.

It can be accessed by:

- First and last name (no middle initials appear) and then the subject identified by DOB, Date of Death, where the SSN was issued and/or the state where the death occurred

- Social Security number

- First name and DOB

- Surname only

Regardless of how it was accessed, a successful search yields all of the above information, including the zip code of the person receiving the benefit (when known). Had Dick found Dr. Mort listed here, he could have then ordered his death certificate had it been publicly available in that state and, failing that, checked the appropriate paper for a news item or obit and/or called the local funeral parlor for more information. Unfortunately, according to SS's Master Death Index, Dr. Mort had not, in fact, taken a dirt nap.

But being the astute fellow he is, Dick knows that does not mean that Dr. Mort is definitely among the upright since the index does not include bodies identified as a John Doe, those folks with their own pension plans, people who died before the index was compiled in 1962 or children who passed away before being eligible for any benefits.

EXAMPLE OF NATIONWIDE DEATH INDEX

Soc Sec Num	Last Name	First Name	Birth Date	Death Date	Resi	Zip1	Zip2
228-12-1418	PLOTKIN	MORTIMER	09/13/1912	03/17/1978	(KY)	40391	24277

24277 VA Pennington Gap . . . . 40391 KY Winchester

Simple Surname Search

Compiled from telephone directories, real property records and even magazine subscriber lists, online name searches contain a good number of listings that do not appear on phone discs since they, obviously, take listed telephone numbers as their base. Also, the information is continually updated whereas a CD remains paralyzed at the time it was compiled. Metronet, the industry's primary provider, is slow and jumps uncomfortably between fields (for example, if one touches "enter" when "tab" would have been appropriate, there's hell to pay) but remains a staple in a PI's online collection mainly because searches can cost as little as $.50 and yield a lot of information. A crude copy of Metronet is available on CompuServe and labeled PhoneFile, and also marketed directly to public via an 800 number entitled "The National Look-up Service." Still, your detective should definitely have his own online account, or he'll be laughed out of the business. And this is a pretty tough business to get laughed out of.

The Surname Search—because it does not allow for differentiation by YOB—is not, except for uncommon names, very effective for global searching. Mortimer Plotkin qualifies, however, so Dick types in Plotkin and then types in Mort, covering all contingencies nationwide from Mort to Mortimer to Morticia. No instance of Mort or Mortimer occurs, but he does locate a Mortabella in Podunk, Idaho.

EXAMPLE OF ONLINE SURNAME SEARCH

	HOH	LOR
1 MORTABELLA PLOTKIN (208) 555 - 5227	X	
24808 NE 50TH AVE PODUNK ID 83214		09

(HOH = Head of Household; LOR = Length of Residence)

The Personal Profile

This can be accessed by name; name and DOB; first name and DOB; name and zip code; city, state and name; address;

street name only; phone number or SSN, taking its information from over one billion records. Whew! In return, it yields literally a full dossier on the person, including:

1. Past and present addresses, some unlisted phone numbers
2. AKAs, SSN, DOB, DL#s and vehicles
3. Relatives and associates, their past and present addresses, AKAs, SSNs, DOBs and DL#s
4. Neighbors of all the above

One of the most powerful searches on the market today, the Personal Profile quite often comes up with addresses not even registered in header information. It is, quite often, the only search needed prior to segueing into the gumshoe portion of the investigation.

Dick runs Dr. Mort's profile and finds no data beyond the disappearance date but notes a San Francisco residential address dated just prior. The name associated with the condo is Mary Jo Mason.

National Driver Licenses by Name

Last Name - First Name - MI			Age	Address	City	State
MASON	MARY	J				

3 exact matches. 3 match first 13 characters

MASON,	MARY	J	82	820 PAMELLA ST	HARTFORD	CT
MASON,	MARY	J		123 CONDO HEIGHTS	JUPITER	FL
MASON,	MARY	J	31	BX 3802 FIRST ST	ATLANTA	GA

Nationwide Driving Records

Ninety-four million entries from (at the time of this writing) nineteen states: CO, DE, IA, IL, KY, LA, MD, ME, MI, MN, MO, MS, ND, NH, OH, OR, SC, WI and WV. Records can be accessed by first and last name; last name and DOB; first name and DOB; last name and zip code; or DL#. The search can be run through all simultaneously or individually by state.

Since Doc is so recently disappeared, Dick is not surprised there is no record. By comparing middle names and issue dates,

```
─────────────────── Florida Driver License ───────────────────
│                                                              │
│  Driver License Number :          Original Issue : 3/30/97   │
│                                                              │
│       Issued in :FLORIDA          Expires On :               │
│                                                              │
│  Class :OPERATORS LICENSE                                    │
│                                                              │
│  Restrictions :No Restrictions                               │
│──────────────────────────────────────────────────────────── │
│                                                              │
│  Driver :MASON, MARY JO           DOB :10/31/60 Age: 37      │
│                                                              │
│  Address :123 CONDO HEIGHTS       Height :5'06"              │
│                                                              │
│        JUPITER, FL 33468-6813     Weight :120                │
│                                                              │
│                                   Hair Color : BLONDE        │
│                                                              │
│                                   Eye Color : BLUE           │
│                                                              │
────────────────────────────────────────────────────────────────
```

Dick is able to sort through all the Mary J. Masons of the world to find the Mary Jo who applied for a driver's license just weeks after Dr. Mort's leap to freedom. Her description suggests she is a thirty-seven-year-old, blonde-haired, blue-eyed, 5'6", 120-pound woman. A follow-up search for vehicles shows her registered auto, a Ferrari.

Lexis/Nexis

Lexis is the legal division and *Nexis* is the news division of a mainstream database maintained by Reed Elsevier and used extensively by investigative journalists and attorneys in the course of their everyday jobs. Anyone can sign up for Lexis (as the service is collectively known), and many detectives do, finding their nationwide sweeps of civil and criminal files, bankruptcies, news clippings, property, professional licensing and corporation records, judgments and tax liens irresistible.

Since his quick 'n cheap fixes have wrought zip, Dick decides to go fishing via Lexis, although these searches are generally considered way too pricey for such nonsense. Dick calls and ups his fee, evoking a side of Mrs. Plotkin he has not seen, obviously she received the caterers bill.

Lexis comes in a DOS or Windows format, Dick's password coded in for easy access. He clicks on the Lexis icon and up comes the menu asking which of the libraries he elects to search.

- The FINDER Library is a collection of 145 million persons, 88 million households and 70 million telephone numbers, all obtained from 3,400 white page directories, Social Security's Master Death Index, census data and other public records—kind of a Metronet with attitude. Dick, being uncommonly smart, knows much of this attitude he's already acquired from Metronet and saves his money.

- The ASSETS Library is compiled from:

    1. Tax assessors' rolls and county recorders' deed transfer records in thirty-eight states: AL, AK, AZ, CA, CT, CO, DC, FL, GA, HI, IL, IN, IA, LA, MD, MA, MI, MN, MS, MO, NV, NJ, NM, NY, NC, OH, OK, OR, PA, RI, SC, TN, TX, UT, VA, WA, WV and WI.

    2. Aircraft registration from the FAA.

    3. Watercraft ownership from the Coast Guard and Florida's Department of Natural Resources.

Dick clicks on ALLOWN and finds Dr. Mort lacking in real property and personal property equipped with wings or rudders.

- The INCORP Library is a compilation of:

    1. Active and inactive corporations, as well as limited partnerships registered with the secretary of state (SOS) in forty-four states: AK, AZ, AR, CA, CO, CT, DE, DC, GA, ID, IL, IN, IA, KS, KY, LA, MD, MA, MI, MN, MS, MO, NE, NV, NH, NY, NC, ND, OH, OK, OR, PA, RI, SC, SD, TN, TX, UT, VT, VA, WA, WV, WI and WY.

    2. Fictitious Business Names in AL, AK, AZ, AR, CA, CO, CT, DE, DC, FL, GA, HI, ID, IL, IN, IA, KS, KY, LA, ME, MD, MA, MI, MN, MS, MO, NE, NV, NH, NJ, NM, NY, NC, ND, OH, OK, OR, PA, RI, SC, TN, TX, UT, VT, VA, WA, WV and WI. (Command ALLBIZ searches all SOS and FBN files.)

    3. Professional licensing info in CA, NJ and PA.

- The LIENS Library is a compilation of:

1. UCC filings in all states. (Command ALLUCC searches all.)

2. Judgments and tax liens in thirty-six states: AZ, AR, CA, CO, CT, FL, HI, ID, IL, IN, IA, KS, KY, LA, ME, MA, MN, MO, NE, NV, NH, NM, NY, ND, OH, OK, OR, PA, RI, SD, TX, UT, VT, WA, WI and WY. (Command ALLJGT searches all.)

Dick finds Dr. Mort has not, in fact, taken his proctology business to any of the contributing states, nor does he have any judgments or liens in the states providing that information.

The NEWS Library is made up of full-text articles from over two thousand magazines, newspapers, journals, newsletters, wire services and broadcast transcripts worldwide. They can be searched en masse or by a specific periodical and/or date.

Dick chooses to search all and types in "Dr. Mort or Mortimer w/2 Plotkin." He has asked the system to find a Dr. Mort or Mortimer Plotkin, allowing or disallowing for his middle initial by narrowing the search to only those articles citing the word Mort or Mortimer within two words of Plotkin. Easily he finds the three-month-old article in which Dr. Mortimer Plotkin appears to have catapulted himself off the Oakland Bay Bridge en route to his office in the city. (Commuting across town to the Golden Gate Bridge to commit suicide is considered redundant.) It seems that Dr. Mort began walking at Treasure Island and was chased by cops halfway to Oz before losing them in traffic. His wallet and a suicide note were found bridgeside, but nobody saw the poor man flop over.

A follow-up article stated that a motorist, upon reading the previous day's *Chronicle*, called the Bridge Patrol to report seeing a red Ferrari pulled over with its hood up and an attractive blonde sitting patiently behind the wheel. A man whom he couldn't describe (most likely, because he had his eye on the blonde) popped down the hood and climbed into the passenger side, and together they sped off. No other articles appeared nationwide concerning the Dr. Mort or Mortimer w/2 Plotkin combo.

A Ferrari. Hmmm.

- The INSOLV Library contains bankruptcy files contributed from forty-five states: AK, AZ, AR, CA, CO, CT, DE, DC, FL, HI, ID, IL, IN, IA, KS, KY, LA, ME, MD, MA, MN, MS, MO, MT, NE, NV, NH, NJ, NM, NY, ND, OH, OK, OR, PA, RI, SD, TN, TX, UT, VT, WA, WV, WI and WY. (Command ALLBKT searches all.)

Here appears some info Mrs. Plotkin either doesn't know or doesn't want Dick to know. Dr. Mort declared bankruptcy just days before his leap, either overboard or in auto.

- The DOCKET library contains:
    1. Civil and criminal court dockets from selected counties in twelve states: AL, CA, CT, FL, IL, ME, MA, NY, OH, PA, RI and TX. (States must be searched individually.)
    2. Formal sanctions against members of financial and health care services by regulatory agencies such as Securities and Exchange Commission (SEC); National Association of Securities Dealers (NASD); Commodity Futures Trading Commission (CFTC); Department of Veterans Affairs; HUD; FHA; Department of Justice; Federal Deposit Insurance Corp. (FDIC); Former Federal Home Loan Bank Board; Federal Reserve Board; Health and Human Services; National Credit Union Administration; Office of the Comptroller of the Currency; Office of Thrift Supervision; Resolution Trust Corp.; State Real Estate and Mortgage Regulators. (Command SANCTN searches all and provides the name of individual and institution, jurisdiction, agency, date, case number, action taken, incident description, status and disposition.)

By clicking on CACIVL, Dick searches all superior court civil filings in Los Angeles, Orange, Sacramento, San Bernardino, San Diego, San Francisco, Santa Barbara and Santa Clara counties. In Frisco, he finds a malpractice suit filed by Mary Jo Mason, along with a satisfaction of judgment by Dr. Mort's insurance company.

Now what are the chances, muses Dick, of a woman who co-owns a property with a man also suing him for malpractice, winning a huge settlement from his insurance company and disappearing about the same time he does?

A lot to one, figures Dick. Unless, of course, they're in it together.

Statewide Searches

With nothing to go on but Mary Jo Mason's new driver's license information, Dick decides to segue into a statewide search of Florida. (OK, I know you're thinking that since Dick's got Mary Jo's new address off the DMV search, why not just go directly there. Well, for plot purposes, let's just say that address turns out to be a mail drop; otherwise, I've got no reason to tell you about the Statewide Comprehensive Search. See how that plot thing works?)

Kinds of Records Available

This differs by state. Luckily for Dick, Florida is one of the most generous in its offerings of public records, and he is able to explore the following chronicles in one comprehensive search:

- Accident reports, attorney listings, banking and financial licenses, beverage licenses, boats owned, concealed weapons permits, condominiums and co-op records, corporation records, criminal histories and incarcerations, divorces, driver's licenses and driver history, fictitious names, handicap parking permits, hotel and restaurant owners, insurance agents, marriages, notary certificates, nursing licenses, private investigators, professional regulations, real estate owned, real estate brokers licenses, sexual predators, sweepstake registrations, teachers, UCC lien filings, vehicles, workmen's compensation claims.

What a Comprehensive Search Can Yield

Again, Dick's inquiries regarding Dr. Mortimer K. Plotkin have brought zip, but as it turns out, Mary Jo Mason's just recently acquired a real estate broker's license in Florida. The company: Mary Jo's Mansions of Jupiter. The address: the same mail drop gleaned from DMV records.

Additionally, the Comprehensive search confirms:

- Mary Jo is a thirty-seven-year-old, 5′6″ white female, born in Florida on the same DOB provided in the Nationwide Drivers Search. Her SSN's prefix indicates it was issued in Florida in 1973.

- Mary Jo's DL#, its issue and expiration dates, along with the registration of the Ferrari.

- Dick is cheered to learn Mary Jo is not a sexual predator, although he doubts Mrs. Plotkin will see it that way.

- He's also delighted that she possesses no permit to carry a concealed weapon.

- And that she has not been criminally incarcerated in Florida.

- And that no workmen's claims have been filed by her.

- Other persons using her SSN, you might ask. Well, Mortimer K. Mason for one. Oh my.

- Mary Jo has several previous Florida addresses, ignoring the span from 1993 to 1997, presumedly when she was out of state.

- Three vehicle accidents are noted for Mary Jo Mason, the last dated just a few weeks prior. Further inquiry reveals the passenger in the car with Mary Jo was Mortimer.

- Property for Mary Jo consists of a condo assessed at $273,980, purchased in August. No past properties are shown.

- She has no UCC filings.

- A new Fictitious Business license was issued for Mary Jo's Mansions of Jupiter, its status active.

- Her broker's license is her only active professional credential.

- Telephone listings are provided for one hundred other folks now or once associated with the condo's address but none with the last name of Mason or Plotkin. Similar findings are dispensed regarding Mary Jo's past Florida addresses.

- A May 3, 1982, marriage appears for Mary Jo Mason and Leonardo Garcia in Dade County. The bride was twenty-two at the time of the union; the groom twenty-six. A divorce record is recorded six months later. No additional marriages were located for either party.

- No relatives were found for Mary Jo, but Possible Associated Persons brought forth William Robert Austin, a white, 5'10", 170-pound male born July 4, 1946, his Florida DL# given along with a veterinary license, his past addresses and three accidents of his own. By comparing commonalities, Dick notes they undoubtedly spent some time together both at a business location and in an automobile, presumedly no longer in mint condition. Since Dick finds no recent linkage, he concludes Billy Bob is merely an old beau whom Mary Jo undoubtedly worked with. He tucks the info away in case his most direct leads don't pan out.

- Vehicles registered to the condo's address show the Ferrari along with a Mazda Miata, including plate numbers, tag expiration dates, legal and registered owners, makes, models and VINs, original values, insurance carriers, policy numbers, lien holders and number of accidents recorded for each vehicle.

- No vehicles were ever registered to Mary Jo at any of her previous addresses.

- Mary Jo has no pilot's license.

- No aircraft is associated with her.

- No documented vessels are found in her name, either at her present or past addresses.

- Under possible corporations, the only entry was Mary Jo's Mansions of Jupiter, Inc. at the mail drop address Dick already had. Mortimer was listed as President and Director, and Mary Jo as Secretary and Agent of Service. The filing date: a month previous.

- Neighbors for all addresses were upchucked by the search and duly noted by Dick for possible follow-up.

Dick ran a comprehensive report on Mortimer K. Mason,

Plotkin's new persona as well, but found nothing beyond what had come up under his association with the accident-prone vamp.

Databases Where You Have to Know Where to Look

Review: Databases fall into two categories, those that can be searched globally and those that must be accessed by some criteria other than name, address, business name, DL#, VIN, etc. Now that Dick has acquired many of these things, he can retrieve information specific to the newly renamed Mortimer K. Mason and his partner in flight, Mary Jo Mason.

Business Credit Raters

Dun & Bradstreet and TRW are the two top firms providing business payment history. Expect to find company name, address, phone, the year the first report was filed, products, state and date of incorporation, the average time it takes for an invoice to be paid, the total owed in the last six months, the current outstanding debt, the credit risk factor, any bankruptcies, tax liens, UCC filings, accounts sent to collection, background information, banking relationships, inquiries from other firms, government contracts, and profit and loss (P&L) statements.

Dick inquires about Mary Jo's Mansions with some skepticism. He, himself, was once approached by D&B and was stunned at the process involved in analyzing his own business. D&B sent him a form to fill out, asking about pretty much everything listed above, including the number of his employees. Dick, for the heck of it, lied through his teeth and was later amazed to see much of his fiction recited in D&B's official report.

Three-month-old Mary Jo's Mansions of Jupiter, however, had not as yet been rated by TRW or Dun & Bradstreet, so there was nothing for her to lie about.

Address Profile

According to this search, Mary Jo's Mansions was located in a multiunit structure, the mail delivered by city delivery carrier #C001. Also present was its zip+4 designation, the streets surrounding the actual address, all other building occupants along with their addresses and phones.

Property

Dick already knows Mary Jo Mason owns the condo, but he does not yet know who owns the multiunit business address. A property search discloses the owner's name, address and phone.

Credit Header

Since Dick now has enough information to access Mary Jo's file—name and address, or SSN—he does that, and back comes her entire residential history dating back to the mid-1980s. Using those residences as a guide, Dick attempts to establish the genesis of Mortimer K. Mason's new persona and finds the only hit comes when matched up with the mail drop. Dick notes Mortimer's "new" SSN and inputs that into TRW's header system, finding it linked to an Ohio man with an established credit history.

EXAMPLE OF TRW CREDIT HEADER

MASON K MORTIMER SSN: 268-78-7025

2643 CLIPPER ST

JUPITER FL 33468

RPTD: 5-97

BARRY L ZEPHER SSN: 268-78-7025

862 MANHART DR

HEATH OH 43056

RPTD: 4-93 TO 3-97

BARRY L ZEPHER SSN: 268-78-7025

1010 W 30TH AVE #7

WELLINGTON OH 44090

RPTD: 10-92 TO 3-93

Demographic Address Search

As you've just seen, as new information is gathered, databases must be revisited in order to flush out the whole story. At the beginning of this search, Dick surname-searched for

Mortimer Plotkin and found only Mortabella of Podunk, Idaho. Now that same database is reaccessed, this time inputting the condo's address rather than Plotkin's name. No matter how the database is accessed—by name, address or phone—all the information will appear.

Dick can now see that had he known Mary Jo's name and her significance at the genesis of his search, this database would have easily found her. Her condo is there (since it includes assessor's data) as are the Clipper Street mail drop (change-of-address info); the median neighborhood income (derived from the last census); the designation of an "A" local (median income measured against local cost of living); Mary Jo's month and year of birth; the 101 percent probability that she owns her duplex, valued at 273.9K; and that she has lived there less than a year (assessor's records).

EXAMPLE OF DEMOGRAPHIC SEARCH
Returned Name/Address

#1–CURRENT RESIDENT/ADDRESS

MARY JO MASON

123 CONDO HEIGHTS

JUPITER FL 33468

(407) 000-0000

#2–COA NAME/ADDRESS

MARY JO MASON

2643 CLIPPER ST

JUPITER FL 33468

(407) 000-0000

GENDER:	FEMALE	LENGTH OF RES:	00
MEDIAN INCOME:	067.9K	HOME OWNER PROB:	101
WEALTH RATING:	A	HOME VALUE:	0273.9K
DATE OF BIRTH:	10/60	HOME VALUE INDEX:	141
		DWELLING TYPE:	DUPLEX

Street Atlas

Dick's ready for a look-see and itching for a Florida vacation. He pulls up Condo Heights on his trusty CD-ROM and pinpoints the address, noting from his address search the cross streets. He prints out a map to the joint, books a reservation to Humidtown and calls Mrs. Plotkin with the news.

Alas, Mortimer's home! Seems he was halfway out the upstairs window, Ping clubs in hand, when Mrs. Plotkin, alerted by her newly installed alarm system, mistook him for a burglar and shot him full in the buttocks. Dr. Mort is resting comfortably (on his stomach, no doubt), and doctors are working around the clock to discover the source of his post-botched-suicide amnesia. Mrs. P. couldn't be happier but refuses to pay Dick's bill since he didn't really *do* anything.

Not to be undone, Dick flies to Jupiter and offers his services to the lithesome Mary Jo, who, in the wake of her lover's sudden hankering for his four iron, is herself in need of a private detective.

What You Cannot Get

You've seen the kind of information just one computer search can yield, and, I think you'll agree, it is aplenty. As earlier stated, any information that exists on paper, in computer or by personal knowledge can conceivably be gotten, and Appendix B shows you where. There are, however, some resources that will *never* (never say never) be available via an online database.

So you don't make that embarrassing blunder, keep this rule of thumb in mind: Databases that are sold or leased to a variety of businesses outside an industry—credit information comes to mind—are basically "out there." Data that is only dispensed within an industry—health records are a prime example—will never be available online, but only through an inside, confidential source.

RESOURCE FIVE: GUMSHOEING

I know nobody wants to read (or write) a book about somebody who sits around all day typing names into a computer (which is why my biography remains unpenned). The truth is, 95 percent of the time, this is what we do. It's the other 5 percent that people want to write (and, hopefully, read) about.

It's called "gumshoeing," a term that came about, I imagine, from the state of one's soles after a hard day of hitting the streets. Its components are legitimate interviewing; illegitimate interviewing—AKA scams; surveillance; and picking through the trash. Gosh, the glamour! Gumshoeing, of course, is the information-gathering technique most frequently used in mysteries because only then has one the potential of meeting people, of having conversations, an occasional adventure and/or car chase, a quick shoot-out, a hot romance and possibly of even making a buck in the end.

So, in reality, you'll probably use the other informational

resources—client debriefing, public records, private and confidential confidants, online databases and in-house CD-ROMs—to impart quick data necessary for propelling the plot, and this resource, for the "guts" of your story. Even though, of course, gumshoeing is the sort of thing we hardly ever do.

Legitimate Interviewing

You know who they are. They know who you are. So what's the point? The point is, every once in a while, the truth works best. Many PIs spend their entire careers scamming from the very people who would gladly spill their guts if they only knew what the PI was really up to.

Example: I was once trying to make a case against a beautiful but wicked gypsy girl who had her hooks into an old man she was pumping full of heart medicine in hopes he'd kick the bucket a bit sooner. (I might have mentioned it.) Anyway, simultaneously, the gentleman's family had been paid a visit from the happy couple and couldn't quite believe their ninety-year-old Uncle Richard had snared such a beauty with his pleasant personality alone. So they hired a private eye to check out Miss Angela.

The PI did the usual, including running Miss Angela's name through the San Francisco County courthouse where he found a document recanting a Joint Deed of Trust. Apparently, a little old lady first "gave" Angela her property (upon the lady's eventual demise, of course) and then rescinded the offer. Behind the latter maneuver was daughter Jocylyn, a lady I'd already had the pleasure of meeting. I knew about her, by the way, the same way this detective had.

Well, now obviously, Jocylyn was on the same side we were, having wrestled her mother's million-dollar home—and her own inheritance—out of Angela's formidable grip. But instead of approaching her truthfully, this PI had a female cohort call with the story that she, too, was an elderly victim about to be scammed by Angela. Could Jocylyn tell her all she knew?

Jocylyn, thoroughly suspicious, instructed the woman to phone me, as I had a complete rendering of Angela's malfeasance. Because the cohort was not truthful with an obvious victim, she got a fraction of the information I had from Jocylyn, and since she didn't have the nerve to follow up by calling me, she missed out on the benefit of my experience as well.

So who should PIs be straight with? Bottom line, everybody they can be, *especially* folks who are inherently on their side.

Interviewing Witnesses

Many times, of course, finding the MP is not the point of your story but just a means to an end. Your readers know where the suspects are and even where the victim is buried. But, as it turns out, the only person who can testify as to who did it is the groundskeeper who happened to run off with the chambermaid just as the investigation was kicking off. (I hate when that happens.)

So your PI logically scours the courthouse, runs a few online searches and comes up with a list of folks likely to know the groundskeeper's whereabouts: a plaintiff desperate to collect his court-ordered judgment (gleaned from the superior court clerk's files); a defendant whom the groundskeeper sued following a hit-and-run golf-carting incident on the fourth hole (muni court); an old landlord with an ax to grind (small claims); former neighbors of that residence (assessor's office, CD-ROMs such as phone disc and online databases such as Metronet); past business associates (FBN Index); relatives (marriage application, voter's registration files); ex-wives (divorce records, marriage index); kids (DA's support files); and so on and so forth.

All these folks, potentially, can be interrogated by your detective in hopes they'll have pertinent knowledge of the habits, and even whereabouts, of the groundskeeper. And all of them, whether pro-MP or con, or as yet unknown, must be approached by an interviewer "sympathetic" to their particular situations. If that is not possible, then certainly a scam is in order.

- *Pro-MP* means they're on his side. Wives, kids, plaintiffs in lawsuits, neighbors—all should be assumed to be pro-MP, unless the detective has found documentation to prove otherwise. These folks' natural inclination is to protect the MP's privacy and only impart information that would be in his best interest. Is your detective hoping to inform the

MP of his old girlfriend's acceptance of his decade-old proposal? Then, that's like a good thing. (Except, perhaps, when approaching the wife.) Is the PI looking to lay paternity papers on the unsuspecting fellow? Not so good. In either instance, these people's loyalty lies with the MP, so the interviewer should at least *appear* to be pro-MP as well. If that cannot be accomplished in a truthful manner, then please proceed to the section on scams.

- *Con-MP* means they dislike the guy perhaps even more than your client does and would do pretty much anything to contribute toward his comeuppance. These folks can definitely be told the truth; the more detail, the better. Opposing parties in legal actions, especially those unable to collect their court judgments, come under this category.

- *Don't know where they stand?* Your detective has found his kids, ex-wives and former neighbors and associates but has no idea of their feelings toward the MP. How are these folks approached? *Gingerly* is a word I've been dying to use, and I think this is the spot. Your detective starts out with a pleasantly neutral attitude but one that can turn "conspiratorial" at any moment, ready to jump aboard the I-Hate-the-MP-Too Express.

How does your detective know who's friend and who's foe? That's what took him so long to get to the door. In a perfect world, an investigator should *never* make that final approach until he's researched every single point at which the person about to interviewed and the MP have interacted. Legal lawsuits, divorce papers and restraining orders tell a lot.

Interviewing the Missing Person

Then, if this is any kind of a book at all, your detective will actually locate the MP at some point. What's he gonna say? It's a problem in real life that I encounter daily, and mostly, believe it or not, I tell the truth. Maybe I'm just not very creative.

Take the case of the seventeen-year-old kid who ended up in the backseat of his friend's car with Marquita, a lusty teenager from a neighboring town. Now, five years later, I'd been hired to search him out and question him about that long-ago encounter.

When we first started looking, this kid didn't even have a

name; he was just a rumor that had spread throughout the company after Marquita brought a sexual harassment lawsuit against one of her co-workers. It was our job to track down the source of the rumor and find out if there was any validity to it. The bottom line was not so much the alleged victim's sexual history but her truthfulness about it. What made this particular guy so special was not that theirs had been such a spectacularly memorial jostle, but because out of it, according to the rumor, Marquita had bore a child (now adopted).

From Marquita's subpoenaed diaries, we learned the name of her then-boyfriend, coincidentally, the man she'd originally named as the pop. After interviewing him, we discovered that after stringing him along for the entire pregnancy, Marquita then admitted he was not the dad at all but that she was date raped. Had charges been brought against this fellow? we asked. The old boyfriend didn't think so. Got a name? we pressed. A guy named David, from another school. Any way to find him? Yeah, he was a friend of so-and-so's.

So we tracked down so-and-so. (As you can imagine, none of these young men were anxious to talk.) With a summons in one hand, we promised so-and-so that he *probably* wouldn't have to attend the deposition if he cooperated during the interview. He did, and gave up his old pal's name.

Poor David we tracked down at his brand-new place of employment. He was such a nice fellow, and having just finished college was fixing to propose to his girlfriend that very weekend. Now came the news that not only was he likely to be the father of a five-year-old adopted child, but that he'd stood—although, happily, not officially—accused of date rape! Although back in high school, David had heard Marquita was pregnant, he'd sighed with relief when her boyfriend took the rap, and he quickly put the incident out of his mind.

Scamming this poor man would have been cruel. Our news was a shocker, as we knew it would be, but at least we were able to assure him that although giving a deposition would probably not be the most pleasant experience, there was no reason it should affect the rest of his life. Except, of course, that someday his child might seek out her biological father. But, I might have forgotten to mention that.

Interviewing for Court Evidence

Now we find the MP, at last, safely in your detective's clutches. What *will* your poor hero do or say now? The answer to that, of course, depends upon why the MP was being sought in the first place; just as every plot differs, so does every case. Getting to the point might be appropriate. But then, maybe not.

Criminal Cases. In the real world, unless a detective is government sanctioned, he often passes on interviewing a suspect in a criminal case. Since the official position of a licensed private investigator in such an instance is a "witness" at best, and "informant" more often than not, his testimony carries little more weight than the average man on the street's. Given that lack of conviction in his ability, both from a safety and liability aspect as well as from simply screwing up the case, many investigators, myself included, prefer to simply hand these scoundrels over to the authorities so they can screw up the cases themselves. If your detective chooses to move forward into this thankless arena, you'd best read Russell Bintliff's *Police Procedural* in the Howdunit series.

Civil Cases. These are a whole other animal. Basically, all that is involved here is talking to the subject, dragging out the conversation as long as possible, thereby both garnishing as much detail as can be gotten as well as upping the bill to the top end of the credibility limit. The session can be tape-recorded—with the subject's approval clearly voiced at the onset—or notes taken by hand, the interview typed up at a later time and then a signature obtained on the newly created document.

Tape Recording Laws and Techniques

States differ, of course, regarding their tolerance toward the taping of telephone conversations. In some states, only one party must have knowledge of the activity; in others, both parties must know (so what's the point?); and in still others, nobody needs to know but the little guy hanging from the telephone pole out behind the house.

So you're probably wondering what happens when two state's laws collide. Say, California decrees, "No taping!" but Nevada says, "Oh, go ahead." When the conversation takes place between a fellow in Sacramento and his lady friend in Reno, which law applies? The short answer is the state where the "crime" occurs. If the taping is executed in Nevada, then there was no crime, since that state's law allows for such basic intrusions on privacy. For a rendering of the current laws regarding taping of telephone conversations, turn to Appendix D.

Since police are governed by the same laws that restrict ordinary mortals, if California says, "No taping!" then must the coppers inform a suspect that their conversation is being recorded? Well, actually, no. The law reads that any ordinary citizen, when contacted by the PD du jour, should *assume* the conversation is being recorded. In short, if he does not, the cop's an idiot and deserves whatever trouble he gets himself into.

So then, must the PD inform a suspect of his rights, thereby alerting him to the seriousness of the situation? Again, no, since if the interview is being conducted by telephone, the suspect is free to bow out at any time with the click of the handset.

So how can your detective document an interview if he resides in a taping-unfriendly state? Well, he could just break the law, but that would be self-defeating since he probably would like to have that conversation admissible in court, as well as to be able to testify as to its occurrence without appearing in an orange jumpsuit. Or he can do what our office does, a technique I like to think I invented, although I'm sure other investigators have simultaneously or even previously invented it as well: To create an authorized document without the knowledge of the interviewee, we place a tape recorder on the desk, thereby taping this end of the conversation while the interviewer takes notes of what is being said at the other end of the line. At the conclusion of the call, the recorder is left on and the interviewer reads back his notes. Then the notes are typed up in transcript form, using the recording as a guide, and signed by the interviewer. Works just great.

Weighing the Accuracy of the Information

This is why your detective spent all that time creating a paper trail. Paper trails don't lie; people lie. When faced with conflicting statements, I opt for the documents every time.

Scams

When it's not in a person's own best interest—or his friend's or relative's—to tell the truth, that is the time at which he is most likely to lie. Duh. When that is the case, approaching the subject in a straightforward manner for an interview would be downright silly and therefore not one's first option. So how does one get the truth out of someone who might suffer ill if the truth were told? By lying to him before he has a chance to lie to you, that's how.

Actually, the word *lie* is not in a detective's vocabulary. We call 'em scams, gags, pretexts, ruses, even whoppers, but never, never do we call them lies. Why should we? Nice people, after all, don't lie.

Why the Scam?

What place has the scam in the second oldest profession on earth? (The oldest, we know. The second oldest is catching someone eliciting the services of the oldest.) Scams are used for all kinds of things in detectivedom: locating people's whereabouts, their assets, their employment; determining their propensity for cheating on their spouses; even eliciting confessions. To cover every scenario would be beyond the scope of this book, so instead, let's concern ourselves with just those scams designed to ferret out the location of a missing person.

The Essence of a Scam

Who knows and who will they tell? These are the top two things to consider when creating a scam. Since pretexts are perpetrated almost entirely upon folks unlikely to respond favorably to the truth, the gag must obviously be beneficial to the target in order to insure a high success rate.

- Who knows where lurks that mysterious MP? Friends, relatives, former landlords, neighbors and co-workers. All of them *might know*, and if they do, then they just might want to help their friend out.

- Who will they tell? Friendly, smiling, nonthreatening folks bearing lavish, tempting gifts. A delivery person laden with a dozen long-stem red roses. An heirfinder firm with a fortune to disperse. An old landlord with a deposit to

deliver. The Publisher's Clearing House's prize patrol under most any circumstances.

The Elements of a Scam

Scams are the closest thing a writer and a detective have
in common. The investigator has a job to do, information to be
found out, and he's determined to find out who knows what and
who they'll tell. So he "writes" a scam, much as one would
pen a play, being careful to think through its beginning, middle
and end. That done, he tries his little play out on the other
unsuspecting actor, knowing that fellow is often taken to impro-
visation, thereby keeping the ending a surprise even to the
playwright.

Now, as a writer, you have a good deal of control over
your characters, but as a writer of scams, we have little control
over the characters we deal with. To minimize that sad fact, we
include as many of the following elements as is possible.

- Making them an offer they can't refuse is a common theme
among good gags. Money's a safe universal choice. A pre-
approved credit card brings unexpected pleasure to those
who can't even pass a check-right test at their local super-
market. A misdirected UPS package from Gumps is another crowd pleaser.

- Getting in and out before they have a chance to think. It
is a proven fact that more people will tell an investigator
things before they've had a chance to think than will blurt
out the same secrets afterward. There have been actual
studies done on this. In our office.

- Taking away more knowledge than one leaves behind.
Your detective should never leave his phone number for a
callback, should always utilize call-blocking, should be
cognizant of the effects of call-return and should consider
felt-tip penning a new license plate for himself if he deliv-
ers the scam in person. In short, he should always, always
leave the target with the Lone Ranger's creed: Who *was*
that masked man?

- Using something you know to find out something you
don't. Let's say your detective has found a fellow with the

right name, the correct DOB, whose Social was issued out of the precise state as was the man's he's looking for. In my book, that's a match, but say your detective is more thorough than I and wants a fourth touchpoint. He knows the guy he's searching for was once married to a gal named Jillian, so he calls asking for her, instead of him, and when he gets a giant hesitation, then he's certain he's found his chap.

- Disappearing without ramifications is the final consideration when perpetrating a successful scam. In the above scenario, we left your PI waiting for the target to stop twitching and inquire as to what he wants with the ex-wife, now in the city jail pending check kiting charges. Now we need to get him out of there so he can live to lie again. To do that, your detective must suddenly realize that the Jillian he's looking for—his fiancée, Jillian Snogerburger—would not have this stranger answering her phone, apologize profusely to the poor befuddled target and hang up.

Simple Scams You Can Pull at Home

So then, let's take the essence of a scam along with the elements and see what they look like.

Getting an address from a phone number. Your detective calls, saying he's from Avis Air and has a package to deliver. The target inquires as to its origin, and the investigator names a company he found on the query line of the MP's credit header. (Using something he knows to find out something he doesn't.) The target recalls the loan he just requested from Pandesto Credit Union, chuckles at that company's gullibility and tells the caller where to deliver the bundle of money.

Obtaining a work address. The investigator knows the target lives in a big apartment complex but doesn't know where he works. He calls the manager, saying he has a melting chocolate Easter bunny to deliver but can never seem to catch his tenant at home. Would he possibly have the address of his employment? Works best around Eastertime.

Getting an apartment number. Same scenario but this time the investigator tells the landlord he doesn't mind leaving the bunny outside the door. If only he knew which door.

Determining where someone's moved. The investigator calls a neighbor or landlord of the last known address, saying he's an old friend of the target's and has just called and found the phone disconnected. Would this person know where the family moved and, by the way, when? If the neighbor offers to pass along the MP's number, the PI explains he's just in town for a few hours and is calling from a phone booth at the airport (thereby evoking two important elements of a scam: not giving the person time to think about how the investigator got his number and not leaving anything to trace).

Getting a phone number. Your detective sends a letter to an address he knows to be correct, asking the recipient to call an 800 number, extension 123, to claim his inheritance from a distant relative, the former queen of Yugoslavia. That done, the caller's own phone number is logged onto the detective's phone bill for posterity. The extension differentiates his call from the other suckers who bought the same act.

Verifying a number is still current. Your detective got the number off a phone disc, but he's not sure it's still current. More troublesome, he knows this MP is such a scoundrel he's unlikely to even admit his own identity. What to do! Happily the detective's got a four-year-old kid he's anxious to break into the biz, so he has him call, asking for one of the MP's kids (whose name he got off a demographic directory database such as Metronet) and then pulling the same wrong-number scenario to back out of it.

Surveillance

It's a pretty simple concept. Basically, your detective just sits around waiting for someone to come out of his house and then the PI follows that person around until he does whatever the investigator suspects the person will do—or until the client's money runs out, whichever occurs first. So if that's all there is to it, why are folks paying us the big bucks? Because it's so *borrrringgg!*

Yes, that's right. Dullsville. Invariably, the client has inferred his spouse is into afternoon dalliances with a local equestrian or someone equally exotic, and even throws in the possibility of a little midmorning devil worship to sweeten the pot. What actually happens is this person's life mirrors our own; it's chockablock full of errands like grocery shopping, retrieving the dry cleaning, even running the family station wagon through the local car wash. Hardly ever do we do anything exciting like going up to the Golden Gate Bridge to drop a gun over, and when we do, it's only because we think we're being tailed.

The Two Positions

There are two basic positions for surveillance: moving and staying put. Whichever one they're doing at the moment, most detectives fervently wish it were the other. That's how bad they both are.

Obstacles to a Successful Surveillance

Whether moving or standing still, each position has its own inherent obstacles hindering the mastery of the maneuver.

Neighborhood watch groups. These are the number one bane of a detective's existence. Do-gooders bent on saving humanity from a crime-filled environment, they never give thought one to the poor schmuck entering his eleventh hour of newspaper reading, coffee drinking and bladder rending. This is what they've been waiting for, a man casing a joint at the speed of snail. Who cares that the neighborhood cat burglar got away? Now here's a guy they can catch! So who do they call?

The cops. Yes, the coppers arrive and the siren inevitably awakens the target from his afternoon nap, which pretty much ends that little moneymaking enterprise. And if that doesn't happen, then the PD goes back and assures the neighbors it's OK, it's just a PI making sure Mr. Henkleburger winds up in jail for bigamy. Of course, what are the chances of a juicy bit like that not circulating through the cul de sac like a firestorm? Before you know it, Mr. H. is out the back door, sprinting through the alley like a gazelle on steroids.

Boredom. It's a proven fact that you can do absolutely nothing for just so long without falling into a seemingly irreversible coma.

Creature comforts. And where does one go? Ever count the number of porta-potties in upper-class suburban neighborhoods? Bet that didn't take long. There is nothing more embarrassing than being caught out watering somebody else's oleanders. And I don't mean with a hose.

Traffic. Who needs it? It only acts as cover for just so long, and then, just like in real life, it gets in your way.

Tailing Techniques

Inevitably, the targets have to move. Sure, nowadays, they can bank at home. Yes, they've got a stockpile of action-packed videos to keep them company. OK, they can even call out to an escort service pretty much anytime they like. But, eventually, just like the Freemen, somebody will run out of Marshmallow Fluff or whatever and will have to leave the compound for reinforcements.

What's a detective to do then? Well, if he's asleep, nothing. The target goes and comes back and the investigator's none the wiser. But if the gumshoe happens to be awake at the time of departure, then it's his God-given duty to follow.

How does one do that? That, my friend, depends upon the budget.

The one-car, economy, why-pay-more, penny pincher's special. Well, not really. At $95 per hour, our going rate, a healthy ten-hour shift adds up to a whole lot more than I personally care about any single other person's daily activities.

I'll never forget the only question I remember from the private investigator's state licensing exam: When following a target, should the investigator (a) stay behind him; (b) stay beside him; (c) stay in his blind spot; or (d) move around a lot? The answer, of course, is (e) all of the above, except for the blind spot bit because then he tends to clip you while changing lanes.

Basically, budget surveillance is the toughest of the lot—and the loneliest—and I'm convinced it is only a matter of time until the investigator, no matter how skilled he is, is "made." The more clandestine the target's activities, the sharper his attention regarding the entire area surrounding him. To elongate the effort, the car should be "swapped" as often as is feasible.

As for technique, suffice to say your detective should just semicircle the backside of the intended prey masquerading as a fellow commuter. He should stay as far away from the target as possible, hiding amongst the traffic, while still being able to exit the freeway should the subject decide to do so. If you want some practical experience, drive onto your local expressway, pick a car, any car, and follow it around a while. You'll get the hang of it.

The midsized two-car convoy. Twice the budget means, simply, twice the time before discovery. Technique is one car hangs with the target while a second follows at a discreet distance, perhaps even traveling on a side street. At frequent intervals, positions are reversed. The advantage is the target's suspicions are greatly alleviated since the car in question disappears entirely at times. Anything over a single vehicle requires communication equipment—walkie-talkies, CBs or cell phones.

The Ford Escort extravaganza. Now we've got an operation worthy of even our finest government operatives. We've got compacts, we've got dark-windowed vans, we've got nondescript vehicles of every make, creed and color. They're moving. They're changing positions. They're slowing down. They're speeding up. Their owners are gabbing away on their radios. In short, everyone (save the target) is having a ball, even indulging in a couple of mild flirtations between operatives and each making more money than any of them dreamed possible. What's not to like?

First, you've got your "point man," the operative with his eye directly on the target. He can be positioned out front of the house, out back with a view of the driveway or driving by on a semiregular basis, depending upon the setup. Then there are the other operatives, positioned at every street leading out of the neighborhood, ready to fall into line when the action starts. When the target moves, they're in convoy, moving around him like a Border collie rounding up standard-sized poodles at an American Kennel Club outing.

High-Tech Help

During those big-budget extravaganzas, your detective might want to slap a very pricey bug under the MP's bumper, utilizing the beeper's intensity to transmit the location of the car. Now he can be blocks away, observing all traffic laws and resulting in stress-free surveillance for both parties. FYI: A PI's worst nightmare is that the bug will fall onto the freeway or that the target will check the car's undercarriage and toss the million-dollar bug in the can.

Signs You've Been Had

It's pretty simple. The target traverses six freeway lanes to make an exit, speeds up, slows down, turns right or left at every block he encounters and/or stops completely, gets out and looks back at the operative. If he continues driving, he spends more time watching the rearview mirror than the road, his passenger turns around and then sharply back just as he starts screaming at her or he even turns around and starts tailing the detective. Trust me, you'll recognize the signs. The *minute* the operative notes any of these aberrant behaviors, it's time to go home, have a beer, swap cars and start up a couple of days later. Remember, it's better to lose the target than to get "burned" and have to abort the entire mission.

The Target's Checking for a Tail

Many times MPs are suspicious sorts. They just expect to be followed—they're mob members, drug runners or compulsive adulterers—so they use a method the experts call "cleaning themselves" to check for a tail. Basically, this means driving into a parking lot or behind a building and then exiting out the other end, watching to see who'll follow. If the detective is flying solo, there's not much he can do but let the target go. If he's in convoy, then the first operative passes on down the street while a cohort circles the lot, catching the MP on the downhill slope.

When to Surveil

So once you've found the MP, why follow him around? Well, maybe your detective just can't let go (or you can't, which means your editor should get out the scissors), or, more likely, your plot requires him to lead the detective to an object or even another person.

Many times, when an MP proves elusive, an investigator can find the person he can't find by following a person he can. Christmas, Thanksgiving and Mother's Day are all good days for that. Not only do most good scoundrels show up at Mummy's house, but it is conceivable one can talk the client into holiday pay.

Staking Out the Joint

Are they really there? Your detective's been out front so long his foot's asleep from the ankle up. There's been no movement for four days, and the ranch-style home is beginning to resemble Waco. How does your detective know the family's not on vacation?

- Check the mail. I'm not suggesting he read it, steal it or even peek in through the window in the envelope. I'm only saying he should just *look* into the box and calculate how many day's worth is there.
- Count the newspapers on the porch.
- Call the house and see if someone picks up.
- Go potty in the bushes and time how long it takes the cops to show.

Bugging the Premises

Of course, I know it's illegal. But it's chapter 137 and your detective's not got a clue as to where resides the MP. What's he gonna do? Well, if he's gutsier than I am—and Mother's Day is still three months off—he could go visit the MP's mum and slip a voice-activated tape recorder beneath her couch. He could then inquire as to the MP, using any number of scams, ruses, pretexts or, gulp, yes, even lies, and then leave, knowing Mumsie will place the call the moment he's got one foot in his Ford Impala. Ten minutes later, Doctor Detecto is back to retrieve his wallet, which, coincidentally, fell out of his back pocket and into the sofa cushions, and out comes the tape recorder as well, into his pocket and out the door with him. (Sleight of hand would be a helpful hobby for him to have developed somewhere along the way.) Then if he's really clever (and at chapter 137, frankly, we're beginning to wonder), he can translate the push-button sounds that came across the speakerphone to decipher the MP's telephone number.

Wiretapping

Now this is *really* illegal. And not only that, it takes some skill, the techniques of which are not taught in any accredited curriculum I've ever found.

Of course, I know very little about this because it's *really* illegal, but if your detective is the sort who finds this activity compelling, I'd suggest he start by having a vast working knowledge of his own instrument. If he doesn't, then he should dismantle someone else's and compare those contents to his own. That done, he can get himself to Radio Shack or the Spy Factory or order through catalogs like Lee Lapin's *Whole Spy Catalog* to find the equipment necessary for the job. From there, it's just a matter of reading the instructions.

The second method of bugging a telephone is to place the wire on the lines coming into the building. But since the farther the tap is from the actual phone, the more expertise required to bug it, obviously wiretapping into an office setup, because of the multitude of lines, would take a professional. Also up a pro's alley would be the technique of going into the main frame of the building, or even an adjacent building, finding the proper "telephone pair" and then leaping the tap across town on "spare pairs" until it connects with the listening device—which could be as far as fifty miles away.

And that's all I know about that.

The Trash

First of all, it's not trash, it's garbage. I wish it weren't, but it is. Secondly, although I'd sooner admit to wearing Tan-In-A-Bottle to my high school reunion, I will concede there are lots of treasures to be found in day-to-day debris.

Legalities

Since it's basically abandoned stuff, taking it, at least in most principalities, is not considered stealing. My sources tell me that once the can hits the sidewalk, the rubbish belongs to no one in particular until it lands at the junkyard. Dumpside, of course, anyone can gleefully pick through anything he'd like— after he's paid the hefty entrance fee and shooed away the seagulls.

Recyclables—aluminum cans, newspapers, bottles—belong to the company who provided the customer with the blue plastic box, so it's best your detective bypass those ex-products. That's OK, because very few clues are found in old bottles.

What he's mostly looking for are envelopes, bank statements, letters and a none-too-ripe banana that can be eaten later—clearly nonrecyclables.

Since this book aspires to a national scope, I cannot answer definitively on the legalities of garbage stealing except to say I think it best not to transport the stuff across state lines. (Yeah, like you'd want to.)

Trespassing

This is where they get you. Yeah, you can have the garbage, but how you gonna get it from back behind the house except to trespass? (And while you're back there, you just might want to peek into a window or two.) Most detectives don't let this sort of technicality stop them. Besides, what's the worst thing that can happen to a private eye found meandering among the cans? Aside from getting shot?

Logistics

Since the can is not yours to keep, unless your PI's prepared to do his sifting then and there, he's got himself a sticky logistics problem. Some sleuths admit to "borrowing" the cans, sorting the contents at their leisure and then returning the containers later. This constitutes a double whammy when their targets find not only their receptacles stolen but returned a few days later. It's further unsettling when the investigator gets the cans confused and replaces theirs with newer, cleaner, greener models.

Equipment

Costume is optional; however, since the maneuver goes most smoothly in the dead of night, one might want to wear dark (even disposable) clothing and rubber gloves. Your detective will want a car to transport the refuse, as well as a disabled burglar alarm and a can of bug spray.

BUILDING A DOSSIER UNTIL IT INCLUDES A CURRENT ADDRESS

The letter read:

> The person I want you to find is Amy Michael. She lived at 2789 Army St. in S.F. with her sister and mother and she was from South Dakota. I have not heard from her since 1953.—Jack Norton

This was in the old days, before computers changed our workaday world and back when I had no idea there were people who, conceivably, could not be found. If I'd gotten this letter today, I'd have surely passed because the office rule is if you can't ID 'em, you can't find 'em. Little did I know this would be a story I'd tell again and again, for finding this MP would take almost every informational resource available in 1992—lots of gumshoeing with a little Metronet and credit header thrown in for good measure.

But I was then, and still am, a sucker for a love story, so

I called Norton and lowballed the job. Soon a $250 check arrived but with scant more information. The sister was older. There was no father around. Dead? Divorced? Jack didn't know. And the mother's and sister's names he couldn't recall. All Jack was sure of was the address and that Amy was in the phone book.

Jack's story was, on his way to the Korean War, he'd met this "beautiful, special girl," written to her all the time he was away, even getting engaged through their letters. Why they split up he wouldn't say, except that he felt awful about it. Then, a few years later, Jack came back to San Francisco, but now, where her house once stood, is a freeway overpass, that bit of Highway 101 just before you come to the crest of the hill and see the skyline beyond.

As is frequently my first stop in finding a long-ago love, I checked the statewide marriage index. Had Amy remained in California and married there any time between 1948 and 1986, she'd have been in that index. Were that the case, obviously I'd have acquired Amy's date and place of birth, her husband's name, parents, witnesses, even the occupations of the newly-weds, certainly enough to find her. That Amy wasn't there told me she'd either married elsewhere or never even wed at all.

So much for the quick fix. Before I did any more research on Amy Michael, I had to establish her legal name. Was Amy short for something? Could Michael actually be Michaels, the more traditional spelling? Jack was sure it was singular, but there simply was no listing for a Michael family living on Army Street.

Polk's cross-directory showed the same thing. Worse still, there was a conspicuous black hole where number 2789 should have been. Jack had insisted the address was correct, that Michael was singular and that the listing had been in the 1953 telephone book, but, obviously, he was wrong about one ingredient, or, horror of horrors, more than one.

Had the Michael family owned property? It took twenty minutes to find someone in the assessor's office who spoke English and another twenty for him to research the four-decade-old data. But the huge map book showed the same thing the city directory had. There was not now, nor ever had been, such a place as 2789 Army Street.

The 1950s sales index showed no Michael family disposing of a property on Army, neither did the grantor/grantee's index for those years. CalTrans informed me that while its relocation department does keep records of where people go when the state buys their properties, that department didn't exist in 1953. Still, the clerk found a George Michaels who lived on Army, about a mile west of where number 2789 should have been—nowhere near the overpass. Wrong spelling, wrong address, husband still alive in 1953. Three strikes, I'm out.

I drove down to that neighborhood which wasn't quite the Mission District and wasn't quite Potrero and found nothing where number 2789 should be except a maze of freeway on-ramps and a bunch of honking cars nipping at my tires. What year did that freeway go up anyway? The people at CalTrans, unbelievably, didn't seem to know. It looked like it'd been there since the Gold Rush.

In the library's California History Room, I found a 1956 article entitled "Traffic vs. Freeways: City Facing a Choice of Evils." The map showed the Bayshore Freeway already existed, as well as a couple of proposed expressways destined to zip through the west side of town; these had never materialized. According to Jack, when he left for Korea, the freeway wasn't there, but it was when he came back. It was there in 1956. It wasn't, supposedly, in 1953. When was the Korean War, anyway? Had Jack actually gone, or was he wrong about that as well? Maybe he was in the Vietnam War. Or World War II. Or perhaps Jack Norton had been sent by a competing detective agency to keep me busy while it got all the good-paying jobs. I was beginning to wonder.

Quickly running out of leads, I began toying with less likely scenarios. Say Amy Michael had stayed in California but never married. I ran the name through Metronet and found two Amy Michaels living in the LA area. Unfortunately, one was way too young, and the other indicated she was not head of household, meaning Michael was her married name.

Jack's Amy Michael was from South Dakota, so I ran a surname search and called every Michael family in that state. None had a branch of the family that had moved to California.

California's death index showed no Amy Michael of the

right age dying in the state. That didn't mean she hadn't passed, of course, it just meant she didn't die single in California. A circumstance I wouldn't wish on anyone.

The answer just had to be in one of the San Francisco telephone directories, years 1950 to 1956. I suspected Jack's memory had huge holes, but unless he just made this girl up, one component in this equation had to be true. He was wrong on the house number, but was he wrong about Army Street as well? What of the spelling of the name? How about the widowed mother and sister? There just had to be something that checked out, an anchor on which I could build further research.

"See Michiel, Michiell, Mitchel and Mitchell," suggested the Polk directory. I was asked to find any number of people; Amy Michael, Amy Michiel, Amy Michiell, Amy Michaels, Amy Mitchell—all but one of whom didn't even exist.

The only possibility came under the deviant spelling, Michiel. Those with addresses on Army Street read:

Michiel, Beth, clk, Cleveland Twist Drill, r2981 Army
Michiel, Esther, (wid wm) slswm, h2981 Army
Michiel, Gloria E, clk, Fraser & Johnston, r2981 Army
Michiel, Hannah W, sten, Hertz Drivurself, r2981 Army

Was Amy, perhaps, the middle name of one of the two women with no middle initial listed? I found it curious that not only had these folks lived just two blocks from the address Jack had given me, but one was a widowed mom, and two of the girls were "clerks" when Jack described Amy as a secretary.

I drove down Army Street and found number 2981 to be a dingy Victorian duplex about a block from the Army/Potrero/Bayshore exchange Jack had described. If this was the right "Michael" family, then Jack had been wrong about the address, the spelling of the last name and, gulp, his girlfriend's first name as well.

This family I tracked through city directories, and then in 1959 they disappeared altogether. Had they simply moved to a suburb, out of state, or in that fateful year, had all four women gotten married and changed their names? Maybe they all died in a huge house fire. Or got the city's first unlisted number. The possibilities were endless.

Unbelievably, the marriage index showed none of the Michiel girls wedding in California. I was far luckier with the death index. Hannah W. Michiel, it seems, had died in Merced County, April 10, 1988, and the first three numbers of her Social Security number indicated she was from South Dakota! I had no idea where Amy fit into this equation, but this just had to be the right family. There were too many coincidences.

I needed to see Hannah's death certificate, her obit perhaps, and hopefully even her probate papers. The latter would require a two-hour drive to Merced, so hoping to avoid that, I checked the *San Francisco Chronicle*'s news morgue for a possible obit.

Instead, I found a 1959 listing for Esther Michiel that read, "Sixty-year-old Woman Victim of Kidnapping by Mental Patient." It seems Esther Michiel and her daughter Hannah, forty-three (I did the calculations; Hannah wasn't "Amy," she was much too old), went to visit a Bernard Willis at Agnew State Mental Hospital, and as they were chatting, Bernard asked if they could take a drive. Once out the gate, he suggested stopping for a milk shake. Then while Hannah was in getting the goods, Bernard slipped behind the wheel and took off with Hannah's mum. "I'm getting away, and I'm taking you with me," he told her.

Bernard drove north toward San Francisco, erratically and up to speeds of seventy miles an hour. When they reached the Bayshore Freeway, Esther clambered into the front seat and begged Bernard to drop her off at home. No can do, said the madman. As they approached the Ninth Street off-ramp, Bernie said, "Give me a quarter. I'm going to call Oakland."

At Church Street, Esther yelled to a bystander, "Call an officer! This car is stolen!" The bystander didn't. They careened past the University of San Francisco, onto Fulton, back around and pretty much covered that end of town. Willis was probably looking for that freeway that was supposed to have been built in 1959. Finally, Esther was able to leap from the car, taking the keys with her. She ran to a stranger's home and called the police.

Without the keys, Willis didn't get far. He persuaded a taxi driver to give him a push, but apparently it wasn't a battery thing, it was a key thing. Bernard was captured and taken back to Agnew, his head hung low. No more milk shakes for you, Bernard.

A few weeks after reading this, I had occasion to be in Sacramento, so I checked out the California State Library's extensive newspaper collection, kept on microfilm. Nothing on Hannah's obit.

What I did find was a 1988 index of real estate records that showed she owned a place in Atwater, fifteen miles north of Merced. Great! Whoever now owned that property had probably bought it from the estate and might, conceivably, know what had happened to the rest of the family.

Metronet showed no listing for the Rancho Circle residence, which meant the phone was either unlisted, the place was vacant or, by some further cosmic joke, there was no such place as 36 Rancho Circle. I ran a list of neighbors, found that the next-door neighbors had resided there six years—two years before Hannah died.

I grabbed a friend, some shorts and a case of Calistoga and drove into the blazing Central Valley. Fifteen miles short of Modesto, we pulled into a mobile home park. The manager said that number 36 was out of town. There would be no talking to him today and, since his phone was unlisted, possibly not ever.

The next-door neighbors couldn't have been nicer. The Falks said Hannah should have never been living there alone with her mother; Hannah was much too sick, having to call the ambulance every third night or so, toward the end. Beth and her husband came out the last month. When the Falks returned from vacation, Hannah was dead and the rest of the family was gone. Wherever they were, said Mrs. Falk, she'd bet it was near an Air Force base. Beth's husband was a war vet, had medical problems and would most likely be taking advantage of the health care services.

What were they like? I asked. Nice people?

A hesitant yes. The women, definitely. But Mr. Falk had a few guarded words to say about the husband. He drank too much. Didn't do anything, just sat around. Mr. Falk had to come over and light the pilot on the stove for the ladies two or three times, and the husband wouldn't even watch so he could learn how to do it. Breaking under our intense questioning, Mr. Falk finally managed to call the husband a dud.

What about the other daughters? I asked. Did they meet

them as well? Gloria used to drive out from Merced in a big fancy car, said Mrs. Falk. As for Amy, Mrs. Falk couldn't recall any talk of her at all.

On to Merced and Hannah's probate papers and the gold mine I'd been itching for. For once, I wasn't disappointed. The executer of the estate was Hannah's sister Beth, and her husband's name? Bob Smith! Yes, indeedy, I was looking for a Mr. and Mrs. Bob Smith, a circumstance that clearly eliminated at least half the people in America.

Unfortunately, there was no further address beyond Hannah's for the Smith family, and her death certificate rendered little else except the attorney who'd handled the probate. Unfortunately, he was now retired and nowhere to be found.

Back in San Francisco, I attacked the computer with new gusto, having, for the first time, the actual name of the person I was looking for and an address, a scant four years old.

I ran a credit header on Robert Smith at the Atwater address, got a hit and list of where he'd been and where he'd gone.

August 1980 - Lake Havasu City, AZ
August 1989 - Atwater, CA
October 1991 - Hanover, IN
April 1992 - Lincoln, CA

Running Beth, I found her addresses to be the same, save for the Lincoln entry. Could it be? Had the Smith's split, leaving Beth lonesome and vulnerable in Indiana? Hang on Jack, we're coming!

Metronet showed the Lincoln, California, Bob to be born in 1948, making him way too young. True he might have dropped Beth, but he couldn't have dropped twenty years as well. It looked like a simple case of mixing of the credit files.

Beth Smith's Indiana number was disconnected, so I ran a list of neighbors and called the woman next door. Beth and Bob Smith? Sure, she knew them. They'd moved just two weeks ago to Pensacola, Florida. Did she have the address or phone? Of course not. What of Esther, the mom? She was in her nineties and in a nursing home, right there in Hanover. They graciously supplied me with Beth's Pensacola phone.

Now for the big moment. I was finally going to talk to

Beth Smith, possible AKA of Amy Michael. I knew she was the same Beth who lived on Army Street, but I still didn't know how Amy fit into any of this. What would I say?

"Is this Beth Smith?" seemed like a good start.

"Yes."

"I'm hoping you can help me. I'm researching the Michiel family tree and trying to see if your branch of the family ties into mine. Now I know you have a sister named Gloria and one named Hannah, and your mother is Esther, right?"

"Yes, that's right."

"Would you have another sister, or perhaps a relative named Amy?"

"Let me think. Hmmm . . . No. I don't recall anyone in our family named Amy."

Rats! I don't know how much you've gotten out of this book so far, but trust me, this is not a good sign.

Still, Beth was the warmest, most open woman imaginable. When she heard I was from San Francisco, she said she still considered it her home. What were the rents like? Were there any jobs? She said she was sixty-three years old, but everybody said she looked forty. She'd been married for twenty-four years, and the marriage was miserable. Her plan was to go to college, get a job and then leave her drunken dud of a husband. She described him as never staying in any one place too long. Arizona, Indiana, California—It seems they'd been everywhere. She called him "One-week Joe."

I hung up but I couldn't get Beth off my mind. When she first answered, her voice was low and lifeless, but she quickly came alive and became warm, funny and full of life. I sensed my call was a welcome lifeline in a house where the phone hardly ever rang.

Mentally, I did the calculations. If Beth was sixty-three, she would have been twenty-two in 1953. Exactly the right age to be Jack Norton's Amy Michael. Oh Beth, I do hope you're Amy. But how can I find out for sure?

I called Jack and told him that I couldn't find Amy but I did have a perfectly nice Beth he might like. I had a hunch she was Amy but the only way to find out for sure was to ask if she knew him. He OK'd it.

I called Beth back and told her I lied. I wasn't a genealogist, I admitted, but was a private investigator hired by a man to find his first girlfriend from over forty years ago. I thought she might be her.

"What is his name?" asked Beth.

I took a breath and let it rip. "Jack Norton."

There was a moment of silence and then a confused, "Who?"

I said the name again, without much conviction.

Another spot of silence and then an excited, "Oh, Jack!"

Later, Beth wrote me a letter, telling all about where she'd been and what had happened to her during "the missing years." Here is part of that letter:

> *I was born in the Black Hills of South Dakota. Life on the ranch was primitive—taking baths in an old, round galvanized tub, cooking with kindling along with kerosene. How our family stood these conditions was anyone's guess. The people in California would look at you as if you were from "out of space" as they had no idea what life was like on the plains and the severe hardship my mother went through.*
>
> *In 1941, my family moved to California. I'd planned to become a psychologist, but my father passed away and I had to help my mother. Instead of college, I graduated from the Dorothy Ferrier School of Modeling and became a runway model at the Emporium, Macy's and City of Paris. I also worked at the Cleveland Twist Drill Company as an executive secretary. It was a ball working there.*
>
> *When the Korean War was on, there used to be a bar across from the Sir Francis Drake called The Yankee Doodle. It was always wall-to-wall officers—Army, Navy, Marines—and for all young girls that was the place.*
>
> *One night I met a tall, nice-looking officer, Lt. Jack Norton. He'd way too much to drink and was on his way to Korea. We had a very, very strong chemistry although nothing sexual happened between us. That kiss good-bye lingers and lingers. I never got over him. I wrote to him and we fell in love through letters. My office was planning*

a wedding shower and I had already given notice.

When Jack returned, he had changed, very nervous, very strange. He came to dinner and met my mother and sister. What a shock when he left to go home. No warning, no good-bye, no explanation, no nothing. Talk about hurt. I called his home but he did not want to talk to me. He will never know what he did to me. I felt betrayed. I felt complete and total devastation, and I walked around in a fog.

When I returned to work, everyone was as shocked as I was. I just couldn't seem to shake it. I became bitter and never went out with any lieutenant, whether in Air Force, Navy or Marines. They used to ask me what I had against lieutenants. I said forget it, not interested, end of conversation.

A few years passed, but the memory, the hurt, and most of all the extreme bitterness was still there. I was doing a show at the Fairmont Hotel. Afterward, I sat at the bar and ordered a martini while waiting for a table. The bartender said that a man wanted to buy me a drink. I told him to thank him, but that I did not accept drinks from strangers. He asked me, "Do you know who he is?" I said no and who cares.

Eventually, though, we talked. His name was Duke and he wanted my phone number. He said he would see I got home. I said no way, this girl does not go home with strangers. When I went upstairs to catch a cab, there was a limo there. Duke appeared and said, get in, tell the driver your address and you will get home safely at this late hour. I went home, got in bed about 1 A.M. and forgot the whole thing.

This relationship lasted eight years. No marriage was ever mentioned as Duke led a sordid life. He took out girls for one reason, but he treated me like a queen. He was on the board of the bank, Union Oil, Standard Oil, etc. I found out later he was a retired bird colonel and a POW—he had horrible pictures, one where they cut someone's head off piece by piece.

In December of 1962, Duke asked me to marry him. I found out he was going to die. I took his ring but still I told him no. His son was very upset with me. How could I do this to his father, as much as he loved me? Finally we flew to Las Vegas, got married, came home, lived in Hillsborough in one fancy home. One month later, he took a sip of his martini and passed out. He was in a coma for nine months. He passed away and I was presented with the folded flag. Still have it.

In 1968, I had an auto accident in which my face, my arms and my legs were severely injured. I thought I was going to say hello to St. Peter. I was on morphine for the pain. I was depressed, hurt, etc.

It was in this state I met Bob Smith. He had just returned from Vietnam. We knew each other for only a month. I told Bob in order to marry him I would have to have a three to four carat ring. He got it, a cluster, so off to Las Vegas again. As soon as the thing was over, I knew I really messed up.

Why I have stayed twenty-four years, who knows. He has a temper and we have nothing in common. Year by year I get more unhappy. He goes through money like water. He gets sick in every place we lived. It's a long story. I feel I'm in a hole, clawing my way out, getting more depressed year in and year out. The violent battles we've had and have. The yelling and screaming he did and does.

Now Jack wants me back. I am worried, r-e-a-l worried as Bob wants everything and nothing for me. Jack wants to pay for everything, but I have too much pride, and I feel like a complete failure, a washout, a has-been, and disgraced, humiliated and any other descriptions you can think of. One has to go through this to know what it is all about. I've been to hell and back.

Unfortunately, this story does not have a happy ending. Beth couldn't leave her husband because she was a sixty-three-year-old woman with no money and no job skills. Jack couldn't leave his wife because it would cost him too much in the divorce. (Oh, yes, Jack was married. A fact he failed to mention.) After several years of this torture, Beth's husband died, not from his many ailments but, ironically, in an automobile accident. Now free at last, and with a small insurance policy and Social Security to see her through, Beth wanted a commitment from Jack.

He was never able to give it.

Appendix A

PI Licensing Requirements by State

The following are "current" licensing standards and offices to contact for acquiring a private investigator's license in each of the fifty states. I say "current" because laws and addresses are always subject to change. For the latest data, it would be best to write to verify the information.

ALABAMA Requirements: None. *Dept. of Public Safety, P.O. Box 1511, Montgomery, AL 36192-0501.*

ALASKA Requirements: None. *Dept. of Public Safety, P.O. Box 20, Juneau, AK 99802-0020.*

ARIZONA Requirements: 3 years of investigative experience, U.S. citizen or legal resident, good moral character, not convicted of a felony or any crime involving a dangerous weapon, not have defaulted on payment of money collected, not have a prior license that was suspended or revoked. *Arizona Dept. of Public Safety, P.O. Box 6326, Phoenix, AZ 85005-6638.*

ARKANSAS Requirements: Proof of liability insurance and examination. *Arkansas Board of Private Investigators and Private Security Agencies, #3 Natural Resources Dr., P.O. Box 5901, Little Rock, AR 72215.*

CALIFORNIA Requirements: 6,000 hours of qualifying investigative experience with law enforcement, military police, insurance adjusters, PI firm, collection or repossession agency arson investigator. (Police science and/or criminal law or justice from an accredited college equals up to 1,000 hours). Exam. *Dept. of Consumer Affairs, Bureau of Collection and Investigative Services, 1920 Twentieth St., Sacramento, CA 95814-6873.*

COLORADO Requirements: None. *Dept. of State, 1560 Broadway, Ste. 200, Denver, CO 80202.*

CONNECTICUT Requirements: 4 character references, 4 credit references, a letter from psychiatrist (if applicable), U.S. citizen or legal resident, proof of 5-year eligibility requirement with dates, duties, addresses and telephone numbers. *State of Connecticut, Dept. of Public Safety, 294 Colony St., Meriden, CT 06450-2098.*

DELAWARE Requirements: 25 + years old, 5 years experience as an investigator or a police officer, 5 in-state references, fingerprinting. *Delaware State Police, P.O. Box 430, Dover, DE 19903.*

DISTRICT OF COLUMBIA Requirements: Completion of application packet, fingerprinting, not convicted of a felony within the past ten years, ninety day waiting period. *Security Office Branch, 2000 14th St. NW; Washington, DC 20009.*

FLORIDA Requirements: Full-time (40 hours per week) 2-year internship, verified before and after internship. *Dept. of State, Division of Licensing, P.O. Box 6687, Tallahassee, FL 32314-6687.*

GEORGIA Requirements: 2 years experience working with licensed PI or law enforcement. *Secretary of State, Examining Boards Division, 166 Pryor St., SW, Atlanta, GA 30303-3465.*

HAWAII Requirements: Provide employment records for past 10 years, criminal abstracts for past 10 years, corporation or partnership papers, 4 years investigative experience. Exam. *Board of Private Detectives & Guards, DCCA, PVL Licensing Branch, 1010 Richards St., P.O. Box 3469, Honolulu, HI 96801.*

IDAHO Requirements: None. *Statehouse, The Capitol, Boise, ID 83720-1000.*

ILLINOIS Requirements: 21 + years old, U.S. citizen, 3 of last 5 years working for licensed PI or law enforcement. Exam. *State of Illinois, Dept. of Registration & Education, 320 W. Washington, 3rd Floor, Springfield, IL 62786.*

INDIANA Requirements: 21 + years old, 1 + years in-state resident, prior experience under a licensed PI, law enforcement or criminal justice schooling, have not been convicted of a felony or certain misdemeanors or been refused a license or had a license revoked or have aided and abetted in an act for which a license is required. *Indiana Professional Licensing Agency,*

Private Detective Licensing Board, 100 N. Senate Ave., Rm. 1021, Indiana Government Center North, Indianapolis, IN 46204-2246.

IOWA Requirements: 18+ years old, not a peace officer, never been convicted of a felony or aggravated misdemeanor, not an abuser of alcohol or a controlled substance, no history of violence, of good moral character, not convicted of a crime or illegal possession of a dangerous weapon, has not been convicted of fraud. Exam. *Dept. of Public Safety, Administrative Service Division, Wallace State Office Bldg., Des Moines, IA 50319.*

KANSAS Requirements: Experience taken into account when applying, but no specific amount set. Exam. *Office of the Attorney General, 2nd Floor, Kansas Judicial Center, Topeka, KS 66612-1597.*

KENTUCKY Requirements: None. *Justice Cabinet, Bush Bldg, 2nd Floor, 403 Wapping St., Frankfort, KY 40601.*

LOUISIANA Requirements: None. *Secretary of State, P.O. Box 94125, Baton Rouge, LA 70804-9125.*

MAINE Requirements: 6 years work experience and/or education in the criminal justice field, no criminal conviction or pending charges, no civil violation, reckless or negligent conduct or family abuse for past 5 years, no drug use, not a fugitive from justice. *Statehouse Station #164, Augusta, ME 04333.*

MARYLAND Requirements: 5 years experience working in a PI firm, as police officer or 3 years experience as a police detective or in any unit of a U.S., state, county or muni law enforcement agency. *Dept. of Public Safety and Correctional Services, Maryland State Police, Pikesville, MD 21208-3899.*

MASSACHUSETTS Requirements: 3 references, 3 years experience as "a detective doing investigative work, a former member of an investigative service of the U.S., a former police officer, of a rank or grade higher than that of patrolman, of the Commonwealth, any political subdivision thereof or an official police department of another state, or a police officer in good standing formerly employed for not less than 10 years with the Commonwealth or any political subdivision thereof or with an official police department of another state." *Dept. of Public Safety, Licensing Section, Rm. 1310, One Ashburton Pl., Boston, MA 02108.*

MICHIGAN Requirements: U.S. citizen, 25 + years old, good moral character, high school education, state resident, not convicted of felony or misdemeanor involving dishonesty or fraud, not dishonorably discharged from military, 3 years experience "lawfully engaged in the private detective business on his or her own account" or as an employee in a PI firm or as an investigator, detective, special agent or police officer of a government entity or a graduate of an accredited police administration program. *Michigan Dept. of State Police, Private Security & Investigator Section, 7150 Harris Dr., Lansing, MI 48913.*

MINNESOTA Requirements: 6,000 hours of employment with a licensed PI firm, a U.S. government investigative service, a city police department or sheriff's office. *Private Detective and Protective Agent Services Board, 1246 University Ave., St. Paul, MN 55104-4197.*

MISSISSIPPI Requirements: None. *Secretary of State, P.O. Box 136, Jackson, MS 39205.*

MISSOURI Requirements: None. *State of Missouri, P.O. Box 720, Jefferson City, MO 65102.*

MONTANA Requirements: 18 + years old, U.S. citizen, not convicted of any felony, not declared mentally incompetent, not suffering from habitual drunkenness or narcotics addiction, of good moral character, 3 years experience in PI firm, with a U.S. government investigative board, has completed the training requirements of the certified board. Trainees must be licensed. Exam. *Board of Private Security Patrolmen and Investigators, 1424 Ninth Ave., Helena, MT 59620-0407.*

NEBRASKA Requirements: 21 + years old, each case judged and decided individually as to experience. *Secretary of State, Ste. 2300, State Capitol, Lincoln, NE 68509.*

NEVADA Requirements: 21 + years old, U.S. citizen or resident, resident of Nevada, 5 years experience as a PI, repossessor or patrolman or two years as a process server. Exam. *Private Investigator's Licensing Board, 198 S. Carson St., Carson City, NV 89710.*

NEW HAMPSHIRE Requirements: U.S. resident, 18 + years old, no record of violent misdemeanors, theft, fraud or felony convictions, 4 years investigative experience with law enforcement or licensed PI firm or a degree in criminal justice from an accredited college or university and employment with PI firm for 2 years. *Dept. of Safety, 10 Hazen Dr., Concord, NH 03305.*

NEW JERSEY Requirements: 25 + years old, 5 years experience "as an investigator or police officer with an organized police department of the state or a county or municipality thereof, or with an investigative agency of the U.S. or any state, county or municipality thereof." *Dept. of Law and Public Safety, Division of State Police, Special and Technical Services Section, P.O. Box 7068, West Trenton, NJ 08628-0068.*

NEW MEXICO Requirements: 3 out of last 5 years involved in investigative work. Exam. *Bureau of Private Investigators, P.O. Box 25101, Santa Fe, NM 87504.*

NEW YORK Requirements: 3 years experience. *Dept. of State, Division of Licensing Services, 162 Washington Ave., Albany, NY 12231.*

NORTH CAROLINA Requirements: 3 years (within last 5) experience with a security company, PI firm or in an investigative capacity with government entity or 2 years criminal justice education and 2 years of the above. Exam. *North Carolina Private Protective Service Board, P.O. Box 29500, 3320 Old Garner Rd., Raleigh, NC 27626-0500.*

NORTH DAKOTA Requirements: 18 + years old, high school diploma, 3 years training and experience in law enforcement or with licensed PI, not convicted of a felony or class A misdemeanor involving violence, not mentally ill or ever confined for such. Exam. *Private Investigation & Security Board, P.O. Box 7026, Bismarck, ND 58502.*

OHIO Requirements: Good reputation, 2 years experience. Exam. *Dept. of Commerce, Division of Licensing, 77 S. High St., Columbus, OH 43266.*

OKLAHOMA Requirements: 18+ years old, U.S. citizen, experience evaluated on a case-by-case basis, 3 references. No exam. *Council on Law Enforcement Education and Training, P.O. Box 11476, Cimarron Station, Oklahoma City, OH 73136-0476.*

OREGON Requirements: None. *Dept. of State Police, 107 Public Service Bldg., Salem, OR 97310.*

PENNSYLVANIA Requirements: None. *State Police, Dept. Headquarters, 1800 Elmerton Ave., Harrisburg, PA 17110.*

RHODE ISLAND Requirements: None. *State of Rhode Island and Providence Plantations, 345 Harris Ave., Providence, RI 02910.*

SOUTH CAROLINA Requirements: 18+ years old, U.S. citizen, 2 years experience with licensed PI, industrial security or law enforcement. *South Carolina Law Enforcement Division, Regulatory Services Dept., P.O. Box 21398, Columbia, SC 29221.*

SOUTH DAKOTA Requirements: None. *Dept. of Commerce and Regulation, 500 E. Capitol, Pierre, SD 57501-5070.*

TENNESSEE Requirements: 3 years experience. *Dept. of Commerce & Insurance, 500 James Robertson Pkwy., 2nd Floor, Nashville, TN 37243-1167.*

TEXAS Requirements: 18+ years old, U.S. citizen, letters of recommendation from local police, no exam or experience. *Texas Board of Private Investigators and Private Security Agencies, P.O. Box 13509, Capitol Station, Austin, TX 78711.*

UTAH Requirements: None. *Dept. of Public Safety, Division of Law Enforcement and Technical Services, 4501 S. 2700 W., Salt Lake City, UT 84119.*

VERMONT Requirements: 21+ years old, 2 years of related experience. Exam. *Board of Private Investigative and Armed*

Security Services, Office of Professional Regulation, 109 State St., Montpelier, VT 05609-1106.

VIRGINIA Requirements: 18 + years old, 3 years investigative experience. Exam. *Dept. of Commerce, P.O. Box 11066, Richmond, VA 23230-1066.*

WASHINGTON Requirements: Errors and Omissions Insurance. Exam. *Professional Licensing Services, Private Detective Section, P.O. Box 9045, Olympia, WA 98507-9045.*

WEST VIRGINIA Requirements: 18 + years old, 3 years experience with licensed PI or law enforcement. *Secretary of State, State Capitol, Charleston, WV 25305.*

WISCONSIN Requirements: 18 + years old, 3 years experience or law enforcement degree. Exam. *Dept. of Regulation and Licensing, P.O. Box 8935, Madison, WI 53708.*

WYOMING Requirements: None. *Division of Economic & Community Development, 2nd Floor W., Herschler Bldg., 122 W. Twenty-fifth St., Cheyenne, WY 82002.*

Appendix B

Where to Find Identifying Information

Below is a guide as to where one would find identifying information, such as legal name and date of birth, location, associates, background data, personal income, business income, assets and liabilities, in public record and databases. The character "*" preceding an item indicates public access varies according to the state and/or the situation. The "**" symbolizes the information is available only to law enforcement but might be obtained through a subpoena, informant or scam. No character denotes public access.

IDENTIFICATION

Full Name:
Assessor; Civil Files; County Tax Collector; Telephone Directories
*Birth Certificate; County Criminal Files; Credit Reporting Agencies; DMV; Post Office; Registrar of Voters
**Banks and Finance Companies; Dept. of Justice, Bureau of ID; Gas and Electric Companies; Telephone Company; Water Companies

Date of Birth:
Credit Header Information; Divorce Records; Newspaper Morgue
*Birth Certificate; Death Certificate; Marriage License Application
**Dept. of Justice, Bureau of ID; FBI; State Dept. Passports;

Place of Birth:
Newspaper Morgue; SSN
*Death Certificate; Registrar of Voters

Social Security Number:
Abstract Judgments; Divorce Files; SS's Master Death Index; Tax Liens; UCC Filings
*Children's Birth Certificates; Credit Header Information; Death Certificate
**IRS Returns

Description:
Associates; Eyewitnesses; High School Yearbook; Neighbors; Newspaper Morgue; Opposing Party in Civil Lawsuit
*DMV; Marriage License Application
**Dept. of Justice, Bureau of ID; FBI; State Dept. Passports

Photograph:
High School Yearbook; Newspaper Morgue
*County Criminal Files; DMV

**Dept. of Justice, Bureau of ID; FBI; State Dept. Passports

Thumbprint:

*County Criminal Files; DMV

**Dept. of Justice, Bureau of ID; FBI; State Dept. Passports

Signature:

Civil Court Files; Divorce Records; Grantor/Grantee Index

*DMV; Marriage License Application; Registrar of Voters

LOCATION

Address:

Assessor; Civil Files; County Tax Collector; Newspaper Morgue; Telephone Directories

*Birth Certificate; County Criminal Files; Credit Reporting Agencies; DMV; Post Office; Registrar of Voters

**Banks and Finance Companies; Dept. of Justice, Bureau of ID; Gas and Electric Companies; Telephone Company; Water Companies

P.O. Boxholders:

*Post Office

Forwarding Address:

Metronet

*Credit Reporting Agencies; DMV

**Post Office; Moving Companies

Death:

Funeral Parlors; Newspaper Morgue; SS's Master Death Index

*Death Certificate

Where He Is Right Now:

Trapline

**Credit Card Company Charges; Telephone Company Records

ASSOCIATES

Children:

Divorce Records; Metronet; Newspaper Morgue

*Birth Certificate

Other Occupants and Relatives:

Metronet

*Marriage License Application

Friends, Business Associates, Etc.:

Civil Lawsuits; County FBN Index; Secretary of State Corporate Records

**Telephone Company's Toll Call information

BACKGROUND

Prior Addresses:

Newspaper Morgue

*Credit Reporting Agencies; Marriage License Application

Demographics of Addresses:
Metronet
Political Party:
Newspaper Morgue
*Registrar of Voters
Student Records:
*School Dept.
Civil Suits:
Superior, Muni and Small Claims Civil Files
Immigration Information:
*County Dept. of Naturalization
**Federal Immigration & Naturalization; State Dept. Passports
Criminal Records:
Newspaper Morgue
*County Criminal Files; Dept. of Corrections
**FBI's NCIC Computer; Interpol

PERSONAL INCOME

Occupation:
Dun & Bradstreet; Newspaper Morgue; TRW Business Reports
*Credit Reporting Agencies; Registrar of Voters
**Banks and Finance Companies; Gas and Electric Companies;
    State Dept. Passports; Telegraph Companies
Professional Licensing:
Consumer Affairs
Inheritances:
Public Administrator; Probate Files
Welfare:
**Welfare
County Employees:
*County Auditor

BUSINESS INCOME

Corporation and Partnership Records:
Secretary of State, Corporate Division
Sole Proprietor Records:
Business Licenses; County FBN Index
Bar Owners:
Alcoholic Beverage Control
Business Reputation, Worth, Associates and References:
Better Business Bureau; Dun & Bradstreet; TRW Business Reports
**Bonding Companies

DEBTS

Credit References:
*Credit Reporting Agencies

Expenditures:
  **Credit Card Companies
Money Owed:
  County Recorder's Grantor/Grantee Index; UCC Filings
  *Credit Reporting Agencies

ASSETS

Bank Accounts:
  Divorce Records
  *Credit Reporting Agencies
  **Financial Institutions
Vehicle Information:
  Divorce Records; Surveillance
  *DMV
Real Estate:
  Assessor; Building Dept.; County Tax Collector; Divorce Records;
    Newspaper Morgue; Real Estate Databases
  *Credit Reporting Agencies (for mortgages)
Aircraft Owned:
  FAA
Boats Owned:
  Lloyds Registry of Shipping; Lloyds Registry of Yachts;
    Yacht Harbor
  *DMV; Harbor Patrol
Stocks and Bonds:
  **Stock Brokers
Securities Offered for Public Sale:
  *Securities Exchange Commission

Appendix C

State Requirements for Obtaining Vital Statistics and DMV Records

The information in this section is current as of the time of printing. Because states are continually changing the laws regarding their restrictions, it is imperative you call or write for an update regarding regulations. Information on how to obtain—and who can obtain—vital statistics is deliberately obscured by many states in an attempt to protect the "privacy" of its citizens.

In some states, for example, no index even exists so you would have to know the exact name and DOB to order.

STATE

DMV: Format: Required Data: Address.

Vital Records: Restriction of access. Address.

*Vital Statistic; beginning dates of records at the state level; where to find at the county level

• • •

ALABAMA

DMV: Format: 7 numeric. Required Data: DL#. Driver's Licenses, P.O. Box 1741-H, Montgomery, AL 36192.

Vital Records: Access restricted. Dept. of Public Health, Bureau of Vital Stats., State Office Bldg., 501 Dexter Ave., Montgomery, AL 36130-1701.
*Birth; since Jan. 1908; Court Equity Clerk
*Death; since Jan. 1908; Court Equity Clerk
*Marriage; since Aug. 1936
*Divorce; since 1950; Court Equity Clerk

ALASKA

DMV: Format: 1-7 numeric. Required Data: DL#, last name, DOB. Driver's Licenses, P.O. Box 20020-E, Juneau, AK 99802.

Vital Records: Immediate family. Dept. of Health & Social Services, Bureau of Vital Stats., P.O. Box H-02G, Juneau, AK 99811-0675.

*Birth; since Jan. 1913; County Clerk
*Death; since Jan. 1913; County Clerk
*Marriage; since Jan. 1913; County Clerk
*Divorce; since 1950; Superior Court Clerk, Judicial District

ARIZONA

DMV: Format: 1 alpha, 3-6 numeric; or 2 alpha, 3-5 numeric; or 9 numeric (SSN); or 1 alpha, 8 numeric. Required Data: DL#, last name, first name, middle name or initial, DOB. Driver's Licenses, P.O. Box 2001-L, Phoenix, AZ 85001.

Vital Records: Family, genealogy; photo ID or notarized form must accompany request. Dept. of Health Services, Vital Records Office, 1740 West Ave., P.O. Box 3887, Phoenix, AZ 85030-3887.
*Birth; since July 1909; Superior Court Clerk
*Death; since July 1909; Superior Court Clerk
*Marriage; since 1917; no index; Superior Court Clerk
*Divorce; since 1923; no index; Superior Court Clerk

ARKANSAS

DMV: Format: 8 numeric (DL#) or 9 numeric (SSN). Required Data: DL#, DOB. Driver's Licenses, P.O. Box 1272-L, Little Rock, AR 72203.

Vital Records: Family, legal representative. Dept. of Health, Div. of Vital Records, 4815 W. Markam St., Little Rock, AR 72205-3867.
*Birth; since Feb. 1914; County Clerk
*Death; since Feb. 1914; County Clerk
*Marriage; since 1917; County Clerk
*Divorce; since 1923; Circuit Court Clerk

CALIFORNIA

DMV: Format: 1 alpha, 8 numeric. Required Data: DL#; last name, first name, DOB. Driver's Licenses, P.O. Box 944231-O, Sacramento, CA 94244.

Vital Records: No state office walk-ins. Office of State Registrar, 304 S St., P.O. Box 730241, Sacramento, CA 94244-0241.
*Birth; since July 1905; County Recorder
*Death; since July 1905; County Recorder
*Marriage; since July 1905; County Recorder
*Divorce; since Jan. 1962; Superior Court Clerk

COLORADO

DMV: Format: 1-2 alpha, 1-6 numeric. Required Data: DL#, last name, DOB. Driver's Licenses, 140 W. Sixth Ave., Denver, CO 80204.

Vital Records: Restricted. State Dept. of Health, Health Stats. & Vital Records, 4210 E. Eleventh Ave., Denver, CO 80220.
*Birth; since 1910; County Clerk
*Death; since 1900; County Clerk
*Marriage; since 1968; County Clerk
*Divorce; since 1968; District Court Clerk

CONNECTICUT

DMV: Format: 9 numeric, first 3 digits less than 245. Required Data: DL#, last name. Driver's Licenses, 60 State St., Wethersfield, CT 06109.

Vital Records: Genealogy, immediate family or legal representative. Dept. of Health Services, Vital Records Office, State Dept. of Health, 150 Washington St., Hartford, CT 06106.
*Birth; since July 1897; Vital Stats. Registrar
*Death; since July 1897; Vital Stats. Registrar
*Marriage; since July 1897; Vital Stats. Registrar
*Divorce; since June 1947; Superior Court Clerk

DELAWARE

DMV: Format: 1-7 numeric. Required Data: DL#. Driver's Licenses, P.O. Box 698-M, Dover, DE 19903.

Vital Records: Restricted. Office of Vital Stats., Div. of Public Health, P.O. Box 637, Dover, DE 19903.
*Birth; since 1861; no county records

*Death; since 1861; no county records
*Marriage; since 1861; no county records
*Divorce; since March 1932; County Prothonotary

DISTRICT OF COLUMBIA

DMV: Format: 9 numeric (SSN). Required Data: DL#; last name, first name, DOB. Driver's Licenses, 301 C St., NW, Washington, DC 20001.

Vital Records: Restricted. Vital Records Branch, Rm. 3007, 425 I St., NW, Washington, DC 20001.
*Birth; since 1871; no county records
*Death; since 1855; no county records
*Marriage; since Sept. 1956; Superior Court Clerk
*Divorce; since Sept. 1956; Superior Court Clerk

FLORIDA

DMV: Format: 1 alpha, 11-12 numeric. Required Data: DL#. Driver's Licenses, Neil Kirkman Bldg., Tallahassee, FL 32399.

Vital Records: Public. Dept. of Health & Rehabilitation Services, Office of Vital Stats., P.O. Box 210, Jacksonville, FL 32231-0042.
*Birth; since April 1865; Circuit Court Clerk
*Death; since 1877; Circuit Court Clerk
*Marriage; since 1965; Circuit Court Clerk
*Divorce; since June 1927; Circuit Court Clerk

GEORGIA

DMV: Format: 7-9 numeric. Required Data: DL#, last name, DOB. Driver's Licenses, P.O. Box 1456-I, Atlanta, GA 30371.

Vital Records: Immediate family. Dept. of Human Resources, Vital Records Unit, Rm. 217-H, 47 Trinity Ave., SW, Atlanta, GA 30334.
*Birth; since Jan. 1919; County Ordinary
*Death; since Jan. 1919; County Ordinary
*Marriage; since June 1952; County Ordinary
*Divorce; since June 1952; Superior Court Clerk

HAWAII

DMV: Format: 9 numeric. Required Data: DL#, full name, DOB. Driver's Licenses, 530 King St., Honolulu, HI 96813.

Vital Records: Restricted. State Dept. of Public Health Research, Stats. Office, Vital Records, P.O. Box 3378, Honolulu, HI 96801.
*Birth; since 1896; Circuit Court Clerk
*Death; since 1896; Circuit Court Clerk
*Marriage; since 1896; Circuit Court Clerk
*Divorce; since July 1951; Circuit Court Clerk

IDAHO

DMV: Format: 9 numeric (SSN). Required Data: DL#, last name, DOB. Driver's Licenses, P.O. Box 7129-T, Boise, ID 83707.

Vital Records: Immediate family or legal representative. Vital Stats., 450 W. State St., Boise, ID 83720.
*Birth; since July 1911; County Recorder
*Death; since July 1911; County Recorder
*Marriage; since May 1947; County Recorder
*Divorce; since May 1947; County Recorder

ILLINOIS

DMV: Format: 1 alpha, 11 numeric. Required Data: DL#. Driver's Licenses, 2701 S. Dirksen Pkwy., Springfield, IL 62723.

Vital Records: Immediate family, legal representative. Dept. of Public Health, Div. of Vital Stats., 605 W. Jefferson St., Springfield, IL 62702.
*Birth; since Jan. 1916; County Clerk
*Death; since Jan. 1916; County Clerk
*Marriage; since Jan. 1962; County Clerk
*Divorce; since Jan. 1962; Circuit Court Clerk

INDIANA

DMV: Format: 1 alpha, 9-10 numeric. Required Data: DL#. Driver's Licenses, State Office Bldg., Indianapolis, IN 46204.

Vital Records: Varies, genealogy. Dept. of Public Health, Vital

Records Section, Lucas Office Bldg., Des Moines, IA 50319.
*Birth; since Oct. 1907; Health Officer
*Death; since Jan. 1900; Health Officer
*Marriage; since 1958; Court Clerk
*Divorce; Court Clerk

IOWA

DMV: Format: 9 numeric (SSN); or 3 numeric, 2 alpha, 4 numeric. Required Data: DL#. Driver's Licenses, 100 Euclid Ave., Des Moines, IA 50306.

Vital Records: Dept. of Public Health, Vital Records Section, Lucas Office Bldg., Des Moines, IA 50319.
*Birth; since July 1880; inquiry forwarded to state
*Death; since July 1880; inquiry forwarded to state
*Marriage; since 1906; inquiry forwarded to state
*Divorce; County Clerk

KANSAS

DMV: Format: 1 alpha, 1 numeric, 1 alpha, 1 numeric, 1 alpha, 1 numeric; or 9 numeric (SSN); or 1 alpha, 8 numeric. Required Data: DL#, DOB. Driver's Licenses, Docking Office Bldg., Topeka, KS 66626.

Vital Records: Any relative. State Dept. of Health & Environment, Office of Vital Stats., 900 SW Jackson, Topeka, KS 66612-1290.
*Birth; since July 1911; Circuit Court Clerk
*Death; since July 1911; Circuit Court Clerk
*Marriage; since May 1913; Probate Judge
*Divorce; since July 1951; Circuit Court Clerk

KENTUCKY

DMV: Format: 9 numeric (SSN). Required Data: DL#. Driver's Licenses, State Office Bldg., Frankfort, KY 40622.

Vital Records: Immediate family. Dept. of Health Services, Office of Vital Stats., 275 E. Main St., Frankfort, KY 40621.
*Birth; since 1911; County Court Clerk
*Death; since 1911; County Court Clerk

*Marriage; since 1958; County Court Clerk
*Divorce; since 1958; Circuit Court Clerk

LOUISIANA

DMV: Format: 1-9 numeric. Required Data: DL#. Driver's Licenses, P.O. Box 46886-C, Baton Rouge, LA 70896.

Vital Records: Genealogy. Dept. of Health, Human Resources, Div. of Vital Stats., P.O. Box 60630, New Orleans, LA 70160.
*Birth; since 1914; Parish Court Clerk
*Death; since 1914; Parish Court Clerk
*Marriage; since 1946; Parish Court Clerk
*Divorce; since 1946; Parish Court Clerk

MAINE

DMV: Format: 7 numeric. Required Data: DL#, last name, first name, DOB. Driver's Licenses, State House, Rm. 29, Augusta, ME 04333.

Vital Records: Public. Dept. of Human Services, Office of Vital Stats., State House, Station 11, Augusta, ME 04333.
*Birth; since 1892; Town Clerk
*Death; since 1892; Town Clerk
*Marriage; since 1892; Town Clerk
*Divorce; since 1892; Judicial District Court Clerk

MARYLAND

DMV: Format: 1 alpha, 12 numeric. Required Data: DL#. Driver's Licenses, 6001 Ritchie Highway, NE, Rm. 211, Glen Burnie, MD 21062.

Vital Records: Immediate family. Dept. of Health & Mental Hygiene, Div. of Vital Records, State Office Bldg., P.O. Box 13146, Baltimore, MD 21203.
*Birth; since 1898; State Archives
*Death; since 1898; State Archives
*Marriage; since 1951; Circuit Court Clerk
*Divorce; since 1961; Circuit Court Clerk

MASSACHUSETTS

DMV: Format: 1 alpha, 8 numeric. Required Data: DL#, last name, first name, DOB. Driver's Licenses, 100 Nashua St., Boston, MA 02114.

Vital Records: Any relative. Dept. of Public Health, Registry of Vital Records & Stats., 150 Tremont St., Rm. B-3, Boston, MA 02111.
*Birth; since 1896; County/City Clerk
*Death; since 1896; County/City Clerk
*Marriage; since 1896; County/City Clerk
*Divorce; since 1952 to 1986 (index only); Probate Court

MICHIGAN

DMV: Format: 1 alpha, 12 numeric. Required Data: DL#. Driver's Licenses, 7064 Crowner Dr., Lansing, MI 48918.

Vital Records: Birth records restricted to immediate family, legal guardian, heirs or representative. All other records unrestricted. State of Michigan Dept. of Public Health, Office of State Registrar & Center of Health Stats., 3423 N. Logan, P.O. Box 30195, Lansing, MI 48909.
*Birth; since 1867; County Clerk
*Death; since 1867; County Clerk
*Marriage; since 1867; County Clerk
*Divorce; since 1897; County Clerk

MINNESOTA

DMV: Format: 1 alpha, 12 numeric. Required Data: DL#. Driver's Licenses, Transporation Bldg., Rm. 108, St. Paul, MN 55155.

Vital Records: Public. Dept. of Health, Section of Vital Stats. Registration, 717 Delaware St., SE, P.O. Box 9441, Minneapolis, MN 55440.
*Birth; since 1900; District Court Clerk
*Death; since 1908; District Court Clerk
*Marriage; since 1958; District Court Clerk
*Divorce; District Court Clerk

MISSISSIPPI

DMV: Format: 9 numeric (usually SSN). Required Data: DL#, last name. Driver's Licenses, P.O. Box 958-H, Jackson, MS 39205.

Vital Records: Varies, restricted, genealogy. State Dept. Health, Public Health Stats. Div., P.O. Box 1700, 2423 N. State St., Jackson, MS 39215-1700.
*Birth; since 1912; Circuit Court Clerk
*Death; since 1912; Circuit Court Clerk
*Marriage; since 1926; Circuit Court Clerk
*Divorce; Chancery Clerk

MISSOURI

DMV: Format: 1 alpha, 15 numeric and 1 alphanumeric or blank; or 1 alpha, 6 numeric; or 9 numeric (SSN). Required Data: DL#. Driver's Licenses, 200-E, Jefferson City, MO 65105.

Vital Records: Birth and death records restricted to legal representative, immediate family. Marriage and divorce records public. Dept. of Health, Bureau of Vital Records, P.O. Box 570, Jefferson City, MO 65012.
*Birth; since 1910; Bureau of Vital Records
*Death; since 1910; Bureau of Vital Records
*Marriage; since 1948; Deeds Recorder
*Divorce; since 1948; Circuit Court Clerk

MONTANA

DMV: Format: 1 alpha, 6 numeric; or 9 numeric (SSN); or 1 alpha, 1 numeric, 1 alphanumeric, 2 numeric, 3 alpha and 1 numeric. Required Data: DL#, last name, first name, DOB. Driver's Licenses, 303 N. Roberts, Helena, MT 59620.

Vital Records: Restricted. Dept. of Health & Environmental Sciences, Bureau of Records, Stats., Cogswell Bldg., Rm. C-118, Helena, MT 59620.
*Birth; since 1907; County Clerk
*Death; since 1907; County Clerk
*Marriage; since 1943; District Court Clerk
*Divorce; since 1943; District Court Clerk

NEBRASKA

DMV: Format: 1 alpha (*A*, *B*, *C*, *E*, *G*, *H* or *V*), 3-8 numeric. Required Data: DL#, last name, first name, DOB. Driver's Licenses, 301 Centennial Mall S., Lincoln, NE 68509.

Vital Records: Restricted. State Dept. of Health, Bureau of Vital Stats., P.O. Box 95007, Lincoln, NE 58509-5007.
*Birth; since 1904; State Dept. of Health
*Death; since 1904; State Dept. of Health
*Marriage; since 1909; County Clerk
*Divorce; since 1909; District Court Clerk

NEVADA

DMV: Format: 9 numeric (SSN); or 10 numeric; or 12 numeric (last 2 are year of birth); or 1 alpha (*X*), 8 numeric. Required Data: DL#. Driver's Licenses, 555 Wright Way, Carson City, NV 89711.

Vital Records: Immediate family. State Health Div., Section of Vital Stats., Carson City, NV 89710.
*Birth; since 1911; County Recorder
*Death; since 1911; County Recorder
*Marriage; since 1968; County Recorder
*Divorce; since 1911; County Clerk

NEW HAMPSHIRE

DMV: Format: 2 numeric, 3 alpha, 5 numeric. Required Data: DL#, last name, DOB. Driver's Licenses, 10 Hazen Dr., Concord, NH 03305.

Vital Records: Immediate family. Div. of Public Health, Bureau of Vital Records, 6 Hazen Dr., Concord, NH 03301-6527.
*Birth; since 1640; Town Clerk
*Death; since 1640; Town Clerk
*Marriage; since 1640; Town Clerk
*Divorce; since 1880; Superior Court Clerk

NEW JERSEY

DMV: Format: 1 alpha, 14 numeric. Required Data: DL#. Driver's Licenses, 25 S. Montgomery St., Trenton, NJ 08666.

Vital Records: Restricted. State Dept. of Health, State Registrar Search Unit, Bureau Vital Records, CN 360, Trenton, NJ 08625-0360.
*Birth; since 1878; County Clerk
*Death; since 1878; County Clerk
*Marriage; since 1878; County Clerk
*Divorce; since 1878; Superior Court Clerk

NEW MEXICO

DMV: Format: 8 numeric; or 9 numeric (SSN). Required Data: DL#, last name, DOB. Driver's Licenses, 1028-L, Santa Fe, NM 87504.

Vital Records: Immediate family. Health & Environment Dept., Public Health Div., Vital Stats. Bureau, 1190 St. Francis Dr., Santa Fe, NM 87503.
*Birth; since 1919; State Vital Records
*Death; since 1919; State Vital Records
*Marriage; no state index; County Clerk
*Divorce; no state index; District Court Clerk

NEW YORK

DMV: Format: 1 alpha, 18 numeric; or 9 numeric (not an SSN). Required Data: DL#. Driver's Licenses, Empire State Plaza, Albany, NY 12228.

Vital Records (except New York City): Immediate family. State Dept. of Health, Bureau of Vital Records, Tower Bldg., Empire State Plaza, Albany, NY 12237.
*Birth; since 1880; Albany Office
*Death; since 1880; Albany Office
*Marriage; since 1915; Albany Office
*Divorce; since 1963; Albany Office

NEW YORK CITY

Vital Records: Immediate family. New York City Dept. of Health, Bureau of Vital Records, 125 Worth St., New York, NY 10013.
*Birth; since 1880; NYC Office
*Death; since 1880; NYC Office
*Marriage; since 1847 to 1865; NYC Office
*Divorce; not at city level

NORTH CAROLINA

DMV: Format: 1-7 numeric. Required Data: DL#, last name, DOB. Driver's Licenses, 1100 New Bern Ave., Raleigh, NC 27697.

Vital Records: Public. Dept. of Human Resources, Div. of Health Stats., Vital Records Branch, P.O. Box 2019, Raleigh, NC 27602-2091.
*Birth; since 1913; Division of Health Services
*Death; since 1930; Division of Health Services
*Marriage; since 1962; Deeds Registrar
*Divorce; since 1958; Superior Court Clerk

NORTH DAKOTA

DMV: Format: 9 numeric. Required Data: DL#. Driver's Licenses, Capitol Grounds, Bismarck, ND 58505.

Vital Records: Restricted. State Dept. of Health, Vital Records, State Capitol, Bismarck, ND 58506.
*Birth; since 1920; County Judge
*Death; since 1893; County Judge
*Marriage; since 1925; County Judge
*Divorce; since 1949; District Court Clerk

OHIO

DMV: Format: 9 numeric (SSN); or 2 alpha, 6 numeric. Required Data: DL#. Driver's Licenses, P.O. Box 7167-L, Columbus, OH 43266.

Vital Records: Public. Dept. of Health, Div. of Vital Stats, Ohio Dept. Bldg., Rm. C-20, 65 Front St., Columbus, OH 43266-0333.
*Birth; since 1908; Probate Court
*Death; since 1908; Probate Court
*Marriage; since 1949; Probate Judge
*Divorce; since 1948; Probate Judge

OKLAHOMA

DMV: Format: 9 numeric (SSN). Required Data: DL#, last name, DOB. Driver's Licenses, P.O. Box 11415-F, Oklahoma City, OK 73136.

Vital Records: Birth records restricted to registrant, next of kin or legal representative. Vital Records Section, Oklahoma State Dept. of Health, 1000 NE Tenth, P.O. Box 53551, Oklahoma City, OK 73152.
*Birth; since 1908; Court Clerk
*Death; since 1908; Court Clerk
*Marriage; no state index; Court Clerk
*Divorce; no state index; Court Clerk

OREGON

DMV: Format: 1-7 numeric. Required Data: DL#, DOB. Driver's Licenses, 1905 Lana Ave., NE, Salem, OR 97314.

Vital Records: Immediate family; must have exact DOB for birth records. Dept. of Human Resources, Oregon State Health Div., P.O. Box 231, Portland, OR 97207-0231.
*Birth; since 1903; County Clerk
*Death; since 1903; County Clerk
*Marriage; since 1907; County Clerk
*Divorce; since 1925; County Clerk

PENNSYLVANIA

DMV: Format: 6-8 numeric. Required Data: DL#, DOB. Driver's Licenses, P.O. Box 8695-L, Harrisburg, PA 17105.

Vital Records: Public. Dept. of Health, Div. of Vital Records, 101 S. Mercer St., P.O. Box 1528, New Castle, PA 16103.
*Birth; since 1906; Dept. of Health
*Death; since 1906; Dept. of Health
*Marriage; since 1941; Marriage License Clerk
*Divorce; since 1946; County Seat Prothonotary

RHODE ISLAND

DMV: Format: 7 numeric. Required Data: DL#, last name, DOB. Driver's Licenses, 345 Harris Ave, Providence, RI 02909.

Vital Records: Immediate family. Dept. of Health, Div. of Vital Records, 101 Cannon Bldg., 3 Capitol Hill, Providence, RI 02908.
*Birth; since 1853; Town Clerk
*Death; since 1853; Town Clerk
*Marriage; since 1853; Town Clerk
*Divorce; since 1962; Family Court Clerk

SOUTH CAROLINA

DMV: Format: 6-9 numeric. Required Data: DL#, last name, DOB. Driver's Licenses, P.O. Box 1498-R, Columbia, SC 29216.

Vital Records: Immediate family; copies of birth and death records are restricted, but events will be confirmed. Dept. of Health & Environment Control, Office of Vital Records & Public Health Stats., 2600 Bull St., Columbia, SC 29201.
*Birth; since 1915; County Treasurer
*Death; since 1915; County Treasurer
*Marriage; since 1950; County Treasurer
*Divorce; since 1962; Court Clerk

SOUTH DAKOTA

DMV: Format: 6-9 numeric. Required Data: DL#, last name, DOB. Driver's Licenses, 118 W. Capitol Ave., Pierre, SD 57501.

Vital Records: Restricted. Dept. of Health, Center of Health Stats. & Vital Records, 523 E. Capitol, Joe Foss Bldg., Pierre, SD 57501-3182.
*Birth; since 1905; County Treasurer
*Death; since 1905; County Treasurer
*Marriage; since 1905; County Treasurer
*Divorce; since 1905; Court Clerk

TENNESSEE

DMV: Format: 7 numeric. Required Data: DL#, DOB. Driver's Licenses, P.O. Box 945-E, Nashville, TN 37202.

Vital Records: Immediate family, legal representative. Dept. of
Health & Environment, Office of Vital Records, Cordell
Hull Bldg., Nashville, TN 37219-5402.
*Birth; since 1914; County Court Clerk
*Death; since 1914; County Court Clerk
*Marriage; since 1945; County Court Clerk
*Divorce; since 1945; County Court Clerk

TEXAS

DMV: Format: 8 numeric. Required Data: DL#, last name, DOB.
Driver's Licenses, P.O. Box 4087-S, Austin, TX 78773.

Vital Records: Immediate family, legal representative. Dept. of
Health, Bureau of Vital Stats., 1100 W. Forty-ninth St.,
Austin, TX 78756-3191.
*Birth; since 1903; County Clerk
*Death; since 1903; County Clerk
*Marriage; since 1966; County Clerk
*Divorce; since 1968; District Court Clerk

UTAH

DMV: Format: 4-10 numeric. Required Data: DL#, last name,
DOB. Driver's Licenses, 1075 Motor Ave., Salt Lake
City, UT 84116.

Vital Records: Immediate family, legal representative. Bureau
of Vital Records, 288 N. 1460 W., P.O. Box 16700, Salt
Lake City, UT 84116-0700.
*Birth; since 1905; County Clerk
*Death; since 1905; County Clerk
*Marriage; since 1978; County Clerk
*Divorce; since 1978; District Court Clerk

VERMONT

DMV: Format: 8 numeric; or 7 numeric. Required Data: DL#.
Driver's Licenses, 120 State St., Montpelier, VT 05603.

Vital Records: Public. Dept. of Health, Vital Records Unit, 60
Main St., P.O. Box 70, Burlington, VT 95402.
*Birth; since 1955; City Clerk
*Death; since 1955; City Clerk
*Marriage; since 1955; City Clerk
*Divorce; since 1969; County Court Clerk

VIRGINIA

DMV: Format: 9 numeric; or 1 alpha (*H, K* or *R*), 8 numeric; or 12 numeric. Required Data: DL#, last name, DOB. Driver's Licenses, 2300 W. Broad St., Richmond, VA 23269.

Vital Records: Birth and death records restricted to immediate family or legal representative. Dept. of Health, Div. of Vital Records, James Madison Bldg., P.O. Box 1000, Richmond, VA 23208-1000.
*Birth; since 1912; Health Dept.
*Death; since 1912; Health Dept.
*Marriage; since 1853; Court Clerk
*Divorce; since 1918; Court Clerk

WASHINGTON

DMV: Format: 5 alpha (last name), 1 alpha (first name), 1 alpha (middle name), 5 alphanumeric. If the last or middle name field falls short of the required spaces, fill with asterisks. Required Data: DL#, DOB. Driver's Licenses, 211 Twelfth Ave., SE, Olympia, WA 98504.

Vital Records: Public, some restricted. State Dept. of Social, Heath Services, Vital Records, P.O. Box 9709, ET-11, Olympia, WA 98504.
*Birth; since 1907; County Auditor
*Death; since 1907; County Auditor
*Marriage; since 1968; County Auditor
*Divorce; since 1968; County Clerk

WEST VIRGINIA

DMV: Format: 2 alphanumeric, 5 numeric. Required Data: DL#, last name. Driver's Licenses, 1800 Washington St., E, Charleston, WV 25317.

Vital Records: Immediate family. Dept. of Health, Div. of Vital Stats, State Office Bldg. #3, Charleston, WV 25305.
*Birth; since 1917; County Court Clerk
*Death; since 1917; County Court Clerk
*Marriage; since 1963; County Court Clerk
*Divorce; since 1968; Circuit Court Clerk

WISCONSIN
DMV: Format: 1 alpha, 13 numeric, 1 alpha (*C*, *P*, *R* or blank). Required Data: DL#. Driver's Licenses, P.O. Box 7918, Madison, WI 53707.

Vital Records: Immediate family, legal representative. Division of Health, Section of Vital Stats., P.O. Box 309, Madison, WI 53701-0309.
*Birth; since 1814; no county indexes
*Death; since 1814; no county indexes
*Marriage; since 1835; no county indexes
*Divorce; since 1907; no county indexes

WYOMING
DMV: Format: 9-10 numeric. Required Data: DL#. Driver's Licenses, 122 W. 25th St., Cheyenne, WY 82002.

Vital Records: Restricted. Div. of Health & Medical Services, Vital Records Services, Hathaway Bldg., Cheyenne, WY 82002.
*Birth; since 1909; County Clerk
*Death; since 1909; County Clerk
*Marriage; since 1941; County Clerk
*Divorce; since 1941; District Court Clerk

Appendix D

State's Laws Regarding Taping of Telephone Conversations

Private parties may legally record their own conversations without the other parties' consent: AL, AK, AZ, AR, CO, CT, DC, HI, ID, IN, IA, KS, KY, ME, MS, NE, NV, NJ, NM, NY, ND, OH, OK, RI, SD, TX, UT, VA, WV, WI, WY.

All parties to a conversation must be aware that it is being recorded: CA, DE, FL, IL, LA, MD, MS, MI, MT, NH, OR, PA, WA (in WA, announcement to record must be recorded also).

Under federal guidelines, private parties may record their own conversations without the other parties' consent, unless the recording is being made for the purpose of violating the law: MN, MO, NC, SC, TN, VT.

State law does not specifically address, but the courts have upheld cases where persons have recorded their own conversations: GA.

Appendix E

Social Security Numbers by State

001-003	New Hampshire
004-007	Maine
008-009	Vermont
010-034	Massachusetts
035-039	Rhode Island
040-049	Connecticut
050-134	New York
135-158	New Jersey
159-211	Pennsylvania
212-220	Maryland
221-222	Delaware
223-231	Virgina
232-236	West Virginia
237-246	North Carolina
247-251	South Carolina
252-260	Georgia
261-267	Florida
589-595	Florida (cont.)
268-302	Ohio
303-317	Indiana
318-361	Illinois
362-386	Michigan
387-399	Wisconsin
400-407	Kentucky
408-415	Tennessee
416-424	Alabama
425-428	Mississippi
587-588	Mississippi (cont.)
429-432	Arkansas
433-439	Louisana
440-448	Oklahoma
449-467	Texas
627-645	Texas (cont.)
468-477	Minnesota

478-485	Iowa
486-500	Missouri
501-502	North Dakota
503-504	South Dakota
505-508	Nebraska
509-515	Kansas
516-517	Montana
518-519	Idaho
520	Wyoming
521-524	Colorado
525	New Mexico
648	New Mexico (cont.)
526-527	Arizona
600-601	Arizona (cont.)
528-529	Utah
530	Nevada
531-539	Washington
540-544	Oregon
545-573	California
602-626	California (cont.)
574	Alaska
575-576	Hawaii
577-579	District of Columbia
580	Virgin Islands
581-584	Puerto Rico
596-599	Puerto Rico (cont.)
586	Guam, Samoa
700-720	Railroad

Appendix F

Reference Books and Catalogs

Books

Bentley, Elizabeth Petty. *County Courthouse Book*. 2nd ed. Baltimore: Genealogical Publishing Co., Inc., 1996.

Easley, Bruce. *Biz-Op: How to Get Rich With "Business Opportunity" Frauds and Scams*. Port Townsend, WA: Loompanics Unlimited, 1994.

Johnson, Richard S. *How to Locate Anyone Who Is or Has Been in the Military*. 7th ed., rev. San Antonio: Military Information Enterprises, 1996.

Kemp, Thomas Jay. *International Vital Records Handbook*. Baltimore: Genealogical Publishing Co., Inc., 1994.

Lapin, Lee. *The Whole Spy Catalog*. San Mateo, CA: ISECO, Inc., 1995.

Loeb, David Ventura, and David W. Brown. *How to Change Your Name in California*. Berkeley: Nolo Press, 1995.

Martin, James S. *Scram: Relocating Under a New Identity*. Port Townsend, WA: Loompanics Unlimited, 1993.

Orion Agency, Inc. Staff. *Obtaining Your Private Investigator's License*. Boulder: Paladin Press, 1986.

Ray, Don. *A Public Records Primer and Investigator's Handbook*. Burbank: Eng. Press.

Richmond, Doug. *How to Disappear Completely and Never Be Found*. Port Townsend, WA: Loompanics Unlimited, 1986.

Sample, John. *Methods of Disguise*. 2nd ed., rev. Port Townsend, WA: Loompanics Unlimited, 1994.

Sands, Trent. *Reborn in the U.S.A.: Personal Privacy Through a New Identity*. 2nd ed. Port Townsend, WA: Loompanics Unlimited, 1991.

Sankey, Michael. *The Librarian's Guide to Public Records*. Tempe, AZ: BRB Publications, Inc., 1996.

———. *The Soucebook of County Court Records*. 2nd ed. Tempe, AZ: BRB Publications, Inc., 1996.

———. *The Sourcebook of State Public Records*. 2nd ed. Tempe, AZ: BRB Publications, Inc., 1995.

Siegel, Warren. *The Criminal Records Book*. Berkeley: Nolo Press, 1996.

Catalogs

"There are two kinds of people in this world," says Rat Dog. "Scoundrels and seekers of scoundrels." (Old press release.) How do they learn their trades? Those who are literate read books and those books they often find in catalogs offered by just a few catalog companies.

Loompanics Unlimited is the main supplier of scoundrels. Their catalog includes the book titles mentioned above as well as periodicals on how to make bombs and assassinate people. Most of their books are both published and distributed by Loompanics Unlimited, P.O. Box 1197, Port Townsend, Washington 98368.

Both Eden Press and Thomas Publications target the "seekers of scoundrels." For their catalogs, contact Thomas Publications at 9501 North IH 35, Suite 007, Austin, Texas 78753, (512) 719-3595 and Eden Press at P.O. Box 8410, Fountain Valley, California 92728, (714) 556-2023.

Intelligence Inc. is on the cutting edge in the marketing of high-tech toys. Contact Intelligence Incorporated, 2228 South El Camino Real, San Mateo, California 94403.

Index